SWEET FARM!

ALSO BY MOLLY YEH

Home Is Where the Eggs Are

Short Stack Vol 32: Yogurt

Molly on the Range

SWEET FARM!

Cookies, Cakes, Salads (!), and Other Delights
from My Kitchen on a Sugar Beet Farm

MOLLY YEH

PHOTOGRAPHS BY
CHANTELL AND BRETT QUERNEMOEN

WM
WILLIAM MORROW
An Imprint of HarperCollins*Publishers*

To the generations
of farmers that came
before us

CONTENTS

Introduction   xi
Ingredients   xviii
Tools   xxix
General Notes   xxxvii

Cookies   1
Bars   52
Salads   84
Dessert for Breakfast   112
Cakes   168
Pies   250
Frozen and No Bake   272
Drinks   294

Acknowledgments   313
Bibliography   315
Universal Conversion Chart   317
Index   319

RECIPES

COOKIES

Big Craggly Sugar Cookies 2

Chewy Frosted Tahini Cookies 5

Giant Almond Butter Blossoms 8

Pistachio Sandwich Cookies 12

Thick Soft Cream Cheese Cutouts 15

Potato Chip Chocolate Chip
    Cookies 18

Chocolate Chocolate Halva
    Walnut Cookies 22

Earl Grey Black-and-White Cookies 24

Cherry Mahlab Linzers 28

Cinnamon Sugar Chocolate
    Rugelach 30

Red Bean Newtons 34

Big Soft Chocolate Sandwich
    Cookies 38

Chocolate-Dipped Brown
    Sugar Animals 42

Italian Rainbow Cookie Dough 45

Jumbo Thumbprints 47

Larder Cabinet Cookies 49

BARS

Soft Almond Sugar Cookie Bars 54

Sorta Weird Seven-Layer Bars 56

Mandarin Orange and Toasted Sesame
    Bars 58

Rhubarb Rose Bars 62

One-Bowl Any-Butter Cookie Bars 64

S'mores Bars 68

Jam Bars, Three Ways: Raspberry
    Coconut, Plum Hazelnut, Apple
    Marzipan 70

Miso Toffee Crackers 72

Chewy Nutty Fruity Granola Bars 76

Stollen Bars 78

Yellow Cake Cookie Bars 82

SALADS

Classic Cookie Salad 86

Overachiever's Cookie Salad 87

Classic Candy Bar Salad 89

Overachiever's Candy Bar Salad 90

Roasted Rhubarb and Strawberries
    with Yogurt Whip, Pretzel
    Streusel, and Sumac 93

Blueberry Cream Cheese Bagel Chip
    Salad 96

Pistachio Rose Shortbread Delight 100

Grape Salad 103

Black-and-White Cookie Salad 104

Pomegranate Coconut Gelatin Mold ... 106

Ube Fluff 110

DESSERT FOR BREAKFAST

Buttered Potato Dough (An All-
    Purpose Enriched Dough) 114

Marzipan Poppy Seed Babka Muffins .. 117

Puffy Potato Doughnuts 120

Cardamom Buns 124

Chocolate Swirly Buns 126

Black Sesame Babka 130

Strawberry, Raspberry, and
    Elderflower Jam 133

Halva, Walnut, and Chocolate
    Chunk Scone Loaf 134

Jam and Mozzarella English Muffin
    Rolls 138

Mandel Bread Cereal 140

Wild Rice Pancakes with Poached
    Rhubarb 144

Fairy French Toast 146

Orange Chocolate Pistachio Scone
    Muffins 150

Pineapple Buns 152

Challah Hotteok 157

Sprinkle Cake Doughnuts 159

Everything I Can Tell You About Sugar Beets...................162

Chocolate (Sugar) Beet Muffins 166

CAKES

Vanilla Cupcakes with Vanilla Frosting...................172

Coconut Raspberry Rose Pistachio Cake 176

How to Frost a Cake...................178

Hawaij Carrot Cake with Orange Blossom Cream Cheese Frosting....180

Lavender Lemon Loaf 183

Sprinkle Cake 2.0 186

Beet Red-ish Velvet Cake...................191

Pistachio Basbousa 194

Stone Fruit Streusel Cake...................198

Chocolate Tahini Fudge Cake with Tahini Whip and Halva..........200

Marzipan Cake...................203

Naturally Colored Rainbow Cake 206

Coffee Cake with Fresh Mint Frosting...................209

Rosemary Potato Loaf Cake...................212

Rainbow Chip Financiers 215

Chocolate Peanut Butter Cake 216

Roasted Squash Cake with Brown Sugar Frosting...................220

Fresh Mint Olive Oil Cake with Preserved Lemon Yogurt Whip 222

Rose Rose Cake...................225

Grilled Peach Shortcakes 231

Almond Butter Mini Cakes with Berry Glaze 234

This Is Also a Wheat Farm 236

Salted Chocolate Chunk Whole Wheat Snack Cake...................238

Elderflower Strawberry Bløtkake...................240

Toasted Sesame Cake...................244

Big Buttery Chocolate Cake 246

Decorating with Marzipan...................249

PIES

Poppy Seed Hand Pies with Blood Orange Glaze 252

Peanut Butter (or Tahini) Fudge Pie ...256

Blueberry Slab Pie 258

My Dad's Coconut Cream Pie...................262

Mazarin Pie 264

Pumpkin Jam and Goat Cheese Bourekas 268

Chocolate Chunk Cherry Cobbler 270

FROZEN AND NO BAKE

Processed Cheese Fudge 274

Macadamia Pudding Pops 276

Peanut Butter Halva 279

Buttery Cracker Icebox Cake...................280

Furikake Puppy Chow 283

Cashew Coconut Buckeyes...................284

Almond Butter–Stuffed Dates...................286

What Do Sugar Beet Farmers Do in the Winter? 287

Black Sesame Snow Ice Cream...................288

Saffron and Cardamom Tiramisu...................292

DRINKS

Tahini Cake Shake...................296

Grapefruit Slushy Float 297

Marzipan Soda...................300

Cardamom Frozen Coffee...................303

Fresh Mint Coconut Shake...................304

Strawberries and Cream Frozen Cocktail 307

Macadamia Matcha Latte 308

Black Sesame Egg Cream...................311

INTRODUCTION

"Sugar beets are big white root vegetables that are processed into table sugar."

That's about all that Nick was able to say before I started plotting my exit from our conversation. I'd initiated it upon seeing a funny squiggly vegetable-shaped tattoo poking out of my former classmate's T-shirt at a party. It was my first time seeing Nick since we'd been acquaintances in music school years earlier, and it was my first time hearing of this sugar beet, which produces around half of the country's sugar. This factoid didn't resonate with me nearly as much as it should have. Although I wasn't yet a professional baker or cookbook author or Food Network host, I did have, as I'd had since as long as I can remember, a deep love of baking and making sweets. And in my life as a recent music school graduate, I was at a crossroads regarding what my future might look like, paying my rent by playing music gigs around New York City while also taking any opportunity I could get to explore my newfound passion for food writing and recipe development. In that moment, however, I had more important things on my mind, like how this dumb party was absolutely not worth the long subway ride from my apartment in Hell's Kitchen uptown to Inwood, and that my beer was getting warm. I can see now that, as an unimpressed and annoying twenty-three-year-old, I didn't know nearly enough about sugar and farming to feel like I could carry on an intelligent conversation about this topic, but also Nick has no game in talking to girls, so this interaction was destined to fail. I thanked him for teaching me my one new thing I learned that day, then pretended that something important was happening on the other side of the room, figuring I'd probably never see him again in any sort of meaningful context. And I immediately forgot about sugar beets.

Until about two weeks later when we went on one date and realized we were actually destined to get married.

But this story doesn't start in Inwood, New York, or even in the United States. It starts about 140 years before that, in Norway, where Nick's great-

great-grandpa Bernt Jahnsen made the decision to leave his small village and sail west in search of opportunity. At that time, Norway was plagued by crop disease, scarcity of land, and poverty. On top of that, Bernt wasn't the firstborn child in his family, so any farmland they did have likely would not have gone to him. So Bernt did what hundreds of thousands of other Norwegians did at that time and took off to claim the 160 acres of land that was being offered to them by the Homestead Act of 1862, in return for a commitment to farm that land for five years.

He arrived in the United States in 1871 and started spelling "Jahnsen" as "Johnson," likely because it seemed more American, but when he realized how many Johnsons there were, he threw on the last name Hagen, presumably to be more distinctive. And then he and his new names made their way to Spring Grove, Minnesota, where many other immigrants from his part of Norway were settling. After working various jobs in that area for a few years, he decided that he might have better luck finding good farmland if he traveled north, closer to Dakota Territory and Canada. In the Red River Valley, a very flat valley created at the bottom of the long-gone Lake Agassiz, Bernt found rich soil and his choice of location for his farm. Subzero winter temperatures aside, he chose really well when you consider its eventual proximity to a Super Target and Culver's.

Bernt worked the land and began farming a variety of crops that were likely familiar to him from his farming background in Norway, like potatoes and grains. He farmed them by hand and with horses. He built a log house, which burned down, and then another log house, and married another Norwegian immigrant, Dorthea, with whom he had ten children.

Their unimprovably named second son, Thorvald, eventually took over the Hagen farm. Thorvald and his older brother, Olaf, had a dairy business together, and they also farmed potatoes and grains, using horses and a steam engine–powered threshing machine (a wheat-harvesting machine that separates the grain from the chaff). By the 1930s, after the first sugar beet processing plant in the valley opened in East Grand Forks, Minnesota, they began farming sugar beets.

Thorvald must have had some success as a potato and beet farmer, because he and his wife, Mary, had the first indoor flushing toilet in the neighborhood. He closed his dairy business in 1940 but continued with his crops, and eventually passed the farm to their oldest child, Cliff. Cliff is Nick's grandpa, and Nick remembers him as someone who didn't show very much emotion. But he must have shown some when he threatened to leave the farm if his dad didn't get with the times, stop using horses to tend to the fields, and get a dang

tractor. So they got tractors—but obviously not the kind with comfortable
air-conditioned GPS-wired cabs that Nick drives today. They just sat out in
the sun, working one row of crops at a time (versus today's monster machines,
which work forty-eight rows or more at once), sweating and swatting bugs. But
at least it was more efficient than using horses. Another one of Cliff's major
contributions to the Hagen Farm was building infrastructure, like big cylindrical storage units for the grain, a shed to house the tractors, and a workshop
to repair them (the building where Nick and I eventually got married). Cliff
brought the farm into the modern age.

By the time my father-in-law, Roger—the oldest child of Cliff and his wife,
Marie—started farming, the farm was growing wheat, barley, pinto beans,
and sugar beets. Roger expanded the farm's land and saw the progression from
a cabless little tractor to bigger and bigger tractors with buddy seats and radios.
He met my mother-in-law, Roxanne, after she moved to town to become a
music teacher, and over blueberry muffins at a friend's house, they fell in wuv.
A few years later they had Nick and his little sister, Anna, who, as teens, made
a pact to get tattoos together without telling their parents. Anna got a little
running man on her ankle and Nick got a sugar beet on his arm.

Around the time Nick and Anna were kids, building tree houses and
picking rhubarb on the farm while their dad and grandpa grew sugar beets
and wheat, a curious, bowl-cut-sporting three-year-old me was sitting on my
kitchen floor in Glenview, Illinois, playing with pink and blue cake batter,
discovering the magical wonder of watching a from-scratch cake take shape.

Nick's tattoo, a "sugar beet bass clef."

Harvesting pinto beans in 1981.

Nick and his dad, circa the late 1980s.

A sugar beet!

That's the earliest of my many memories involving big messes made of flour and sugar, sneaking bites of cake batter out of the mixer, and engaging in the glorious act of eating baked goods hot out of the oven. For as long as I can remember, baking was seen by my family as the best way to spend a free afternoon and to show someone you care. Making a cake or ice cream or homemade versions of Oreos was seen as far superior to buying them from the store (although we did that, too, of course). Whether we were making brioche by hand or basil-infused vanilla pudding from scratch, my sister and mom and I were always finding reasons to pull out the big tub of sugar.

While my older sister eventually found her way to culinary school for a baking and pastry program, I chose to study music in college. Playing the drums was another passion of mine, sparked by the music I grew up hearing from my dad's clarinet. But as soon as I got my first apartment in New York, in my third year of college, I began spending all my free time in the closet-size kitchen, re-creating rugelach and challah and the like that I'd grown up making with my mom. And while I waited for my few triangle notes in long orchestra rehearsals, I'd daydream about red velvet cupcakes piled with marshmallowy cream cheese frosting. The online life diary I began in 2009 quickly turned into a mostly food blog where I chronicled my restaurant and food truck–chasing adventures around the city as well as my experiments in the kitchen. When I graduated from college, I had no real plan other than to stay in the city and say yes to anything that came my way that had to do with food or music. I truly loved them both, but a more defined course started to take shape as soon as that squiggly sugar beet tattoo appeared in front of me.

When our stories converged, Nick's and my sugar-driven paths accelerated. Once we realized that we were each other's person, we sought out answers to questions like where we should settle down (in the Midwest, closer to both of our families) and what we'd do there for a living (farm sugar, bake with sugar, and blog about it). Although this wasn't his intention while he was in college, Nick found himself excited about committing to farming full-time with his dad, who would eventually pass on the reins to Nick. And anticipating moving out of an expensive city to a place with a bigger kitchen and fewer distractions, I was itching to build a life with more time to blog and bake. As soon as we moved, I got a job at the town bakery where Nick's mom's pastor's friend, the owner, offered me a baking position without even meeting me or confirming that I knew how to weigh butter. (I didn't.)

At the bakery, I learned how to measure butter by the pound, frost cakes with smooth edges, and scoop five hundred cookies of uniform size swiftly and efficiently. When I finished baking muffins and scones for the day, at around five a.m., I'd hurry home so I could work on recipes for my blog and photograph them as soon as the light was bright enough. I would then spend a couple of hours writing blog posts, posting on social media, and figuring out what was resonating most with my blog readers. Conveniently, what did the best on my blog and social media was also what I loved making the most: cakes, more cakes, and sweets in general.

At the same time that I was learning my way around sugar in the kitchen, I was also absorbing what it was like to live on a sugar farm: from how sugar beets are grown, to the smell emitted from the processing plant as the beets are turned into the sugar I'd eventually bake with, to the ways the harvest cycle affects everyday life at home and in the community. Nick and I moved in right before harvest, so he basically peaced out for a good few weeks and I was left to my own accord. It was jarring and confusing, but I threw myself into my blog and the overnight bakery shift, so I have some very fond, albeit sleepy, memories of it all. It took a good few years, but I started to get the hang of making it through the solitary reality of harvest (take a ceramics class, catch up on *The*

Bachelorette, go on a book tour, work a whole lot more, and of course, bake a lot more since there are more mouths to feed with all the extra harvest helpers), and adjust my mindset to associating winter with the carefree traveling that used to occur in the summer. Twelve years in, I'm still trying to become laid-back enough to be flexible whenever the weather makes Nick come in an hour late for dinner or change his weekend schedule at the last minute, making us cancel our day at the lake, but being the cool chill girl is overrated, right? (Right?!) This lifestyle has its very intense moments, because there's no real turning it off until the winter, but living in a place with so much family history (and hopefully a very long future), where I can see my ingredients grown before my very eyes, is special beyond words.

Even though I now cook lots of soups, steaks, and other savory dishes in addition to desserts on my show and in my past books and blog, I have always considered myself a baker first. The part of my dork mathlete brain that laughed in the face of AP Calculus is the same part that understands Bach better than jazz and that finds the precise measurements, details, and ratios of baking completely soothing on a spiritual level. Rolling out cookie dough until it is exactly ⅜ inch thick, frosting perfectly parallel lines on a cake, and cutting uniformly sized square brownies brings me so much pleasure, it's stupid.

In the decade-plus since I moved to East Grand Forks, I have spent my time completely immersed in the world of sugar, both during my work hours in the kitchen tweaking cake recipe after cake recipe and in my after hours, hearing Nick talk about how the beets are growing outside. I have homed in on exactly what I want out of my sweets and not stopped until I got there, feeding test batches to dozens of farmers along the way. Every single thing I bake gets analyzed for its texture, flavor, and aesthetic, and if it's not where I want it, I don't sleep too well that night. This sugar obsession has led us to open a bakery café, Bernie's, which puts the sugar and wheat from our region to use in baked goods that pay homage to our Scandinavian roots and showcase twists on the church cookbook staples that are so ubiquitous here. This obsession has also meant that in my first three books, I had to fight the urge to allow the dessert chapters to completely take over. Luckily, I didn't have to do that here.

The recipes in this book represent the most creative satisfaction I have *ever* had because recipes for sweets pour out of me like any bucket of sprinkles that gets handed to my children: swiftly and with great joy. I'd say I speak fluent sugar, which makes it convenient that I live on a sugar farm.

My style of baking is firmly rooted in my upper Midwest surroundings, where the treats are big, sweet, lovable, and the opposite of precious or dainty. (That's what Paris is for.) I'm also endlessly inspired by my Chinese and Jewish heritage, Nick's Scandinavian heritage, and the people who eat most of my sweets: big burly farmers and tiny, cookie-loving kids. This book has a mix of the type of church cookbook–inspired gems that we feature at Bernie's and from-scratch versions of sweets I ate in my suburban and urban upbringing but can't find anywhere in town. It is a reflection of my love of both rustic beauty and clean lines, unexpected flavors that tell a story, and my relentless search for perfect textures and peak moisture. I love employing secret ingredients to improve upon classics (see the Buttered Potato Dough on page 114) and finding flavor combinations that work but that wouldn't have really been feasible on the farm even one generation ago (see the Ube Fluff on page 110). You will see that I have zero chill when it comes to my loves of marzipan, rosewater, tahini, pistachios, potatoes, black sesame, and coconut. And I am extra proud that there is a whole chapter on salads in this book about sweets. I value efficiency and hate doing dishes, so if I can pass along shortcuts, I will, but if letting your doughnut dough spend the night in the refrigerator really is the key to unlocking your doughnut dreams, I am going to urge you to do that. And last, not every recipe in this book is sweetened by straight-up sugar. Some use honey or maple syrup or fruit juices or a combination, and that's because even though I reach for sugar most often, I consider myself sugar agnostic and believe there's a time and a place for all sweeteners. (Except for monk fruit. Get outta here.)

My goal with this book is to pass along the knowledge that I've picked up on over years of obsessing about texture and flavor, introduce you to some of my versions of classics as well as some unexpected formats and flavor combinations that I love, and help you celebrate special moments big and small. These recipes are meant for birthdays and first days of school, the action-packed days of harvest, and friends visiting from out of town who hopefully bring you Trader Joe's naturally colored candy-coated chocolates. There are one-bowl recipes to make with your kids and goodies to have in the cookie jar to snack on when the craving strikes. If you need an easy five-minute sweet, I've got some of those! If you want to fill a weekend making a sprinkle cake with homemade sprinkles and rainbow chips in the frosting, I've got that too!

So, from our sugar farm to your kitchen, here are more than one hundred ways to sweeten your life.

INGREDIENTS

Just like a great violinist can make even a toy violin sound good, you can make delicious baked goods using generic butter, inexpensive eggs, and imitation vanilla, so long as you are attentive to the process, ingredient amounts, and bake times. Fat and sugar taste great together, and that's just a reality of our human existence, so if the fanciest ingredients are not within your budget, you can absolutely compensate. At the same time, I will inform you when a splurge will indeed make a significant difference. (It's usually where cocoa and chocolate are involved, and sometimes where butter is involved.) But then again, there is a place in my heart for waxy grocery store milk chocolate, so don't let anyone tell you that you must sell your soul to fund a weekend baking activity. All the ingredients in this book are easy to find for me, either at my local grocery store or online, with the exception of the sugar beet in the muffins on page 166, and for that I have provided a substitute. So if I can find these items, I am willing to bet a layer cake that you can, too.

One blanket statement that I'd like to make about all ingredients: Buy the ones with the fewest number of ingredients listed. Nut butters should ideally contain just nuts and maybe a little salt, with no sugar or palm oil unless specifically directed in the recipe; coconut milk, just coconut, water, and some guar gum is okay; yogurt should include just milk, maybe cream, and probiotics—you get the picture.

BUTTER: Bake through this book and you will have kept a dairy farmer very, very happy. All the recipes will be great when made with generic brand unsalted butter. But for recipes like buttercreams, butter-based cakes, and anything with the absence of very many other ingredients and flavoring agents (like the Big Craggly Sugar Cookies on page 2), splurging on good-quality grass-fed European-style butter, which has a higher percentage of fat and a lower percentage of water, will give you the buttery flavor you deserve and take things to an otherworldly level. Brands I turn to are Kerrygold and Plugrà.

Salted butter is for toast and corn on the cob. Unsalted butter is what you want to bake with, so you can control the amount of salt that's going into your recipe. If a recipe calls for room temperature butter, know that this is critical. Leave your sticks out on the counter for a few hours or overnight. To speed this up if you're in a hurry, chop the butter into small pieces, scatter them on a plate or cutting board, and place in a sunny spot in your kitchen. Butter that is cold and cubed should be cut into roughly ½-inch cubes, which can easily be done by cutting your stick in half lengthwise, turning it on its side and then cutting it lengthwise again, and then cutting it widthwise in finger-size slices. The cubes should be uniform so that they incorporate evenly into your dough. You can always go the extra mile by cubing your butter first and then sticking it in the freezer while you assemble the rest of your ingredients.

CHOCOLATE AND COCOA: While there are certainly times when the waxy inexpensive grocery store chocolate achieves the mood you need (e.g., Hershey's milk chocolate in a s'more or on the Giant Almond Butter Blossoms on page 8), in general, bad semisweet, bittersweet, or dark chocolate can taste raisiny and derail your efforts to bake a good cookie. *So if there was one ingredient that I would urge you to splurge on in terms of your search effort and money, it is good chocolate and cocoa powder.* Milk chocolate is generally the exception, since inexpensive milk chocolate still tastes smooth and sweet. Most things that chocolate chips can do, hand-chopped chocolate chunks can do better. They take a little extra effort, but you earn an exciting variation of shards and pools of chocolate that taste great and look super cool.

Unsweetened cocoa powder and unsweetened Dutch-process cocoa powder can *sometimes* be used interchangeably (mainly in no-bake applications, such as in glazes and frostings) but not always, so do pay attention and use what's called for in the recipe's ingredients list. I prefer Dutch process for its bolder flavor and darker color, but it's also more expensive and a little harder to find. Unsweetened cocoa powder is acidic and reacts with baking soda for super-fluffy chocolate cakes. My chocolate and cocoa brands of choice are Valrhona, Guittard, Callebaut, and Tony's Chocolonely.

COCONUT MILK: Coconut milk is tasty, fatty, and a great alternative to dairy in cakes and as whipped cream. The only weird part about the world of coconut milk is that sometimes the ingredients lists are as long as novels. Avoid those. Get coconut milk that contains mostly just coconut and water; some guar gum is okay and makes for easier mixing. Unless you're directed to do otherwise (as in the Chocolate Peanut Butter Cake on page 216), measure coconut milk by opening up the can, mixing the solids and the liquids together until smooth, and then measuring. This way, everything comes out evenly.

COCONUT OIL: Over the years I have felt butter's self-confidence lessen, because more and more I won't allow butter to go anywhere without coconut oil babysitting it. Butter doesn't have anything to worry about, though, because its flavor remains one-of-a-kind perfect. But when it comes to texture, enhancing a butter-based baked good with oil is often a very good idea, since oil is 100 percent fat, and butter, at best, has a fat percentage in the mid-80s. More fat means more moisture. Coconut oil is also solid at room temperature, so it functions very similarly to butter when you're whipping it up with sugar, and it provides a touch more structure in the final result.

The subtle warm flavor of unrefined coconut oil also complements the flavor of butter without overpowering it. My taste buds have grown used to this depth, and now I sometimes feel like something's missing if I use refined coconut oil, but if you're anti-coconut flavor, then I won't hold your use of refined coconut oil against you. Store coconut oil in a dark spot at room temperature. Unless a recipe specifically asks that it be melted, coconut oil should be used at its softened room temperature state, which is similar in consistency to butter's room temperature state.

CREAM CHEESE: Acidity is as important in baking as it is in cooking, and cream cheese is my favorite way to get there because, unlike lemon or vinegar, it has a way of adding depth without steering you in an unwanted flavor direction. Cream cheese might be the single best ingredient to ever happen to baking. Its tang brings life and balance to sweets, and its texture keeps dough soft after it bakes. And of course, cream cheese frosting is the easiest, most direct way to make everyone love the layer cake you made, even if it looks like a four-year-old decorated it.

The only drawback of cream cheese is that it has the potential to spoil easily and so the official recommendation from the FDA is that cream cheese frosting should be stored in the refrigerator. Unfortunately, cakes lose their nice soft texture when cold, so it's important to plan ahead to bring your leftover cake to room temperature before serving.

I typically use blocks of Philadelphia cream cheese, or a generic brand. If you overbeat cream cheese, it can get runny, so pay attention to the directions when you're making cream cheese frosting. Usually you'll add it at the very end of the mixing process (versus at the beginning, as with the butter), then stop mixing when it's all combined and smooth. Also, applying this frosting on a freezer-cold cake is the least frustrating way to go, since cream cheese frosting is significantly droopier than buttercream.

EGGS: For my everyday baking I use inexpensive large eggs, because I go through so many of them and can't really detect the difference between a chocolate cake made with inexpensive eggs and one made with pricier organic eggs. I reserve the few eggs that our elderly chickens produce for omelets and egg sandwiches, where you can really taste the difference. Baked goods come together and bake up more evenly when you bring your eggs to room temperature first, but it's usually not as crucial as bringing your butter to room temperature (I have, however, specified "room temperature" when it is especially helpful), so if you forget to do it, don't fret. If you've got a few minutes, stick the eggs in their shells in warm water to take the chill off. Any time you're beating egg whites, give your bowl and whisk a wipe down and then make sure that absolutely no yolk gets into the mixture, because the yolk or any oil residue on a bowl or whisk could prevent the whites from beating up fluffily.

EXTRACTS: If I had a (literal) money tree or, just as good, a vanilla bean plant, I'd invest in vanilla bean pods for every single thing, even for schmearing onto my body as perfume. The warmth and flavor that vanilla bean provides is like cashmere for the soul. But, alas, my ability to keep plants alive is abysmal at best, so we make do. Vanilla beans earn their keep when they can be used in multiple forms. You can use the tiny dots in the pod and then throw the whole scraped pod into the pot when you're making things like jam or soda syrup so it infuses even more flavor, or repurpose it into homemade vanilla extract. But on a regular basis, I typically go with vanilla bean paste, which is a little less intense than whole vanilla beans but still very good. Vanilla extract is nice as a supporting or casual flavoring agent, and clear imitation vanilla has its place, too, for when you're wanting to mimic the nostalgic flavor of a boxed cake mix.

FLORAL SITUATIONS: Floral flavors are the best because they make you feel fancy and special without having to shave your legs and put on a nice dress. The main quirk I've found with using floral flavors in the kitchen is that each flower seems to have its own preferred form. Rosewater and orange blossom water are straightforward; you can find them in specialty stores or online and you can use them like extracts. (Store them in the dark cabinet with your extracts, too.) Lavender seems to be easiest to find in its dried form, in the tea or bulk section. Be very careful if you're buying it from a craft store because it might have been treated with nonedible chemicals and not be suitable for culinary use. Elderflower is consistently easy to find in its liqueur form (St-Germain is great) or as a cordial, which

is alcohol-free. And while I don't use violet very often except sometimes splashed into buttercream, I keep a bottle of Monin brand syrup on hand. If you're looking to use fresh flowers as decor, be sure to use only edible flowers that have not been treated with any chemicals. You can also always go about growing your own flowers to make flower waters and syrups and the like, but it requires a lot of patience.

FLOURS: The thought of lugging home an extra sack of flour for the sake of just a tiny percentage more of protein content might seem silly at first, but consider how you would feel if, say, the barista accidentally made your latte with skim milk instead of the whole milk you ordered. Depending on your personality, you might still just drink it; it would taste similar, it would still caffeinate you and do the job, but it would be a solid B- job, with definite room for improvement. That's the difference between using bread flour in an enriched dough versus all-purpose, what almond flour can do to a cookie bar, or what potato flour can do to a doughnut.

Getting specific about flours satisfies my need to find the absolute best textures out there. I typically use Dakota Maid or King Arthur (two places where Nick's wheat ends up!) and Bob's Red Mill (I particularly love their specialty flours, like potato flour and almond flour). Since I go through flours quickly, I keep them at room temperature in airtight containers. But if you anticipate you'll go through them slowly (more than a couple of months for whole wheat flour and nut flours, or more than six months for all-purpose), you can extend their lifespan in the fridge or freezer—just try to remember to bring them to room temperature before using.

FOOD COLORING: While I love using ingredients that contribute natural pretty colors whenever I can, including matcha powder, finely ground freeze-dried berries, beet juice, and turmeric, I also have all too much fun with food coloring. Opening up a new box of Americolor's Heavenly Seventy gel food coloring set is the grown-up version of ripping into a new big box of crayons on the first day of school. What joy! You don't need the Heavenly Seventy set if you're not looking to make a profession out of it, but I would recommend you order a few gel colorings online or get some from your craft store because they come in prettier colors than the grocery store liquids, and the fact that they're gels means that they're a bit more forgiving and won't alter the texture of your final product. My favorite Americolors are Pumpkin, Dijon, Peacock, Olive, Cypress, Wedgwood, Eggplant, Dusty Rose, and Chili Pepper.

FRUIT AND VEGGIES: Bake with apples, pumpkin, and squash in the fall; strawberry and rhubarb in the early summer; stone fruit in the late summer; and citrus in the winter. Using produce in its optimal season tastes best, celebrates the passing of time, and makes you all the happier when a new season comes around. Dried, freeze-dried, and jams are seasonless and always fair game.

HALVA: "Halva" simply means "sweet" in Arabic and can refer to a number of different confections. The style I refer to in this book is the one I grew up seeing at delis and in candy stores, a combination of sesame and sugar cooked into a crumbly situation that is my kryptonite. Eat it on its own, add it to cookies, sprinkle it in between cake layers, or crumble it into pies. The options are endless—but keep in mind that it will totally melt at high-enough temperatures, making it kinda disintegrate into a baked good and lose its texture. So if you're baking it into cookies, it's usually a good idea just to place larger chunks on the top before baking. I can find the standby Joyva brand at my local grocery store (in the fancy cheese section, randomly), which makes for a fine ingredient. If I'm eating halva on its own, I'm going with an online order to Seed + Mill or Hebel & Co, which take halva to a whole new level and stock a variety of flavors. Or you can make a peanut butter variety—see page 279.

MARZIPAN AND ALMOND PASTE: Marzipan and almond paste are Play-Doh-textured combinations of ground almonds and sugar. The only difference is the ratio of almonds to sugar; almond paste has more almonds and thus a purer taste. Because of this I prefer to use almond paste as an ingredient over marzipan, since whatever I'm making likely includes additional sugar. Although marzipan is usually a bit too sweet for me when used as an ingredient, it takes food coloring very easily and can be molded as decor. (Almond paste gets oily and weird if you try to add food coloring and mold it.)

Unless I'm serving just straight marzipan dipped in chocolate (which is delightful and should definitely be made from scratch), I buy marzipan and almond paste from the store. Both items can be found in the baking aisle. Odense and Solo are the most common brands sold in the United States, and they have yet to communicate on standard sizing: one is 7 ounces and one is 8 ounces. So if you're left with 1 ounce of stray almond paste, you now know why. Snack on it or be a rebel and add it to the recipe. If you have any trips to Germany planned, bring an extra suitcase to stock up on Niederegger, and plz bring some back for me.

MILK AND BUTTERMILK: Get outta here with your skim milk! Success in this book is defined by rich, moist delights, and to do that you've gotta use some fat. There are definitely instances where nondairy milks are okay, and even preferred, since they're so tasty. But in doughs and batters, fatty whole milk and tangy buttermilk and—if you're really going for it—heavy cream are what you want. That said, anytime the stand-alone word "milk" is listed in an ingredients list without specifying the fat percentage, you can assume that you can get away with using whatever milk you have on hand, dairy or nondairy. Unless otherwise specified, dairy for dough and batter is typically best when used at room temperature, but if you don't have the time, that's okay.

NUTS, SEEDS, AND THEIR BUTTERS: If you like nutty flavors, you have come to the right place! If you're allergic to nuts, you've also come to the right place, because my love for nuts is matched only by my love for sesame seeds. Plopping ground nuts, seeds, and their butters into cake batters and frostings is the best because they add flavor and moisture, usually without really altering the structure of the cake or frosting. In cookies, I love the chewiness they lend. For nut and seed butters, always use unsweetened for these recipes, and ideally those that have no added other stuff like palm oil (unless otherwise noted). If a recipe calls for unsalted nut butter but you only have salted, you can use it but reduce the added salt in the recipe by about half (or omit it entirely if it's a small quantity, like ⅛ teaspoon or a pinch). The brands of nut and seed butters I use are Crazy Richard's, Smucker's Natural, Target Good & Gather Natural, Ground Up PDX, and Justin's. For tahini, I use Seed + Mill, Soom, Whole Foods 365, Wild Harvest, and Al Arz. All nut and seed butters should be used at room temperature. (Store them that way, too, so they're easy to scoop and spread, unless you anticipate you'll go through them very slowly, in which case you can store in the fridge and then bring to room temperature before using.) For nuts and seeds, store them in the freezer to extend their lifespan. In some cases, I prefer using salted nuts since they add their own brand of flair; just don't dump the nuts out of the bag directly into the batter or dough, because all the salt from the bottom of the bag will come out, too, and oversalt whatever you're making. (I learned that one the hard way.)

Toast nuts in a 350°F oven until fragrant; begin checking around 6 minutes. Toast seeds in a skillet since they're smaller and can burn more easily, so you want to keep an eye on them (toast on medium-low heat, stirring frequently).

OIL: When using neutral oil in batters and doughs, use one that fits your preference and price point. It's providing texture, not flavor, and baked goods don't get so hot that you need to worry about a smoke point, so you could really use anything. I typically use canola oil, but soybean, peanut, and grapeseed are also reliable options (and they also have high smoke points, making them good options to deep-fry and pan-fry with as well). You could use olive oil in baked goods, but unless you're actually meant to taste the olive oil flavor, it's not worth the higher price. Vegetable oil can sometimes contain a blend of different oils, which is fine for baking, but for frying, double-check the ingredients to make sure that the specific oils it contains have a sufficiently high smoke point.

SALT: Salting your sweets is just as important as salting your savories, because salt brings out flavor and balances out sugar. It's incredible what a good pinch of salt can do to an otherwise cloying buttercream frosting. We are all at the mercy of Diamond Crystal kosher salt because it is the best salt with the purest flavor, and it should be used pretty much at all times always. It enhances everything without standing out with its saltiness, and if you happen to accidentally add a little too much to whatever it is you're making, all is not lost; it's forgiving in that way. The disadvantage to living out here on the farm is that I need to order Diamond Crystal online; luckily I have the sort of storage space that allows me to stockpile enough of it that I'd be okay in a zombie apocalypse. Hoard it. It won't go bad; it's literally thousands of years old. *If you must use a saltier salt (table salt or Morton), you will need to reduce the salt in these recipes (by half for table salt, a third for Morton). But avoid this if possible.*

The other salt you'll find in this book and in my pantry is Maldon flaky salt. Its strength is as a topping, because it adds tasty salty crunch and looks sparkly. Use flaky salt when you want to experience salt as soon as whatever you're eating hits your tongue. This is especially tasty when you're dealing with melted chocolate (which loves salt as much as caramel does).

SOUR CREAM: As someone who grew up in a household that only ever saw sour cream on latkes, I am now making up for lost time. It's *soooo* fatty, which brings so much moisture to your cakes. If your '90s upbringing has ingrained in you a deep fear of fat, too, you can explore subbing Greek yogurt, but consider giving the real thing a shot.

SPICES: Buy spices in small quantities because they lose their flavor over time. That bulk bag of cinnamon at the back of your spice cabinet is not aging like a fine wine or leather; it's getting weaker. Weak doesn't mean the spices are spoiled or anything, so they are safe to use; it just means that whatever you make with them won't have the flavor that it should, or you'll have to add so much of that spice that you'll end up noticing its unpleasant grainy texture. So try to replace them about every six months to a year. Spice brands I love are Burlap & Barrel, Diaspora Co., and New York Shuk.

SWEETENERS: The sugar I get at my grocery store is made from sugar beets since that's what we're surrounded by, and it's processed right in our area. The sugar you have access to might be made from sugarcane, it may be a blend of the two, or you might not even know. (Nutrition labels are not required to make the distinction between beet and cane sugar.) Beet sugar and cane sugar act essentially the same and can be used interchangeably. If you have a good nose or especially acute taste buds, you may be able to detect slight variations in smell and flavor, and you may notice very slight differences in performance. But in general, these differences are as subtle as can be. One perk of beet sugar is that, while cane sugar is sometimes processed using bone char from animal bones, beet sugar is not, making it 100 percent vegan friendly.

The three main sugars I use are granulated, powdered, and light brown sugar. In the colder months the vibe is also sometimes right for dark brown sugar and molasses. I also keep honey, corn syrup, date syrup, and maple syrup on hand for their different identities, sweetness levels, and strengths.

YEAST: Instant yeast is the most user-friendly yeast, period. End of discussion. You don't need to dirty up a whole additional vessel and sprinkle it over warm water and wait for five minutes and then wonder if the stuff on top is foamy enough. You just add it straight to all the other dry ingredients and move on with your day. If you bake a lot, get a big jar and keep it in the back of your fridge. If you bake a little, go with the packets, and still keep them in your fridge.

Make sure whatever you're preparing with yeast never comes into contact with hot liquid, because that will kill the yeast. Rather, the liquid should be assertively warm, between 105° and 110°F, which is actually warmer than you might expect. (I recommend using a thermometer to check the temp of your water for yeasted doughs just to be sure. Even just a few degrees can make a big difference.) If you have active dry yeast and want to use it up before converting yourself to the instant yeast lifestyle, proof it in whatever warm liquid (water or milk) is called for in the recipe along with a pinch of sugar, and add that mixture when you mix in the other wet ingredients.

YOGURT: In baking, yogurt does a swell job at enriching and balancing. It doesn't contribute as much fatty richness as sour cream, but it brings along its great tart flavor and slight bit of virtue by way of probiotics. Like milk, you'll get the tastiest results when you use full-fat yogurt. And when buying yogurt, peep at the ingredients list to ensure that there aren't added thickening agents such as pectin, which could throw off the texture of the final result. Chobani and Fage are my go-tos.

TOOLS

ACCORDION PASTRY CUTTER: Not so fast with that knife. Before you cut those bars, you've got to score them with an accordion pastry cutter (a bunch of pizza cutters on an adjustable attachment to give you evenly spaced parallel lines) so that all your bars will have perfect 90-degree angles and uniform sizing. This is 100 percent the most satisfying job in the kitchen there ever was. Swing by Bernie's to pick one up? Or order one online.

BENCH SCRAPER: Bench scrapers are great for dividing dough into portions (I prefer this over using a sharp knife directly on my countertop) and scraping up dough residue when I'm cleaning. They also assist in achieving smooth frosting edges on cakes. I typically prefer metal bench scrapers that have rulers on the end, because those come in handy.

BIG LIGHTWEIGHT MIXING BOWLS: Vintage glass bowls look so cute, but when you go to lift them to pour batter or wash them out, they start to feel clunky. And when you do that many times in a baking day, you'll start to understand the value of lightweight metal bowls. These inexpensive workhorses are very good at what they do, and you can find them easily online. They can also be inverted on the floor to make a drum set for your toddler.

BLENDER: A high-speed blender, of which Vitamix is the most reliable brand, is a completely different species from your average smoothie maker because it can eliminate any graininess from your purees. This is important when grinding fresh mint into the cake batter on page 222 and the shake on page 304. A high-speed blender is also better at making extra-creamy nut milk and blending ice and other frozen ingredients than its lower-powered counterpart. For recipes that don't require a lot of frozen ingredients or complete pulverization, like the tahini milkshake on page 296, a regular blender will suffice.

COOKIE SCOOP: Cookie scoops, ice cream scoops, dishers—whatever you want to call them—they're the scoops with the levers that come in all different sizes. They are very handy in the kitchen to help you easily get uniformly sized cookies, cupcakes, muffins, and so on. I use the ¼ cup scoop most often, as well as the 2 tablespoon and the ⅓ cup.

FINE ZESTER: A Microplane, which is the brand name for the best fine zester, is a specific but highly useful tool because it's very hard to mimic its job with a regular grater. Use it for zesting citrus and grating nutmeg (and Parmesan, ginger, and garlic). That's pretty much it. Like I said, very specific, but you'll use it a lot.

FOOD PROCESSOR: Many things that I often make in a food processor, like buttery pie crusts and scones, can be made by hand in a manner that is more time consuming yet therapeutic. Some jobs, though, like blending cookies or nuts into fine crumbs, ought to be done in a food processor. Cuisinart's Custom 14-Cup food processor is a standard powerful workhorse that I'd recommend to anyone who bakes regularly. If that's not in the cards yet, then a smaller lower-cost processor will blend your nuts and cookies just fine.

INSTANT-READ DIGITAL THERMOMETER: Bread that is beautifully golden on top might still be raw in the middle. Or it could be overbaked and dry. Or it might be perfect! How do you tell? An instant-read digital thermometer that you can stick right down into the center of that loaf and get a magic number is how you tell. Even just a few degrees can be the difference between a good loaf of bread and a fantastic moist loaf that is so soft but still fully baked. So stop standing there in front of your open oven burning your hands by trying to pick up a loaf and tap it on the bottom. Take the guesswork out of it and get a digital thermometer. I also reach for a digital thermometer when I'm temping warm water for yeast, confirming that doughnuts are cooked through in the fryer, cooking egg whites for meringue, and boiling jam. And of course, outside of sweets, it comes in handy for meat and fish. ThermaWorks makes quick-reading accurate digital thermometers at a range of price points, and I love them.

KITCHEN RULER: A simple ¼ inch is the difference between a thin, crispy cookie and a thick, soft cookie, and baking a cake in a 9-inch pan when you're supposed to bake it in an 8-inch pan will mean a different bake time, a sadder, shorter cake, and a worse eating experience. Don't leave anything up to chance, and don't trust your ballparking skills unless you're willing to bet your television on it. Put a metal ruler in your utensil crock and refer to it regularly, no matter how much the person standing next to you pokes fun at it.

KNIVES: The sharper the knife, the safer the knife. You don't typically do as much chopping for sweets as you do for savory cooking, but you should still aim to use a sharp, good-quality chef's knife for accuracy and to prevent slipping. A long serrated knife is also important to have for leveling cakes. I love Misen knives for their durability, price point, and sharpness.

MEASURING SPOONS AND CUPS: First of all, weigh your ingredients. But do have measuring spoons on hand for tiny amounts of ingredients (see page xxvi). Measuring cups are most often used in my kitchen not to actually measure but to scoop flour into the bowl that is set on the scale. Don't get fancy here; you'll be happier with multiple cheap plastic or metal sets than with one nice set.

OFFSET SPATULAS: Offset spatulas are the go-to for frosting cakes, but they also have so many other uses, like dislodging muffins from the pan, spreading brownie batter evenly, and just making a peanut butter and jelly sandwich. (Seriously, using a small offset for PB&J makes the process so ergonomically satisfying.) I also strongly prefer using them over a knife to loosen bars and cakes from the pans because the metal pans will dull your knives. A large offset and a small offset are both convenient to have on hand.

OVEN THERMOMETER: Ovens are like people with perfect skin who say their only secret is sunscreen and Vaseline. Don't trust them; they're lying. When you set the dial on your oven to 350°F, it aims for 350°F, and I believe that in its heart it wants to hit 350°F. But just like a baby aiming for their mouth with the spoonful of hummus, it regularly misses the mark, and that's how we get hummus in our belly button. No oven is immune to inaccuracy. My electric oven is on the mark 90 percent of the time, but she occasionally gets a hot flash (she's about fifty years old), so when that happens I need to turn the temp down to 325°F in order for her to hold at 350°F. I have a gas oven that regularly runs 100°F too hot. *One hundred!!!* It drives me bonkers. The dial is merely a suggestion; it's up to you to make sure you're baking your things at the proper temperature.

Luckily the solution costs just a few dollars. An oven thermometer, which you can get at a grocery store, home goods store, or hardware store, should be placed as close to the center of your oven as possible every time you use the oven, and you should refer to that, not the built-in dial, to determine your oven temperature.

PANS: Bake with sturdy, light-colored metal pans for the best, most consistent, evenly baked, and nicely shaped results. Glass and ceramic pans make fine casserole vessels and are acceptable to use in no-bake situations or layered dishes when you want to see the layers through the clear glass, but for cakes, bars, cookies, pies, muffins, and buns, your go-to should be light-colored metal. Any mention of a "sheet pan" in this book refers to a standard rimmed half sheet pan that is 13 × 18 inches; "quarter sheet pan" refers to a 9 × 13-inch rimmed baking sheet. I recommend only ever keeping and using standardized rimmed sheet pans because they stack and store easily, are sturdy, and don't curve over time. For square, rectangular, and loaf-shaped pans, I stick to pans that have corners that are as close to 90-degree angles as possible for aesthetic reasons; the corner slices will look way more uniform when baked in these. USA Pan and Nordic Ware make excellent baking pans.

In the case of cakes, bars, pies, rolls, and anything else where a batter or dough fills up the pan, it is super important to use the exact size of pan that is specified in the recipe. Even a 1-inch difference will drastically throw off your baking time and end results. (A vast majority of the pans required in this book are standard common sizes, and if they're not, I've provided alternatives.) For cookies, pan size is more forgiving since you're spacing out the cookies anyway. So if what you have is a little bigger or smaller than 13 × 18 inches, you can absolutely still use it. I will specify when a rimmed sheet pan is important; otherwise, flat sheets are fine.

PARCHMENT PAPER: Precut parchment sheets are one of the best-kept secrets of bakeries. They fit perfectly flat on standard rimmed sheet pans. Order them online, keep some in both quarter sheet and half sheet size, and never again wrestle with parchment paper that is curling or not the perfect size. If you make a lot of layer cakes, you can also look into getting precut circles. Also, parchment paper can and should be reused if it's clean and unburned.

PIPING BAGS: Piping bags are useful to have on hand even if you're not planning to pipe fancy buttercream roses anytime soon. They're the easiest way to pipe frosting neatly into the centers of sandwich cookies and onto cupcakes, and to fill doughnuts. Reusable and disposable piping bags can be found at craft stores and online.

PIPING TIPS: Piping tips are not truly necessary if you're just using piping bags to fill sandwich cookies and doughnuts. But if you're looking to pipe

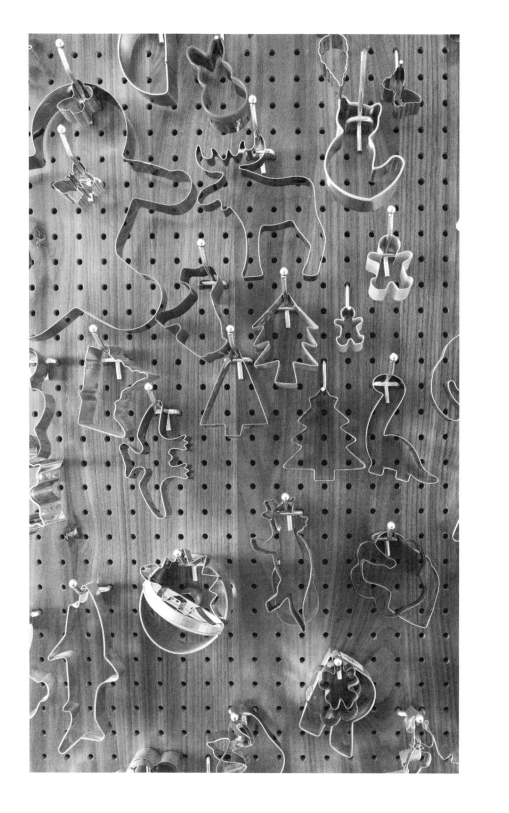

cake decorations, they are very fun to play around with, even if you have just a couple. Peruse your local craft store, start off with some round and star tips, and expand into petal and leaf tips if you want to explore further.

ROLLING PIN: I feel I can get the most power and control with my small 11-inch tapered rolling pin, but any rolling pin, or a wine bottle, will do.

ROTATING CAKE WHEEL: This is the first tool you should consider if you're looking to up your cake-decorating game. It will help you get super-smooth edges and uniform decor all the way around. You're likely to find inexpensive plastic varieties at your local craft store, but if you can spring for the heavy-duty metal variety, like Ateco brand, which is more likely found online or in specialty cooking stores, it will help your decorating confidence soar.

SCALE: See page xxxvii for my passionate plea that you weigh your ingredients. I don't care what scale you use as long as you use it, but a digital Taylor brand scale will make it more enjoyable. Weigh any quantity that is more than a tablespoon or two; for quantities less than that, I recommend measuring spoons because scales are not always accurate enough to differentiate between, say, ¼ and ½ teaspoon of baking soda, which can make a world of difference in your end result.

SIEVE OR SIFTER: I hate any step that even hints at being superfluous, but there are some occasions—such as when you make thicker butter-based cake batters that absolutely shouldn't be overmixed—when sifting the dry ingredients goes a long way in helping them incorporate into the batter swiftly and easily. It also helps to break up any clumps of leavening agents. If you've ever accidentally eaten a chunk of baking powder, you know that sifting is worth it just to avoid that situation. Since some digital scales will automatically turn off in the time it takes you to sift the full amount of your ingredients, here's what you should do: Set your bowl on the scale with the sieve sitting securely on the rim (oh yeah, ideally stick to long-handled sieves that have a little notch on the end that will facilitate this), then hit Tare. Scoop all the flour and other dry ingredients (except salt) into the sifter, so you're weighing before it's actually sifted, and then pick up the sifter and sift. Salt will not go through the little holes, so add it after sifting, and have a light touch when you quickly mix it in so you don't cause more clumps to form.

SPECIAL EQUIPMENT: Occasionally, special equipment is required to achieve the best results, but I have tried to keep these items to a minimum or limited them to items you can either substitute with success or inevitably find other uses for in your kitchen: A set of nesting circle cookie cutters have nice sharp edges to get clean-cut circles (other shapes or a drinking glass can stand in). Nut milk bags for straining out fine pulp from nut milk (a clean kitchen towel can also get the job done). Ice pop molds (I can never find mine so I usually grab a pack of Dixie cups from the grocery store). And a candy thermometer (an instant-read thermometer will work, but having the clip on a candy thermometer is indeed convenient with frying and heating sugar or meringue syrups).

SPICE GRINDER: Electric spice grinders are small, mighty little tools that are experts at grinding small, mighty little seeds, such as poppy seeds and sesame seeds, that would otherwise get passed over in a food processor. They're also useful for blending small quantities of ingredients like freeze-dried berries and Oreos, so you don't have to dirty up your food processor. As for spices, you will get the most flavor and lifespan out of them if you buy them whole and grind right before using them. Frankly, this isn't something that fits into my lifestyle right now, so unless it's nutmeg, mahlab, or cardamom, I'm usually buying my spices preground.

SPOONULAS: Spoonulas are flexible rubber spatulas that are cupped, which allows them to do everything that a regular rubber spatula can do, plus a whole lot more. They've almost completely replaced wooden spoons and regular rubber spatulas in my baking (and most of my cooking), and my prediction is that once everyone realizes how superior these are, regular rubber spatulas will become a thing of the past. The best spoonulas are silicone (so they're heat-safe) and are made from one long piece, not a piece of wood stuck into a piece of rubber in a hole that is destined to get icky and moldy. GIR brand, all the way. Get some big ones and some minis.

STAND MIXER: If you don't have a stand mixer, see if you can sweet talk a friend or grandparent into being allowed to babysit theirs for a while, because it's important here. With cake batter, frosting, and whipped cream, you can get by with a hand mixer; with cookie doughs, it's a little sloppy but it can be done. But when it comes to yeasted dough, I want you to make it in a stand mixer and here's why: You end up needing to dust the dough with too much flour when you knead it by hand. Too much flour can lead to dryness, and you know we don't want that.

WHISKS: Whisks that are on the smaller side are good at getting into the curves of bowls and doing a more thorough job of mixing. OXO Good Grips whisks are the best—I love the 9-inch size.

GENERAL NOTES

ON SUBSTITUTIONS: I have written these recipes to taste the absolute best I believe they can taste. That was my number one goal. The decisions I made in these recipes were in the interest of texture and flavor, period. I never thought to myself anything along the lines of "Huh, if I use less butter or sugar in this cake, I can eat a bigger piece." My brain doesn't work like that; I'd take one bite of the richest, most luxurious cake over a whole slice of a less luxurious cake any day. Quality over quantity. I did take reason and convenience into consideration as well to avoid things like, for example, having part of a can of coconut milk left over. If you're out of a certain ingredient or need to make a substitution for whatever reason, there is often a solution somewhere in your fridge or pantry, and if you're unsure whether a certain substitution will work, I recommend turning to reliable resources such as The Kitchn, King Arthur's website, and *Cook's Illustrated*. If you Google "How can I substitute X for Y?" you will find answers!

INGREDIENT TEMPERATURES: The temperature of individual ingredients when they're added to the batter, dough, or other mixture is important for the overall texture of a dish or baked good. Some ingredient temperatures are way more important than others; for example, always pay attention to butter temperature because cold and cubed butter functions very differently from soft or melted butter (one will give you a perfect flaky pie crust, the other a chewy, oily mess). Egg temperatures are more forgiving; while they should usually be brought to room temperature before using, it's not the end of the world if you forget and use them right out of the fridge. I'll specify "room temperature" when you should definitely make the effort, like when you're combining eggs with melted coconut oil or butter (they will seize if they come into contact with very cold eggs). Egg whites will whip best if they're at room temp. Nut butters should always be used at room temperature; they're hard and annoying out of the fridge (see page xxv for more). Heavy cream whips only if it's cold. Milk, sour cream, and heavy cream are also ideally added to a cake batter at room temperature, but, like eggs, it is not the end of the world if they're not.

WEIGH YOUR INGREDIENTS: You know the saying "Two Jews, three opinions"? (If you don't, now you do.) The other version of that is "One measuring cup, six amounts." Scoop 1 cup of powdered sugar six different times and you will, in fact, get six different amounts. Which will yield a cake with six different consistencies of glaze, six different aesthetics and sweetness amounts, an infinite number of inconsistent opinions from the people eating the cake—you get the picture. Flour is another ingredient that is extra prone to inconsistent measurements in cups, and that can leave you with a tough dough, a gummy cookie, or—*gasp*—a dry cake. The easiest way to eliminate this variation—and create a whole lot more ease in general in your baking—is to use a digital scale to weigh all your ingredients. Baking will not only become physically easier, as you no longer have to dig through drawers for a measuring cup (or wash one!) or stoop down to eye level for liquids, but you'll also have an easier time making half batches of recipes, dividing cake batters evenly among cake pans, and creating uniformly sized doughnuts and cookies. Fewer dirty dishes, more accurate results, and an overall more enjoyable baking experience? Have I not sold you???

If you make one big change this year, please let it be that you start to weigh your ingredients. It involves a short learning curve, but I promise you will not regret ripping off this Band-Aid.

To weigh your ingredients, place the bowl on the scale and hit the Tare button. (This takes the weight of the bowl itself out of the equation, so you're weighing just the ingredient.) Add the first ingredient. Hit Tare again and add the next ingredient, and so on and so forth. You can also label your mixing bowls with their weight, so if you've mixed a batch of cake batter and need to divide it up evenly, you can just put the whole bowl of cake batter on the scale and subtract the weight of the bowl to get the weight of the batter. Or if you want all your cupcakes to have the exact same amount of frosting, put each cupcake on the scale, hit Tare, and then frost.

Am I going overboard? I love weighing ingredients.

OVEN RACKS: Unless otherwise specified, the oven rack you're using should be placed in the center of the oven. If you're using more than one rack at once, they should be placed in the upper middle and lower middle of the oven.

BAKE TIMES: While the standard for writing bake times involves supplying a range of minutes, I pretty much always ignore the top end of that time frame, and I'd recommend you do, too. Instead, pay attention to the physical cues (Is it golden? Is it puffed? Has the internal temperature reached a certain number?) to determine whether something is done. If it gets to that top end of the time frame and it's not done, don't take it out of the oven! My format for giving bake times is to say when to start checking for doneness and also give you the physical cue that will tell you it's done. So set your timer and check quickly to see if it's done; don't let all the heat out of the oven. If it's done, pull it out. If it's not, use your best judgment to determine whether it needs another 30 seconds, another minute, or more, and repeat until it's done.

SERVING TEMPERATURES: The hotter things are, the sweeter they tend to taste. A cookie right out of the oven or a warm pudding that's about to be frozen into ice pops may taste too sweet—and a cold cake can taste dull. So pay attention to any serving-related directions when it comes to evaluating your baked goods, as tempting as it may be to shove a hot cupcake in your mouth. I mean, that's cool, too. Just know that that's not its final state.

ABOUT THE VERY SWEET ELEPHANT IN THE ROOM: I am well aware that sugar isn't the healthiest ingredient. But I also firmly believe that a life without sweet celebrations and special little treats simply lacks joy. I wholeheartedly strive for balance every day. I love my salads and my green juice, but I will also always cherish the moments in the evening when Bernie asks me for a treat and we sit down on the kitchen floor together, split a cupcake, and giggle about whatever funny thing happened that day. I am no nutritionist, but I believe that putting love and energy into making your own sweets and truly enjoying them with people you love is a whole lot healthier than restricting yourself in an extreme way or trying to become satisfied with artificially sweetened soda. These recipes represent probably only 4 percent of what I actually consume, but, in more ways than one, that is a very, very sweet 4 percent.

COOKIES

As a general rule, cookies should be big. Borderline comedic in size. They should be big enough that they bring you on a journey through their true range of textures: crispy edge, firm crust, and the promised land of a soft, chewy middle, with an expanse that can handle at least four full uninterrupted glorious bites before your teeth find those firm and crispy outer rings again at the other side. You should have time to settle in and immerse your mind and mouth in full cookie joy for long enough to forget about the stresses of the world around you before it's time to wrap things up. Cookies should be Mahler symphonies, not nursery rhymes.

Of course delicious exceptions exist, typically cookies that are meant to be texturally homogeneous throughout, such as crispy shortbreads and those Mexican wedding cookies that melt on your tongue as soon as you pop them into your mouth. There's even an exception in this chapter, the Red Bean Newtons. But as a texture-first person who is always chasing chewiness, it's the big, craggly, rustic disks and the thick-as-hockey-pucks soft cutouts that make me remember why I'm grateful to be alive during a time that stand mixers exist.

Making really big cookies presents some logistic considerations. Someone will inevitably say, "Oh my, these are big, I couldn't possibly eat this much." I'm sorry. To them you can explain that the other half will still be good tomorrow because, thanks to its large size, it has enough moisture that it can sit for a bit on the counter. They're built for gnawing on over the course of a couple of days. Or you can plan to have them ready after long days of physical work (such as farming!) when you have room in your stomach and need the extra calories. Or you can consider splitting a cookie with a friend, because a huge gooey chocolate chip cookie broken down the equator is better than a small cookie, for the reasons I just mentioned. Just please don't bake these smaller and put the soft, chewy, expansive middle at risk.

Following are a handful of favorites from the two areas of my life that contain the most cookies: harvest time, when I keep a stock of cookie dough in the freezer to bake off daily and send out in tractors to be gobbled by dirt-dusted hands; and Bernie's, where our Potato Chip Chocolate Chip Cookies fly out the door.

BIG CRAGGLY SUGAR COOKIES

These cookies look dumb and boring, and they're going to be last to get picked for the team. Look at them. They're just, like, nothing cookies. But stay with me, please. The farmers who eat them every year for harvest in their tractor lunches will be the first to tell you that they're quite the opposite of nothing cookies. They are your childhood, but thicker, butterier, and better.

I'm not always going to expect you to splurge on the nice European-style grass-fed butter, but it's going to make a difference here since there are so few other ingredients. You'll notice the butter flavor. Also, before you make these, forget everything you know about making cookies. Or rather, promise to read these directions carefully and trust them when they say don't let the butter soften, don't cream the butter and the sugar to incorporate air, don't give them enough space on the pan, and don't be alarmed when the mixture looks all wrong. *Do* plan some time because even though butter doesn't need to soften, the dough still needs a rest period before baking in order for the cookies to maintain their outrageous thickness. The resulting cookie for giants is crisp on the outside, chewy on the inside, and almost scone-like (perhaps his grandma was a scone).

MAKES 6 GIGANTIC (*GIGANTIC*) COOKIES

1 cup (226 grams) cold very-good-quality, ideally European-style, unsalted butter, cut into ½-inch cubes

1½ cups (300 grams) granulated sugar

2 large cold eggs

2 teaspoons pure vanilla extract

3 cups (390 grams) all-purpose flour

1½ teaspoons baking powder

1 teaspoon kosher salt

1 tablespoon (13 grams) turbinado or coarse sanding sugar, for sprinkling (totally fine to sub granulated sugar if that's all you have)

IN a stand mixer fitted with a paddle, combine the butter and granulated sugar and mix on low until just combined and pasty, 1 to 2 minutes. A few butter bits that are still intact are totally okay. You want to avoid beating any unnecessary air into this mixture so the end result is extra dense and delightful. Add the eggs one at a time, continuing to mix on low until they're just incorporated, scraping down the sides of the bowl occasionally with a rubber spatula, and then mix in the vanilla. The mixture will look curdled

and weird; it's supposed to look this way. Stop the mixer and sprinkle in the flour. Sprinkle the baking powder and salt evenly over the flour and give the dry ingredients a rough little whisk to combine, then turn the mixer on low to incorporate the dry ingredients into the wet ingredients. Use the spatula to scrape down the sides as needed to ensure all the ingredients get combined evenly.

LINE a rimmed sheet pan with parchment paper. This pan needs to fit in the freezer, so if you can make room for a standard half sheet pan, use that; otherwise go with a smaller sheet pan for now and plan to transfer the cookies to a half sheet pan to bake.

DIVIDE the dough into 6 large (170-gram) balls and flatten them slightly into 3-inch disks. Place them on the sheet pan, spacing them evenly apart, and sprinkle with the turbinado sugar. Freeze for at least 2 hours or up to 3 months. If you plan to bake these within a day, there's no need to cover the pan, but if you plan to keep the dough frozen for longer, then wrap tightly with plastic wrap.

WHEN ready to bake, preheat the oven to 375°F. If you froze the cookie dough disks on a small sheet pan, transfer them to a parchment-lined half sheet pan, spacing them evenly apart. They'll seem close, a little too close, but cookies that smooch in the oven have a special charm.

BAKE until the bottoms are golden and the tops are lightly golden; begin checking for doneness at 26 minutes. If you have an instant-read thermometer handy, aim for an internal temperature of around 180°F. Let cool on the pan for 10 minutes and then transfer to a wire rack and/or your mouth.

STORE in an airtight container at room temperature. These are best within a few days of baking. After that they'll be okay for a few more days, but if you think you won't finish the batch in that time, I'd recommend keeping unbaked disks of dough in the freezer and baking one or two at a time whenever the craving strikes.

OKAY, fine, you can make these smaller. They will be less good. Just scoop 12 slightly rounded ¼-cup (85-gram) balls, flatten, sprinkle with turbinado sugar and freeze them as instructed above, and bake them all on one sheet for like 22 minutes. Don't say I didn't tell u so.

CHEWY FROSTED TAHINI COOKIES

Dessert textures, ranked:

1. Chewy
2. Moist, dense cakey
3. Buttery flaky
4. Moist, fluffy cakey
5. Bready
6. Ice creamy
7. Crumbly
8. Liquid/drinkable
9. Creamy fruity or creamy cheesy
10. Crunchy
11. Saucy
12. Soaked
13. Airy

Dessert toppings, ranked:

1. Frosting
2. Streusel
3. Glaze
4. Whipped cream
5. Crunchy sugar
6. Syrup
7. Chocolate, chunks or shaved
8. Chocolate ganache
9. Sauce, like fruity ones or caramelly things

Dessert flavors, ranked:

1. Tahini, halva, marzipan, pistachio (tie)
2. All other nuts and seeds
3. Rose and chocolate (tie)
4. Other florals
5. Coconut, cardamom, cinnamon (tie)
6. Mint, other fresh herbs
7. Fruits that are cherry, plum, strawberry, peach, blueberry
8. Vegetables like sweet potato, squash, and corn
9. Citrus
10. Coffee
11. Other fruits except bananas, which are unranked because they are so gross

Put the three number ones together and what do you get? Chewy frosted tahini cookies. So, am I saying that these knockout tahini-laced cookies are my favorite recipe in this book? Maybe!!

MAKES 14 BIG COOKIES

1 cup (226 grams) unsalted butter, room temperature

1 cup (224 grams) tahini (peanut butter or almond butter would also work)

1 cup (200 grams) plus 6 tablespoons (75 grams) granulated sugar, divided

1 cup (200 grams) packed light brown sugar

2 large eggs

2 teaspoons pure vanilla extract

3½ cups (455 grams) all-purpose flour

1 teaspoon ground cinnamon

2 teaspoons baking soda

1½ teaspoons kosher salt

Frosting and assembly

¾ cup (170 grams) unsalted butter, room temperature

2 cups (240 grams) powdered sugar

Good pinch of kosher salt

4 ounces (113 grams) cream cheese, room temperature

Toasted sesame seeds, for sprinkling

PREHEAT the oven to 375°F. Line two sheet pans with parchment paper.

IN a stand mixer fitted with a paddle, combine the butter, tahini, 1 cup (200 grams) of the granulated sugar, and the brown sugar and mix on medium until creamy and combined, 1 to 2 minutes. Add the eggs one at a time, mixing well after each addition, followed by the vanilla, scraping down the sides of the bowl with a rubber spatula as needed to ensure that everything combines evenly. Stop the mixer and sprinkle in the flour. Sprinkle the cinnamon, baking soda, and salt evenly over the flour and give the dry ingredients a rough little whisk to combine, then turn the mixer on low to incorporate the dry ingredients into the wet ingredients.

PLACE the remaining 6 tablespoons (75 grams) granulated sugar in a shallow bowl or rimmed plate. Scoop out heaping ¼-cup (100-gram) balls, roll them in the sugar to coat, and place them on the sheet pans, 3 inches apart, spacing out 5 balls of dough per pan. (You'll need to bake in batches.) No need to flatten the balls.

BAKE until lightly browned and set around the edges but still a little gooey in the middle; begin checking for doneness at 13 minutes. Let cool on the pans for 5 minutes and then transfer to a wire rack to cool completely. For the best results, bake one pan at a time in the center of the oven. If you're short on time, you can bake two pans at a time, on the upper middle and lower middle racks, switching each pan to the other rack and rotating the pans 180 degrees a little over halfway through the bake time.

TO make the frosting, in a stand mixer fitted with a paddle, combine the butter, sugar, and salt and mix on low until you're confident that sugar won't fly everywhere, then gradually increase the speed to medium high and continue to mix until smooth and fluffy, 1 to 2 minutes. Reduce the speed to medium, add the cream cheese, and mix until just combined. Scrape down the sides of the bowl as needed to ensure that everything combines evenly.

FROST the cookies with big rustic swoops. Sprinkle with sesame seeds.

STORE in an airtight container in the refrigerator for up to a week or so. Unbaked balls of dough that have been rolled in sugar can be stored in an airtight container in the freezer for up to 3 months. Bake from frozen and add a few minutes to the baking time.

GIANT ALMOND BUTTER BLOSSOMS

My unattractive trait of tinkering with perfection is on full display here because if there ever was a cookie that didn't need reinventing, it is the object of Bernie and Grandma's annual holiday tradition, Grandma's peanut butter blossoms. Bernie unwraps the Hershey's kisses and does so well at not eating them all while Grandma makes the dough. They stick the kisses onto the cookies together, then deliver a few to me when Bernie comes home for naptime. It's the most pure and joyful holiday tradition, and like I said, there was no reason for me to tinker—other than that I wanted more chewy innards in every bite. And an even distribution of chocolate. And then I accidentally made them with every single kind of nut butter in our pantry and realized I craved the almond butter ones the most. See? This is why I don't sleep.

MAKES 14 BIG COOKIES

1 cup (226 grams) unsalted butter, room temperature

1 cup (224 grams) unsweetened unsalted almond butter (peanut butter or tahini would also work)

1 cup (200 grams) plus 6 tablespoons (75 grams) granulated sugar, divided

1 cup (200 grams) packed light brown sugar

2 large eggs

2 teaspoons pure vanilla extract

3½ cups (455 grams) all-purpose flour

1 teaspoon ground cinnamon

2 teaspoons baking soda

1½ teaspoons kosher salt

Seven 1.55-ounce milk chocolate bars, halved (preferably Hershey's)

PREHEAT the oven to 375°F. Line two sheet pans with parchment paper.

IN a stand mixer fitted with a paddle, combine the butter, almond butter, 1 cup (200 grams) of the granulated sugar, and the brown sugar and mix on medium until creamy and combined, 1 to 2 minutes. Add the eggs one at a time, mixing until combined after each addition, followed by the vanilla, scraping down the sides of the bowl with a rubber spatula as needed to ensure that everything combines evenly. Stop the mixer and sprinkle in the flour. Sprinkle the cinnamon, baking soda, and salt evenly over the flour and give the ingredients a rough little whisk to combine, then turn the mixer on low to incorporate the dry ingredients into the wet ingredients.

PLACE the remaining 6 tablespoons (75 grams) granulated sugar in a shallow bowl or rimmed plate. Scoop heaping ¼-cup (100-gram) balls and roll them in the sugar to coat. Place them on the prepared sheet pans, 3 inches apart, spacing out 5 balls of dough per pan. (You'll need to bake in batches.) No need to flatten the balls.

BAKE until lightly browned around the edges; begin checking for doneness after 11 minutes.

REMOVE from the oven and carefully top each cookie with a chocolate bar half, pressing firmly so the cookies crack around the edges. Return to the oven and bake for another 2 minutes. Let cool on the pans for 5 minutes and then transfer to a wire rack to cool completely. For the best results, bake one pan at a time in the center of the oven. If you're short on time, you can bake two pans at a time, on the upper middle and lower middle racks, switching each pan to the other rack and rotating the pans 180 degrees a little over halfway through the bake time.

STORE in an airtight container at room temperature. These are best within a few days of baking. After that they'll be okay for a few more days, but if you anticipate that you won't finish the batch in that time, I'd recommend freezing unbaked balls of dough and baking one or two at a time whenever the craving strikes. Unbaked balls of dough that have been rolled in sugar can be frozen in an airtight container for up to 3 months. Bake from frozen and add a few minutes to the baking time.

PISTACHIO SANDWICH COOKIES

These are basically a pistachio variety of homemade Nutter Butters. You could do your morning weight workout with these heavy cookies and promptly balance it all out by eating the cookies. But it would be worth it, obviously, for the chew and the nuttiness and the big, satisfying mouthful. These are cookies that mean it. You could make this recipe with other nuts, but the love story between the pistachios and creamy lemon filling here is real. Add to it the pretty green color in both the cookie and the nuts around the filling and you've got A-plus tone-on-tone aesthetic.

MAKES 14 BIG SANDWICH COOKIES

Cookies

1 cup (226 grams) unsalted butter, room temperature

1 cup (200 grams) plus 6 tablespoons (75 grams) granulated sugar, divided

1 cup (200 grams) packed light brown sugar

2 large eggs

1 teaspoon pure vanilla extract

½ teaspoon pure almond extract

1 cup (128 grams) finely ground unsalted roasted pistachios (if you only have salted, reduce the added salt to 1 teaspoon)

3½ cups (455 grams) all-purpose flour

2 teaspoons baking soda

1½ teaspoons kosher salt

Filling and assembly

1 cup (226 grams) unsalted butter, room temperature

½ cup (64 grams) finely ground unsalted roasted pistachios (if using salted, reduce the added salt to just a pinch)

2 cups (240 grams) powdered sugar

⅛ teaspoon kosher salt

Zest of ½ lemon

½ teaspoon pure almond extract

About ¼ cup (32 grams) coarsely or finely ground pistachios, for rolling

PREHEAT the oven to 375°F. Line two sheet pans with parchment paper.

IN a stand mixer fitted with a paddle, combine the butter, 1 cup (200 grams) of the granulated sugar, and the brown sugar and mix on medium until creamy and combined, 1 to 2 minutes. Add the eggs one at a time, mixing well after each addition, followed by the vanilla and almond extracts, scraping down the sides of the bowl with a rubber spatula as needed to ensure that everything combines evenly. Stop the mixer and sprinkle in the pistachios and flour. Sprinkle the baking soda and salt evenly over the pistachios and flour and give the ingredients a rough little whisk to combine, then turn the mixer on low to incorporate the dry ingredients into the wet ingredients.

PLACE the remaining 6 tablespoons (75 grams) granulated sugar in a shallow bowl or rimmed plate. Scoop out rounded 2-tablespoon (50-gram) balls, roll them in the sugar to coat, and place on the prepared sheet pans, 3 inches apart, spacing out 7 cookies per pan. (You'll need to bake these in batches.) Flatten to a ½-inch height with a fork to create a crosshatch pattern.

BAKE until very lightly browned; begin checking for doneness at 9 minutes. Let cool on the pans for 5 minutes and then transfer to a wire rack to cool completely. For the best results, bake one pan at a time in the center of the oven. If you're short on time, you can bake two pans at a time, on the upper middle and lower middle racks, switching each pan to the other rack and rotating the pans 180 degrees a little over halfway through the bake time.

TO make the filling, in a stand mixer fitted with a paddle, combine the butter, pistachios, powdered sugar, salt, and lemon zest and mix on low until you're confident that sugar won't fly everywhere, then gradually increase the speed to medium high and continue to mix until smooth and fluffy, 1 to 2 minutes. Add the almond extract and mix to combine. Scrape down the sides of the bowl as needed to ensure that everything combines evenly.

SPREAD or pipe the undersides of half the cookies with a thick layer of filling going almost all the way to the edges and sandwich with the underside of the remaining cookies, pressing so the filling smooshes to the edges. Roll the edges in the ground pistachios.

STORE in an airtight container in the fridge for up to a week or so. Unbaked balls of dough that have been rolled in sugar can be stored in an airtight container in the freezer for up to 3 months. Bake from frozen and add a few minutes to the baking time.

THICK SOFT CREAM CHEESE CUTOUTS

There are two secrets that make these cutout cookies not just your typical cutout. One is that you are going to promise me you'll make these with a kitchen ruler. Never is a need for a kitchen ruler more crucial than when making cutout cookies, because the difference that just a ¼ inch of thickness makes to a sugar cookie is like the difference between mashed potatoes and a potato chip: same bones, two totally different animals. There is a place in this world for a thin crispy cutout cookie, but this farm and this book aren't it. The other secret, the cream cheese, contributes a brightness that is not always as present as it should be at the cookie swap. It also helps keep the cookies soft.

I like to decorate these with a thick glaze and chocolate frosting in the style of my childhood favorite, the iconic smiley face cookie, but they're also great with just a thick layer of straight cream cheese frosting.

MAKES ABOUT 12 BIG COOKIES

Cookies

1 cup (226 grams) unsalted butter, room temperature

4 ounces (113 grams) cream cheese, room temperature

1 cup (200 grams) sugar

1 large egg

1 teaspoon pure vanilla extract

½ teaspoon pure almond extract

3⅔ cups (477 grams) all-purpose flour, plus more for dusting

1 teaspoon baking powder

¾ teaspoon kosher salt

Glaze

2 cups (240 grams) powdered sugar

2 tablespoons (40 grams) light corn syrup

3 tablespoons (45 grams) milk, plus a little more as needed

½ teaspoon pure vanilla extract

¼ teaspoon pure almond extract

Pinch of kosher salt

Yellow food coloring

Frosting

2 tablespoons (28 grams) unsalted butter, room temperature

1 ounce (28 grams) cream cheese, room temperature

½ cup (60 grams) powdered sugar

2 tablespoons (10 grams) unsweetened cocoa powder

Pinch of kosher salt

¼ teaspoon pure vanilla extract

IN a stand mixer fitted with a paddle, combine the butter, cream cheese, and sugar and mix on medium until pale and fluffy, 2 to 3 minutes, scraping down the sides of the bowl occasionally with a rubber spatula. Beat in the egg, then add the vanilla and almond extracts. Stop the mixer and sprinkle in the flour. Sprinkle the baking powder and salt evenly over the flour and give the dry ingredients a rough little whisk to combine, then turn the mixer on low to incorporate the dry ingredients into the wet ingredients. Pile the dough onto a piece of plastic wrap, pat it into a disk, wrap it up, and refrigerate it for at least 2 hours or up to a couple of days.

WHEN you're ready to bake the cookies, preheat the oven to 350°F. Line two sheet pans with parchment paper.

ROLL out the dough on a lightly floured surface to just a hair shy of ½-inch thickness (use your kitchen ruler!), dusting with a little more flour as needed to prevent sticking. Using a circle cookie cutter that's around 3¼ inches in diameter, cut out circles and transfer them to the prepared sheet pans, 1 inch apart. Reroll the scraps and cut out more circles.

BAKE until the cookies are just thinking about starting to turn brown around the bottom edges; begin checking for doneness at 12 minutes. Let cool on the pans for 5 minutes and then transfer to a wire rack to cool completely. For the best results, bake one pan at a time in the center of the oven. If you're short on time, you can bake both pans at once, on the upper middle and lower middle racks, switching each pan to the other rack and rotating the pans 180 degrees a little over halfway through the bake time.

TO make the glaze, in a medium bowl, combine the powdered sugar, corn syrup, milk, vanilla and almond extracts, the salt, and a couple of drops of food coloring. Stir in additional milk little by little as needed until the glaze is the consistency of a runny glue. Set a wire rack on a rimmed sheet pan to catch any glaze drips. Dip the cookies into the glaze so it coats the top and sides, let the excess drip off, and place on the prepared rack. Let the glaze set, about 45 minutes.

TO make the frosting, in a stand mixer fitted with a paddle, combine the butter, cream cheese, powdered sugar, cocoa, and salt and mix on low until you're confident that sugar won't fly everywhere, then gradually increase the speed to medium high and continue to mix until smooth and fluffy, 1 to 2 minutes. Add the vanilla and mix to combine. Scrape down the sides of the bowl as needed to ensure that everything combines evenly. Transfer to a piping bag and snip off the end to form an opening that's about ⅜ inch. Pipe smiley faces onto the cookies and . . . smile!

STORE in an airtight container in the refrigerator for a week or so. Bring to room temperature before serving. Frosted cookies can also be stored in an airtight container in the freezer for up to a few months; thaw at room temperature.

SOLO FROSTING OPTION

You might not be in a smiley face mood, or you may very well be in a smiley face mood but simply have more creative aspirations for your cookies. This smooth, sweet, easy-to-make frosting pipes well, spreads well, and takes food coloring well. It does not harden like royal icing, but you will not miss that feature as you bite down on a thickly applied layer of this on a cream cheese cutout. Emphasis on the "thickly."

½ cup (113 grams) unsalted butter, room temperature

2 cups (240 grams) powdered sugar

Good pinch of kosher salt

½ teaspoon pure vanilla extract

¼ teaspoon pure almond extract

Food coloring, optional

4 ounces (113 grams) cream cheese, room temperature

Sprinkles, optional

IN a stand mixer fitted with a paddle, combine the butter, powdered sugar, and salt and mix on low until you're confident that sugar won't fly everywhere, then gradually increase the speed to medium high and continue to mix until smooth and fluffy, 1 to 2 minutes. Reduce the speed to medium, add the vanilla and almond extracts and the food coloring (if using), and mix to combine. Add the cream cheese and mix until just combined. Scrape down the sides of the bowl as needed to ensure that everything combines evenly.

SPREAD or pipe the frosting onto the cookies and decorate with sprinkles as desired.

POTATO CHIP CHOCOLATE CHIP COOKIES

Had I married into the farm two generations earlier, I like to think I would have been potato farmer royalty—a potato princess—because Nick's grandpa was not only a potato farmer but president of the Red River Valley Potato Growers Association. And contrary to what Idaho wants you to think, the potatoes from this region are outrageously tasty. This validates both my rabid potato chip habit and my frequent use of potatoes in baking (see the Buttered Potato Dough on page 114). When we opened Bernie's, we knew we needed a special locally inspired chocolate chip cookie, so we looked straight to the potato. Everyone knows that a salted chocolate chip cookie is ideal, but when the salt is delivered in the form of a potato chip? Forget about it! The chips soften slightly and become a little chewy, so don't worry about scratching the inside of your mouth. This cookie is Bernie's bestseller for a reason.

And I should mention that all the rules of good chocolate chip cookies apply here: Hand chopping your chocolate is much better than using uniform chips because it gives you a variety of shards and melty pools. The better the chocolate, the better the cookie. Unbaked balls of dough can be frozen for cookie emergencies; in fact, their flavor and texture will improve when they chill a bit before baking. (I am rarely that patient.) And chocolate loves an extra boost of salt, so do not interpret the flaky salt on top as optional. Also, this is controversial, but I believe chocolate chip cookies are best not when they're still warm out of the oven but when they're fully set and have arrived at their final texture.

MAKES 14 BIG COOKIES

1 cup (226 grams) unsalted butter, melted and cooled slightly

1½ cups (300 grams) packed light brown sugar

½ cup (100 grams) granulated sugar

2 large eggs

1 tablespoon (13 grams) pure vanilla extract

½ teaspoon pure almond extract

3 cups (390 grams) all-purpose flour

1½ teaspoons kosher salt

1 teaspoon baking powder

1 teaspoon baking soda

12 ounces (340 grams) very-good-quality bittersweet (66% cacao) chocolate, coarsely chopped

2 heaping cups (57 grams) ruffled potato chips, plus a few more for topping

Flaky salt

PREHEAT the oven to 350°F. Line two sheet pans with parchment paper.

IN a large bowl, whisk together the butter, brown sugar, and granulated sugar to combine. Whisk in the eggs one at a time, mixing well after each addition, and then whisk in the vanilla and almond extracts. Sprinkle the flour evenly over the surface of the mixture, followed by the salt, baking powder, and baking soda. Give the dry ingredients a rough little whisk to combine, then whisk them into the rest of the batter until mostly incorporated. (You'll finish up incorporating the dry ingredients as you mix in the chocolate and potato chips.) Switch to a rubber spatula and fold in the chocolate, shards and all (reserving some bigger chocolate pieces for the tops of the cookies), and the potato chips. No need to be careful with the potato chips; they know they're going to get a little crushed.

SCOOP heaping ¼-cup (100-gram) balls of dough onto the prepared sheet pans, 3 inches apart, spacing out 5 balls of dough per pan. (You'll need to bake in batches.) Top with the reserved chocolate, additional chips (broken into pieces), and a little flaky salt.

BAKE until puffed and set around the edges but still gooey in the middle; begin checking for doneness after 12 minutes. If you have an instant-read thermometer handy, aim for an internal temperature of around 175°F. Let cool completely on the pans (or sneak a warm one if you *must*). For the best results, bake one pan at a time in the center of the oven. If you're short on time, you can bake two pans at a time, on the upper middle and lower middle racks, switching each pan to the other rack and rotating the pans 180 degrees a little over halfway through the bake time.

STORE in an airtight container at room temperature. These are best within a few days of baking. After that they'll be okay for a few more days, but if you anticipate that you won't finish the batch in that time, I'd recommend freezing unbaked balls of dough and baking one or two at a time whenever the craving strikes. Unbaked balls of dough can be frozen in an airtight container for up to 3 months. Bake from frozen and add a few minutes to the baking time.

CHOCOLATE CHOCOLATE HALVA WALNUT COOKIES

Even though chocolate cookies predate the invention of chocolate chip cookies, chocolate chip cookies still manage to win the popularity contest, and that's just not right. With chocolate cookies you get more chocolate flavor, a fudgier texture, an edgier appearance, and a good-lookin' color contrast when you add halva, as in this cookie. This version is inspired by the underdog—but best—Levain cookie, chocolate peanut butter, and incorporates walnuts because walnuts are good with chocolate in a cookie. (I'll give the Levain chocolate chip walnut cookie that win.) A tricky thing about putting halva in a cookie is that it melts when baked and becomes invisible (even though you can still taste it). So visually and texturally, you're doing yourself and your Instagram feed a favor by mixing only some of the halva into the dough and then poking big ridiculous chunks of it into the top of the cookies.

MAKES 12 BIG COOKIES

1 cup (226 grams) unsalted butter, melted and cooled slightly

1 cup (200 grams) packed light brown sugar

½ cup (100 grams) granulated sugar

2 large eggs

1 tablespoon (13 grams) pure vanilla extract

2 cups (260 grams) all-purpose flour

1¼ cups (100 grams) Dutch-process cocoa powder

1½ teaspoons kosher salt

1 teaspoon baking powder

1 teaspoon baking soda

8 ounces (226 grams) halva, any flavor, coarsely chopped, divided

4 ounces (113 grams) white chocolate, coarsely chopped, divided

4 ounces (113 grams) roasted unsalted walnuts, coarsely chopped

Flaky salt

PREHEAT the oven to 350°F. Line two sheet pans with parchment paper.

IN a large bowl, whisk together the butter, brown sugar, and granulated sugar to combine. Whisk in the eggs one at a time, mixing well after each addition, and then whisk in the vanilla. Sprinkle the flour and cocoa evenly over the surface of the mixture, followed by the salt, baking powder, and baking soda. Give the dry ingredients a rough little whisk to combine, then whisk them into the rest of the batter until mostly incorporated. (You'll finish up incorporating the dry ingredients as you fold in the mix-ins.) Switch to a rubber spatula and fold in half of the halva, half of the chocolate, and all of the walnuts.

SCOOP heaping ¼-cup (100-gram) balls of dough onto the prepared sheet pans, 2½ inches apart, spacing out 6 balls of dough per pan. Flatten slightly and top with the remaining halva and white chocolate, and a pinch of flaky salt. It'll look a little crowded on top of these cookies but they'll spread.

BAKE until puffed and set around the edges but still gooey in the middle; begin checking for doneness after 12 minutes. If you have an instant-read thermometer handy, aim for an internal temperature around 175°F. Let cool completely on the pans (or sneak a warm one if you *must*). For the best results, bake one pan at a time in the center of the oven. If you're short on time, you can bake both pans at once, on the upper middle and lower middle racks, switching each pan to the other rack and rotating the pans 180 degrees a little over halfway through the bake time.

STORE in an airtight container at room temperature. These are best within a few days of baking. After that they'll be okay for a few more days, but if you anticipate that you won't finish the batch in that time, I'd recommend freezing unbaked balls of dough and baking one or two at a time whenever the craving strikes. Unbaked balls of dough can be frozen in an airtight container for up to 3 months. Bake from frozen and add a few minutes to the baking time.

EARL GREY BLACK-AND-WHITE COOKIES

This is a combination of two of the best Jewish foods of all time, one a bit more niche than the other: black-and-white cookies and the used tea bag.[*] This black-and-white variation maintains 95 percent of its black-and-white identity: It's a cake that's eaten like a cookie, it's got two glazes and the chocolate glaze is slightly thicker than the lighter glaze, and the manner in which you eat it is begging to be overthought. The 5 percent difference, from the addition of Earl Grey, is not a big departure from the vanilla and hint of lemon profile of the classic, since Earl Grey itself has such wonderful sweet citrus notes; it's just different enough to make you tilt your head and notice it in a new light. *Did you do something different to your hair? Have you worn that lip color before?* It's still your old friend the B and W, but with a new and interesting story to tell.

Before you make these, I need you to listen to me. Black-and-white cookies are inherently on a fast track to dryness; these thin, flat cakes will overbake in a matter of seconds. This ingredients list does everything in its power to set you up for moist success by including coconut oil, heavy cream, and sour cream, but *you* have to be the one to bring it home. Watch these like a hawk in your oven, do not let the tops get brown, and remove them as soon as they are *just* set on top. You've got this.

MAKES 14 COOKIES

Cookies

2 cups (260 grams) all-purpose flour

1 teaspoon baking powder

¼ teaspoon baking soda

1 tablespoon (6 grams) Earl Grey tea leaves (from about 3 tea bags)

½ teaspoon kosher salt

½ cup (120 grams) sour cream, room temperature

½ cup (120 grams) heavy cream, room temperature

2 teaspoons pure vanilla extract

6 tablespoons (85 grams) unsalted butter, room temperature

¼ cup (50 grams) unrefined coconut oil, room temperature

1 cup (200 grams) sugar

Zest of 1 orange

2 large eggs, room temperature

[*] *Source: "The 100 Most Jewish Foods: A Highly Debatable List" by Alana Newhouse for* Tablet *magazine*

Glaze

3 Earl Grey tea bags

6 tablespoons (90 grams) hot water

2½ cups (300 grams) powdered sugar

2 tablespoons (40 grams) light corn syrup

½ teaspoon pure vanilla extract

⅛ teaspoon kosher salt

¼ cup (20 grams) Dutch-process or unsweetened cocoa powder

PREHEAT the oven to 375°F. Line two sheet pans with parchment paper.

IN a medium bowl, sift together the flour, baking powder, and baking soda and then lightly stir in the tea leaves and salt and set aside. In a separate medium bowl or large measuring cup, whisk together the sour cream, heavy cream, and vanilla and set aside.

IN a stand mixer fitted with a paddle, combine the butter, coconut oil, sugar, and orange zest and beat on medium high until pale and fluffy, 3 to 4 minutes. Add the eggs one at a time, mixing well after each addition and scraping down the sides of the bowl with a rubber spatula as needed to ensure that everything combines evenly. Reduce the speed to low and add the flour mixture and cream mixture in three alternating additions, mixing until mostly combined. Turn off the mixer and use your spatula to finish up the mixing by hand, making sure to combine thoroughly without overmixing.

USE an ice cream scoop to scoop ¼-cup (65-gram) blobs of the batter onto the prepared sheet pans, 3 inches apart, spacing out 5 blobs per pan. (You'll need to bake in batches.)

BAKE until the bottoms are just beginning to brown and a toothpick inserted into the center comes out clean; begin checking for doneness after 10 minutes. If they're not yet done, check frequently until they are because you want to avoid overbaking at all costs. Let cool on the pans for 5 minutes and then transfer to a wire rack to cool completely. For the best results, bake one pan at a time in the center of the oven. If you're short on time, you can bake two pans at a time, on the upper middle and lower middle racks, switching each pan to the other rack and rotating the pans 180 degrees a little over halfway through the bake time.

TO make the glaze, steep the tea bags in the hot water for 5 minutes, then remove the tea bags, squeezing out any excess liquid. In a medium bowl, whisk together the powdered sugar, 3 tablespoons (45 grams) of the tea, the corn syrup, vanilla, and salt. If the mixture is too thick to spread, whisk in more tea a tiny bit at a time until it's thin enough. Spread a thin layer of the glaze over half of the flat bottom of each cookie. To the remaining glaze, add the cocoa powder and another 2 teaspoons of tea. It should be ever-so-slightly thicker than the first glaze but still spreadable. If the glaze is too thick to spread, add more tea a tiny bit at a time until it's thin enough. Cover the other halves of the cookies with the chocolate glaze (to really get authentic, overlap the white glaze with the chocolate glaze by a hair) and let set at room temperature, at least 30 minutes.

STORE in an airtight container between layers of parchment at room temperature. These are best within a day or two of baking but will keep for up to 3 days.

CHERRY MAHLAB LINZERS

Mahlab is a spice that's made using the pit of a St. Lucie cherry, and it's common in Greek and Middle Eastern cuisine. All I can say is thank goodness that whoever first accidentally ate a nonpitted St. Lucie had a palate that was fine-tuned enough to recognize a good thing, because its flavor, which whispers a subtle combination of almond and cinnamon, is so special. The first time I had it, it tasted unique and comforting at the same time, like the feeling of a soft new sweater that was unfamiliar yet cozy and destined to become a go-to. It's unusual to find it in Western baking (although it can be found easily online and in some international grocery stores), but I hope that changes because it gets along easily with other flavors that we know and love, like almond and vanilla. Hence these linzers! These are just great classic linzers made memorable by your extra effort to track down mahlab.

You'll get the most flavor out of your mahlab if you buy it as whole seeds and grind it fresh in a spice grinder. What will you do with the rest of your mahlab after you make these cookies? Use it like you'd use any other spice, particularly in cookie doughs, cake batters, or yeasted doughs that lean in the direction of vanilla, almond, or cinnamon flavor profiles. Just don't do anything silly like eating a whole big spoonful of it in one sitting because, like apple seeds, mahlab contains small amounts of cyanide. Luckily a little goes a long way (the flavor, not the poison).

MAKES 18 TO 20 SANDWICH COOKIES

1 cup (226 grams) unsalted butter, room temperature

1 cup (200 grams) granulated sugar

1 large egg

1½ teaspoons pure vanilla extract

¼ teaspoon pure almond extract

2 cups (260 grams) all-purpose flour, plus more for dusting

1 cup (112 grams) fine almond flour

1 tablespoon (5 grams) finely ground mahlab

¾ teaspoon baking powder

¾ teaspoon kosher salt

About ¾ cup (240 grams) cherry jam

Powdered sugar, for dusting

IN a stand mixer fitted with a paddle, combine the butter and granulated sugar and beat on medium high until pale and fluffy, 2 to 3 minutes. Add the egg and beat to combine, then beat in the vanilla and almond extracts. Stop the mixer and sprinkle in the all-purpose flour and almond flour. Sprinkle the mahlab, baking powder, and salt evenly over the flours and give the dry ingredients a rough little whisk to combine, then turn the mixer on low to incorporate the dry ingredients into the wet ingredients. Divide the dough in half, shape each half into a disk, wrap tightly in plastic wrap, and refrigerate for at least 2 hours or up to 3 days.

WHEN ready to bake, preheat the oven to 350°F and line two sheet pans with parchment paper.

WORKING with one dough disk at a time, roll it out on a lightly floured surface, until it's about 3⁄16 inch thick (or a scant ¼ inch thick), dusting with a little more flour as needed to prevent sticking. Using a circle cookie cutter that's around 2¾ inches in diameter, cut out circles and transfer them to the prepared sheet pans, 1 inch apart, rerolling the scraps as needed. (You'll need to bake in batches.) Cut little shapes out of half of the circles; these can either be slightly smaller circles or teeny-tiny stars, clouds, or other shapes. These little cutouts can be added to the dough scraps to reroll.

BAKE until golden; begin checking for doneness after 10 minutes. Let cool on the pans for 5 minutes, then transfer to a wire rack to cool completely. For the best results, bake one pan at a time in the center of the oven. If you're short on time, you can also bake two pans at a time, on the upper middle and lower middle racks, switching each pan to the other rack and rotating the pans 180 degrees a little over halfway through the bake time.

SPREAD the flat bottoms of the cookies that don't have the cutouts with a heaping teaspoon of jam. Top with the cookies that do have the cutouts and then dust with powdered sugar.

STORE in an airtight container at room temperature for 4 to 5 days.

CINNAMON SUGAR CHOCOLATE RUGELACH

Rugelach was always my mom's care package cookie when I was in college, which is why I think I now prefer to eat them when they're a few days old and have lost the outer-crisp pep in their step. You can taste the cream cheese in the dough better this way, which is the secret best part about rugelach. My mom always made her rugelach with chocolate chips that hung out in whichever direction they pleased, but when I got my hands on her recipe, I saw the opportunity for a perfect emoji-worthy swirl using melted chocolate. The important steps here are to make sure the chocolate rolled dough has enough time in the fridge to firm up so you can get your very clean cuts, and to use a ruler when slicing the logs. You want the nuggets to be wide enough that they sit firmly upright without tipping over and big enough that they afford you crisp outer edges and a soft buttery interior that is best when just a tad underdone. Toppings here can run the gamut from sugar to sprinkles to nuts, but cinnamon sugar satisfies those like me who occasionally go for the second-best rugelach flavor.

MAKES 24 COOKIES

Dough

2½ cups (325 grams) all-purpose flour, plus more for dusting

¼ cup (50 grams) sugar

1 teaspoon kosher salt

1 cup (226 grams) cold unsalted butter, cut into ½-inch cubes

8 ounces (226 grams) cold cream cheese, cut into rough cubes

2 large egg yolks (reserve the whites for the egg wash)

1 teaspoon pure vanilla extract

Filling and assembly

10 ounces (283 grams) milk chocolate, finely chopped, or 1⅔ cups chips

Egg wash: reserved egg whites beaten with a splash of water

2 tablespoons (25 grams) sugar

1 teaspoon ground cinnamon

TO make the dough, in a food processor, pulse together the flour, sugar, and salt. Scatter in the butter and cream cheese, distributing it all over the dry ingredients, and pulse until the butter and cream cheese are pea size. Add the egg yolks and vanilla and continue pulsing until larger clumps start to form. (You can also do this by hand in a big bowl, using your fingers to incorporate the butter and cream cheese by smashing and rubbing it in with the dry ingredients until it's evenly dispersed and pea size. Add the egg yolks and vanilla and use a spatula to gently mix into a shaggy mass.)

TURN out onto a work surface and press the dough together with your hands. Divide the dough in half, shape each half into a rectangle, wrap tightly in plastic wrap, and refrigerate for at least 1 hour or up to 2 days.

TO form the rugelach, melt the chocolate in a double boiler or in a bowl in the microwave in 30-second increments, stirring after each, until smooth. Set aside to cool briefly while you roll out the dough.

WORKING with one dough rectangle at a time, roll it out on a lightly floured surface into a wide rectangle, 9 × 18 inches, dusting with a little more flour as needed to prevent sticking. Use an offset spatula to spread half of the chocolate on the dough in a thin even layer, leaving a 1-inch border along the long edge that's farthest from you. (Try to work kind of quickly so the chocolate doesn't harden.) Brush the border with a thin layer of egg wash and, starting with the long end closest to you, roll the dough into a long, tight log and set aside seam side down. Repeat with the remaining dough and melted chocolate. (Stick the remaining egg wash in the fridge because you'll use it again before the rugelach slices go into the oven.)

TRANSFER the logs to a cutting board or sheet pan and refrigerate for about an hour to allow the chocolate to get good and firm. (Depending on your fridge space, you might want to cut the log in half so you're dealing with four shorter logs as opposed to two really long ones.)

WHEN ready to bake, arrange oven racks in the upper middle and lower middle positions and preheat the oven to 350°F. Line two rimmed sheet pans with parchment paper.

COMBINE the sugar and cinnamon in a small bowl. Brush the logs with a thin layer of egg wash and sprinkle liberally with the cinnamon sugar. Cut the logs into 1½-inch slices and transfer them to the prepared sheet pans, 2 inches apart.

BAKE until golden brown on top; begin checking for doneness at 25 minutes. Switch each pan to the other rack and rotate the pans 180 degrees a little over halfway through the bake time. (You might notice that the cookies seem to sweat and leak some fat while in the oven; this is completely normal.) Let cool on the pans for 5 minutes and then transfer to a wire rack to cool completely.

STORE in an airtight container at room temperature for 4 to 5 days. I actually like these best a day or two after they're made.

RED BEAN NEWTONS

Although my Chicago suburban upbringing had me as obsessed with Lunchables and Dunkaroos as the next '90s kid, my family's frequent weekend trips to Chinatown introduced me to a whole world of Asian desserts that I find equally nostalgic, like red bean–flavored sweets. The first time I tasted red bean paste was at the dim sum restaurant I always went to with my dad and sister. That inaugural bean paste was buried inside the spherical fried sesame ball that looked like it was having the most fun on the dessert cart. My sister, already a bean-in-dessert aficionado, explained to me that it kind of tasted like peanut butter. After very hesitantly taking a tiny bite, I discovered that she was actually right and not just lying to me like every time she had tried to get me to eat a dried chile pepper out of the kung pao chicken by telling me it was a dehydrated carrot. It was more pasty than peanut butter and pleasantly sweet, and it's a taste I'll always associate with those big jolly weekend dim sum outings.

In a decidedly less deep fried but just as nostalgic situation, here is red bean paste wrapped up in a soft cakey cookie pulled from the Fig Newton. The texture of the cookie and the bean paste feel like they were meant for each other because they are similarly soft, allowing for one clean bite. If modern atrocities like brownie batter hummus have made you anti-beany sweets, forget all of that and start anew with red bean paste, please.

You can purchase red bean paste online or in Asian grocery stores. There are two main types, chunky and smooth. Either works here. You can also make it from scratch, which is what I typically do.

MAKES ABOUT 32 COOKIES

½ cup (113 grams) unsalted butter, room temperature

½ cup (100 grams) packed dark brown sugar

2 tablespoons (42 grams) honey

1 teaspoon toasted sesame oil

2 large eggs

1½ cups (195 grams) all-purpose flour, plus more for dusting

½ cup (67 grams) whole wheat flour

½ teaspoon kosher salt

¼ teaspoon baking soda

1½ cups (390 grams) Red Bean Paste (recipe follows, or store-bought)

Sesame seeds, for topping

IN a stand mixer fitted with a paddle, combine the butter, brown sugar, honey, and sesame oil and beat on medium high until creamy, 2 to 3 minutes. Add one of the eggs and beat to combine. Separate the second egg and add the yolk to the mixer, reserving the egg white for the egg wash. Continue mixing until the mixture is light and creamy, a minute or so. Stop the mixer and sprinkle in the all-purpose flour and whole wheat flour, and then sprinkle the salt and baking soda evenly over the flours. Give the dry ingredients a rough little whisk to combine, then turn the mixer on low to incorporate the dry ingredients into the wet ingredients. Divide the dough in half, shape each half into a rectangle, wrap tightly in plastic wrap, and refrigerate for at least 2 hours or up to 2 days.

WHEN ready to bake, arrange oven racks in the upper middle and lower middle positions and preheat the oven to 350°F. Line two sheet pans with parchment paper. Place the red bean paste in a piping bag or zip-top bag with a 1-inch opening snipped (this is a large opening; measure it with a ruler) and set aside.

WORKING with one dough rectangle at a time, roll it out on a lightly floured surface into a rectangle that is about 14 inches long, 8 inches wide, and ⅛ inch thick, dusting with a little more flour as needed to prevent sticking. Cut down the middle lengthwise into 2 thin rectangles. Pipe a 1-inch ribbon of red bean paste down the center of each. Fold one side over the filling, then fold again in the same direction so the filling is locked in and the seam is face down. Use your hands to gently flatten to ½ inch thick and square off the sides. Repeat with the other rectangle. Carefully transfer the two rectangles to a prepared sheet pan, spacing them 3 inches apart. Repeat to make 2 rectangles with the other half of the dough and set them on the other prepared sheet pan.

BEAT the reserved egg white with a splash of water and brush a thin layer over the logs. Sprinkle with sesame seeds and bake until lightly golden; begin checking for doneness at 16 minutes. Switch each pan to the other rack and rotate the pans 180 degrees a little over halfway through the bake time. Remove from the oven and let cool on the pans for 10 minutes. Carefully transfer the logs to a cutting board and use a sharp knife to slice them into 1½-inch pieces. Let cool and eat.

STORE in an airtight container at room temperature for up to 3 days.

RED BEAN PASTE

Making red bean paste from scratch is a satisfying process that begins with the same steps it takes to cook any other bean and ends with a jam-like step, caramelizing sugar to create a thick substance that you can plop onto ice cream (like the snow ice cream on page 288) or even spread onto toast. If you feel moved to embellish, try adding a pinch of five-spice, some orange zest, or other cozy flavors.

MAKES ABOUT 1½ CUPS

1 cup (200 grams) dried adzuki beans

½ cup (100 grams) sugar

Pinch of kosher salt

PLACE the beans in a medium bowl and cover with a couple of inches of water. Soak overnight at room temperature. Drain the beans, transfer them to a large pot, and cover with a couple of inches of water. Bring to a boil, reduce to a simmer, and cook, covered, until very soft, 1 to 2 hours, adding more water if necessary.

DRAIN the beans, return them to the pot, and mash with a potato masher or fork. Add the sugar and salt and cook over medium-low heat, stirring and mashing continuously with a stiff rubber spatula, until all the liquid has evaporated and the mixture is thick and pasty. Remove from the heat and let cool completely.

MAKE this up to 3 days in advance and keep in an airtight container in the fridge until ready to use.

BIG SOFT CHOCOLATE SANDWICH COOKIES

"Don't be silly; we can make those from scratch," my mom once said in response to my request to buy Oreos at the grocery store when I was a kid. These were the most formative words that anybody ever said to me. Our homemade Oreos were mind-bogglingly good. That one simple sentence set off a lifelong curiosity about making everything from scratch and discovering that, with the exception of Chicago-style deep-dish pizza, homemade is always better. I know that this concept isn't rocket science, and I would have figured it out sooner or later, but this cookie has always symbolized that truth for me. These get their specialness from their mighty size, in both diameter and thickness, and soft cookie texture (thanks, cream cheese dough), which makes for a nice clean bite. I believe these are best when they're cold and kept in the fridge, which extends their lifespan by at least a few days. And, like most things with cocoa powder, they'll be their best selves when they're made with the best cocoa.

Want to try a mint version? Add 1 teaspoon of mint extract to the filling.

MAKES ABOUT 12 BIG SANDWICH COOKIES

Cookie

2¾ cups (358 grams) all-purpose flour, plus more for dusting

1¼ cups (100 grams) Dutch-process cocoa powder

1½ teaspoons kosher salt

1 teaspoon baking powder

1 teaspoon instant espresso powder

1 cup (226 grams) unsalted butter, room temperature

4 ounces (113 grams) cream cheese, room temperature

1¼ cups (250 grams) sugar

1 large egg

1 teaspoon pure vanilla extract

Filling

½ cup (113 grams) unsalted butter, room temperature

2 cups (240 grams) powdered sugar

Pinch of kosher salt

½ teaspoon pure vanilla extract

4 ounces (113 grams) cream cheese, room temperature

IN a medium bowl, whisk together the flour, cocoa, salt, baking powder, and espresso powder and set aside.

IN a stand mixer fitted with a paddle, combine the butter, cream cheese, and sugar and beat on medium high until pale and fluffy, 2 to 3 minutes. Add the egg and vanilla and mix to combine. Reduce the speed to low and add the dry ingredients, mixing until just combined. Divide the dough in half, shape each half into a disk, wrap tightly in plastic wrap, and refrigerate for at least 2 hours or up to 2 days.

WHEN ready to bake, preheat the oven to 350°F. Line two sheet pans with parchment paper.

WORKING with one dough disk at a time, roll it out on a lightly floured surface to just a hair shy of ¼ inch thick, dusting with a little more flour as needed to prevent sticking. Using a circle cookie cutter that's around 3¼ inches in diameter, cut out circles and transfer them to the prepared sheet pans, 1 inch apart.

BAKE until just set and no longer shiny on top; begin checking for doneness at 8 minutes. Let cool on the pans for 5 minutes and then transfer to a wire rack to cool completely. For best results, bake one pan at a time in the center of the oven. If you're short on time, you can bake two pans at a time, in the upper middle and lower middle positions, switching racks and rotating the pans 180 degrees a little over halfway through the baking time.

TO make the filling, in a stand mixer fitted with a paddle, combine the butter, powdered sugar, and salt and mix on low until you're confident that sugar won't fly everywhere, then gradually increase the speed to medium high and mix until smooth and fluffy, 1 to 2 minutes. Reduce the speed to medium, add the vanilla and cream cheese, and mix until just combined. Scrape down the sides of the bowl as needed to ensure that everything combines evenly.

USING a piping bag or a zip-top bag with the corner snipped off, pipe the filling almost to the edges on the bottoms of half the cookies and sandwich with the other half. Press gently to adhere. These will take a couple of hours to set, but you should definitely eat one immediately.

STORE in an airtight container in the refrigerator for up to a week. I love them cold straight out of the fridge.

CHOCOLATE-DIPPED BROWN SUGAR ANIMALS

For a short but suspensefully delicious period of time, the Girl Scouts sold a cookie that had the ability to unseat the Thin Mint as the clear winner of the Girl Scout cookie pack. It was a large chocolate-dipped square with animals embossed in it, and it was Keebler adjacent in flavor. Its crispy texture was balanced by the thin layer of creamy chocolate on the back, and it came in a pack of one column in a hot-pink box. I really liked them. But not enough people did. Or Thin Mints felt threatened. So away they went. I forgot about them until one day when Bernie and I were making cutout cookies and she demanded that we use brown sugar instead of granulated sugar. The result had just enough brown-sugary depth to bring me back to those Girl Scout cookies. They weren't the same; they were thicker and bigger—and they were better!

We tinkered, adding some cinnamon to enhance the brown sugar but stopping before going full-on gingerbread cookie. Some of the gingerbread cookie energy is there, but these should not be exclusive to Christmastime. They are like a secular gingerbread cookie. A nondenominational gingerbread cookie. A gingerbread cookie for basic Jews like me.

MAKES ABOUT 20 LARGE COOKIES

1 cup (226 grams) unsalted butter, room temperature

1⅓ cups (267 grams) packed dark brown sugar

2 large eggs

1 tablespoon (13 grams) pure vanilla extract

3⅓ cups (433 grams) all-purpose flour, plus more for dusting

1⅓ cups (149 grams) fine almond flour

1 teaspoon baking powder

1 teaspoon kosher salt

½ teaspoon ground cinnamon

10 ounces (283 grams) semisweet chocolate, finely chopped, or 1⅔ cups chips

3 tablespoons (38 grams) refined coconut oil

IN a stand mixer fitted with a paddle, combine the butter and brown sugar and mix on medium until creamy and combined, 1 to 2 minutes. Add the eggs one at a time, mixing well after each addition, and then mix in the vanilla, scraping down the sides of the bowl with a rubber spatula as needed to ensure that everything combines evenly. Stop the mixer and sprinkle in the all-purpose flour and almond flour. Sprinkle the baking powder, salt, and cinnamon evenly over the flours and give the dry ingredients a rough little whisk to combine, then turn the mixer on low to incorporate the dry ingredients into the wet ingredients. Divide the dough into two disks, wrap tightly in plastic wrap, and refrigerate for at least 1 hour or up to 2 days.

WHEN ready to bake, preheat the oven to 350°F. Line two sheet pans with parchment paper.

WORKING with one dough disk at a time, roll it out on a lightly floured surface to a scant ½-inch thickness (use your kitchen ruler!), dusting with a little more flour as needed to prevent sticking. Using a large cookie cutter (or cutters) that's somewhere in the ballpark of 3 inches, cut out shapes and transfer them to the prepared sheet pans, 1 inch apart. Reroll the scraps and cut out more shapes.

BAKE until the cookies are slightly puffed up and golden around the bottom edges; begin checking for doneness at 14 minutes. Let cool on the pans for 5 minutes, then transfer to a wire rack to cool completely. For best results, bake one pan at a time in the center of the oven. If you're short on time, you can bake two pans at a time, in the upper middle and lower middle positions, switching racks and rotating the pans 180 degrees a little over halfway through the baking time.

MELT the chocolate and coconut oil in a shallow dish in the microwave in 30-second increments, stirring after each, until smooth. Dip the bottoms of the cookies into the chocolate and place them on parchment paper or a silicone mat. Let set at room temperature for about an hour or in the refrigerator for about 15 minutes. (If it's particularly warm in your kitchen, go the refrigerator route.)

STORE in an airtight container at room temperature for 4 to 5 days.

ITALIAN RAINBOW COOKIE DOUGH

Deep in the far reaches of my freezer—next to the plastic-wrapped piece of Bernie's first birthday cake and the clown cones from *Molly on the Range*—are a few containers of rainbow cookie dough that Cookie DŌ's founder, Kristen Tomlan, sent to me when Bernie was born, after we had collaborated on that flavor a month before. Bernie's face is on the container, so obviously I could never get rid of it, and also the limited-edition dough was so good I was afraid of eating it because then I probably would have eaten it all and then there wouldn't have been any left. That's the logic I followed for four years, until I finally sheepishly asked Kristen for the recipe. She obliged and here it is, in all its sweet, almondy, million-times-easier-to-make-than-actual-rainbow-cookies glory. You can eat it as raw dough, play with it with your kids and not worry about them getting raw flour cooties up their noses, bake them up into thick chewy gooey cookies, or do all three!

Thank you, Kristen!!!!

MAKES ABOUT 3 CUPS DOUGH OR 7 BIG COOKIES

2 cups (260 grams) all-purpose flour

1 teaspoon cornstarch

½ teaspoon baking powder

½ teaspoon baking soda

½ teaspoon kosher salt

½ cup (113 grams) unsalted butter, room temperature

2 tablespoons (25 grams) sugar

½ heaping cup (150 grams) gently packed almond paste

¼ cup (60 grams) pasteurized egg whites (can be found in a carton near the eggs at the grocery store)

1 teaspoon pure vanilla extract

Red and green food coloring

6 ounces (170 grams) semisweet chocolate, coarsely chopped, or 1 cup chips

¼ cup (80 grams) raspberry jam

TO heat-treat the flour, place the flour in a microwaveable bowl. Microwave on high for 30 seconds at a time, stirring well after each interval, until an instant-read thermometer registers at least 165°F when stuck into the flour in several different spots. This should take about 2 minutes total, but all microwaves are different. If some flour sticks to the sides of the bowl, just leave it there (we have extra, don't worry)! Break up any chunks and let the flour cool completely. You can speed up the cooling process in the fridge or freezer.

TO make the dough, measure 1¾ cups (228 grams) of the heat-treated flour and place it in a medium bowl. Discard the rest. Add the cornstarch, baking powder, baking soda, and salt and whisk together. Set aside.

IN a stand mixer fitted with a paddle, combine the butter, sugar, and almond paste and beat on medium high until pale and fluffy, scraping down the sides of the bowl occasionally with a rubber spatula, 5 to 6 minutes. Add the egg whites and vanilla and mix until fully incorporated, 2 to 3 minutes. Reduce the speed to low and gradually add the dry ingredients, mixing until just combined. Scrape down the sides of the bowl with a rubber spatula as needed to ensure that everything combines evenly. Remove the bowl from the mixer and steal a lick right from the paddle. 😋

DIVIDE the cookie dough evenly into three small bowls. Add a few drops of red food coloring into one bowl and mix. Do the same with the green. Leave one bowl as is. Mix in the chocolate, dividing it evenly among the three bowls.

IF you're planning on eating this just as cookie dough, continue with the next step. If you want to bake the dough into cookies, skip ahead to the baking step.

IN a large bowl, place the three colors of cookie dough and dollop in the raspberry jam. With a stiff spoon or rubber spatula, swirl to combine the doughs and jam, but be careful not to mix too much. You want to see the three distinct colors of the cookie dough and ribbons of the raspberry jam. To serve, divide into bowls, add a scoop to the top of an ice cream cone, or dig right in.

STORE in an airtight container in the refrigerator for up to a week or in the freezer for up to 3 months.

TO bake cookies, preheat the oven to 375°F. Line a sheet pan with parchment paper.

GRAB a ¼-cup cookie scoop and scoop a little red, a little white, and a little green dough into the scoop, filling it a little over the top (to yield 100 grams). Use your finger to press a hole halfway through the middle of the scoop. Add ½ teaspoon of jam to the hole and pinch the dough shut so that the jam is completely covered by cookie dough on all sides. Remove the filled cookie dough from the scoop, roll it into a ball, and place it on the prepared sheet pan. Repeat to make more balls, placing them 2½ inches apart.

BAKE until the cookies are set on the outside and your desired gooeyness on the inside; begin checking for doneness at 12 minutes. Let the cookies cool on the pan for 5 minutes, then destroy.

STORE in an airtight container at room temperature (or in the fridge if they're excessively gooey in the center) for up to 3 days.

JUMBO THUMBPRINTS

FOR PEOPLE WITH JUMBO THUMBS LIKE ME

Life with gigantic thumbs can be a total drag on days when all I want to do is hold up a plate of food for Instagram but can't because I'm embarrassed about my gigantic thumbs. It also makes doing the crossword on my phone really challenging. I can't wear cute press-on nails because they never come in my size, and I'm triggered every time I watch the *Mean Girls* scene where they're all standing in Regina George's room talking about their body insecurities. *My dang thumbs!* I think to myself every single time.

But do you know what my thumbs are *so great* at? Big huge soft thumbprint cookies!

These are essentially an improved version of my favorite hamantaschen, which are extra soft, have lots of personality from the cream cheese, and exercise nice restraint when it comes to the sugar. This thumbprint shape is a much better format though, because who wants to wrestle with fussy triangle-shaped cookies, only to have half of them flop open in the oven, when they're not commanded to by a millennia-old tradition? Also, you get a more doughy cookie this way.

1 cup (226 grams) unsalted butter, room temperature

4 ounces (113 grams) cream cheese, room temperature

⅓ cup (67 grams) plus ¼ cup (50 grams) sugar, divided

1 large egg yolk

1½ teaspoons pure vanilla extract

2¼ cups (293 grams) all-purpose flour

½ teaspoon kosher salt

½ cup (160 grams) jam of choice

IN a stand mixer fitted with a paddle, combine the butter, cream cheese, and ⅓ cup (67 grams) of the sugar and mix on medium until creamy and combined, 1 to 2 minutes. Add the egg yolk and vanilla and mix to combine, scraping down the sides of the bowl with a rubber spatula as needed to ensure that everything combines evenly. Reduce the speed to low, add the flour and salt, and mix until just combined.

LINE a sheet pan with parchment paper. This pan needs to fit in the freezer, so if you can make room for a half sheet pan, do that; otherwise you can crowd them onto a smaller sheet pan for now and transfer to a half sheet pan to bake.

PLACE the remaining ¼ cup (50 grams) sugar in a shallow bowl or rimmed plate. Scoop out ¼-cup (60-gram) balls, roll them in the sugar to coat, place them on the sheet pan 2 inches apart, and gently press indentations in the center of each one (about the size of two big thumbs, or roughly 1 inch) almost to the bottom. Freeze for at least 2 hours or up to 3 months. If you plan to bake these within a day, there's no need to cover the pan, but if you plan to keep the dough frozen for longer, then wrap tightly with plastic wrap.

WHEN ready to bake, preheat the oven to 350°F. If you froze the cookie dough balls on a small sheet pan, transfer them to a parchment-lined half sheet pan.

SPOON 2 teaspoons of jam into each indentation and bake until the cookies just start to turn brown on the edges; begin checking for doneness at 22 minutes. Let cool on the pan for 5 minutes and then transfer to a wire rack to cool completely.

STORE in an airtight container at room temperature for 4 to 5 days.

LARDER CABINET COOKIES

These are my take on kitchen sink cookies but rebranded with a name that doesn't make it sound like all the ingredients are bathed in the cooties and gross junk that collects in the bottom of a real kitchen sink. All the best things in a larder cabinet—or rather, does "snack cabinet" make me sound less like I've spent too much time on the deVOL Kitchens website?—are held together by a chocolate chip–adjacent cookie dough that is part coconut oil and rosewater scented, relying on two additional larder cabinet MVPs. Eating them makes you feel slightly more mischievous than when you're eating a chocolate chip cookie, but they scratch a similar itch.

½ cup (113 grams) unsalted butter, melted and cooled slightly

½ cup (100 grams) unrefined coconut oil, melted and cooled slightly

1 cup (200 grams) packed light brown sugar

1 cup (200 grams) granulated sugar

2 large eggs

2 teaspoons pure vanilla extract

1 teaspoon rosewater

3 cups (390 grams) all-purpose flour

1½ teaspoons kosher salt

1 teaspoon baking powder

1 teaspoon baking soda

½ cup (30 grams) coarsely crushed pita chips

½ cup (45 grams) shredded sweetened coconut

6 ounces (170 grams) semisweet or bittersweet chocolate, coarsely chopped

4 ounces (113 grams) halva, any flavor, coarsely chopped

½ cup (64 grams) roasted salted pistachios, coarsely chopped

⅓ cup (8 grams) freeze-dried raspberries

Flaky salt

PREHEAT the oven to 350°F. Line two sheet pans with parchment paper.

IN a large bowl, whisk together the butter, coconut oil, brown sugar, and granulated sugar until combined. Add the eggs one at a time, whisking well after each addition, then whisk in the vanilla and rosewater. Sprinkle the flour evenly over the surface of the mixture, followed by the salt, baking powder, and baking soda. Give the dry ingredients a rough little whisk to combine, then whisk into the rest of the batter until mostly incorporated. (You'll finish up incorporating the dry ingredients as you fold in the mix-ins.) Switch to a rubber spatula and fold in the pita chips, coconut, chocolate (reserving a handful of bigger chunks for the top), halva (reserving a handful of bigger chunks for the top), pistachios (reserving a handful for the top), and the raspberries (reserving a few for the top).

SCOOP heaping ¼-cup (100-gram) balls of dough onto the prepared sheet pans, 3 inches apart, spacing out 5 dough balls per pan. (You'll need to bake in batches.) Top each with a few chunks of the reserved chocolate, halva, and pistachios and a pinch of flaky salt. (Don't top with the reserved raspberries before baking; otherwise they may burn or discolor in the oven.)

BAKE until puffed and set around the edges but still gooey in the middle; begin checking for doneness at 12 minutes. If you have an instant-read thermometer handy, aim for an internal temperature of around 175°F. While the cookies are still hot, carefully press in the reserved raspberries. Let cool completely on the pans (or sneak a warm one if you *must*). For the best results, bake one pan at a time in the center of the oven. If you're short on time, you can bake two pans at a time, on the upper middle and lower middle racks, switching the racks and rotating the pans 180 degrees a little over halfway through the bake time.

STORE in an airtight container at room temperature. These are best within a few days of baking. After that they'll be okay for a few more days, but if you anticipate that you won't finish the batch in that time, I'd recommend freezing unbaked balls of dough and baking one or two at a time whenever the craving strikes. Unbaked balls of dough can be frozen in an airtight container for up to 3 months. Bake from frozen and add a few minutes to the baking time.

BARS

Around here, any dessert that is baked in a pan and cut into squares, such
as a brownie, blondie, or lemon square, is lumped into the category of "bar."
Marge could be bringing a pan of bars to the potluck and you know it will
be something sweet, but only Marge knows if it will be fruity, nutty, layered,
chocolaty, or some combination of those.

The best bars come with stories. "Hannah's mom's are the absolute best,
but she *must (!)* make them using her red plastic Tupperware bowl; otherwise
they're not as good." Or "Soccer games simply could not begin without
confirmation that Ellie's mom made the Special K bars for halftime." And
their recipes are scribbled on old stained notecards with just barely enough
clues to get you by. Bakers of yore didn't need to be directed to preheat the
oven or line a pan with parchment—they just knew.

The strengths of bars are that they feed a crowd, travel well to potlucks,
are quick to make since they usually don't require that anything be chilled
before baking, and, my personal favorite, deliver the chewiness of good cookie
innards with the kind of geometrically pleasing 90-degree angles and parallel
lines that fantasies are made of. Since the ingredients are contained by the
walls of the pan, you have options for layers upon layers and thinner batters
that would otherwise be too oozy for their free-form cookie counterparts,
opening up delicious new worlds in which to play.

ALMOND
COOKIE BAR

SOFT ALMOND SUGAR COOKIE BARS

If ever there were a treat fit for a fairy princess tea party, it would be these bars. (In my mind they're actually called fairy princess bars, but "soft almond sugar cookie bar" is more descriptive and less embarrassing for big burly farmers to obsess over.) I had these bars developed and ready to go in time for Bernie to hit her tea party phase, which has been every bit as magical as I always imagined it would be. Almost as magical as when she hit her back massage–giving phase.

These bars are sweet, moist, cakey, and almondy, a combination I dream of on a regular basis, and they actually stay great for a good few days because of their moisture content, so I'm prone to keeping these out on the counter and cutting off a corner every time I walk by. The secret to success here is taking care not to overbake them; pull the bars from the oven as soon as they're set and try not to let them get any color on top.

MAKES 15 LARGE BARS

Bars

Nonstick spray

1 cup (226 grams) unsalted butter, room temperature

8 ounces (226 grams) cream cheese, room temperature

1½ cups (300 grams) sugar

Zest of 1 lemon

2 large eggs

2 teaspoons pure vanilla extract

1 teaspoon pure almond extract

1 cup (112 grams) fine almond flour

2 cups (260 grams) all-purpose flour

1½ teaspoons kosher salt

Frosting and assembly

¾ cup (170 grams) unsalted butter, room temperature

2 cups (240 grams) powdered sugar

¼ teaspoon kosher salt

½ teaspoon pure almond extract

1 teaspoon lemon juice

2 tablespoons (30 grams) heavy cream (or 1 tablespoon/15 grams milk)

Pink food coloring, optional

Sprinkles, optional

PREHEAT the oven to 350°F. Grease a 9 × 13-inch metal baking pan and line with enough parchment paper to allow for 1-inch wings on the long sides. (If you only have a glass or ceramic pan, that's okay; just prepare to bake these a little longer!)

IN a stand mixer fitted with a paddle, combine the butter, cream cheese, sugar, and lemon zest and beat on medium high until pale and fluffy, 3 to 4 minutes. Add the eggs one at a time mixing well after each addition. Beat in the vanilla and almond extracts. Reduce the speed to low and add the almond flour, mixing to combine. Then add the all-purpose flour and salt and mix until just combined. Scrape down the sides of the bowl with a rubber spatula as needed to ensure that everything combines evenly. Transfer the batter to the prepared pan, spreading it out evenly. (It's easiest to use an offset spatula for this but a rubber spatula or spoon will work, too.)

BAKE until the edges are golden and a toothpick inserted in the center comes out with just a few crumbs; begin checking for doneness at 22 minutes and try very hard not to overbake. Let cool completely in the pan.

TO make the frosting, combine the butter, powdered sugar, and salt in a stand mixer fitted with a paddle and mix on low until you're confident that sugar won't fly everywhere, then increase the speed to medium and continue to mix until smooth. Add the almond extract, lemon juice, heavy cream, and food coloring (if using), increase the speed to medium high, and continue to mix for a few more seconds until combined and fluffy. Scrape down the sides of the bowl with a rubber spatula as needed to ensure that everything combines evenly.

SPREAD the frosting all over the cooled bars and top with sprinkles if desired. Cut into 15 large squares (or smaller ones if you'd like).

STORE in an airtight container at room temperature for 4 to 5 days or in the fridge for up to a week.

SORTA WEIRD SEVEN-LAYER BARS

One of the best restaurants in the world is a Scandinavian Jewish deli in Fargo (can't make that one up!) called BernBaum's. They once had this seven-layer bar type thing that included matzo meal and everything bagel chips that I couldn't stop eating because I was so enchanted by its delicious weirdness. The unique nature of this bar didn't just come from its good sweet-and-salty combination, it also exercised some beautiful restraint in the sweetness department, a welcome change from the candy bar sweetness of a typical seven-layer bar. This inspired-by-BernBaum's version limits the sweetness to just a few ingredients: the chocolate, the butterscotch, and the condensed milk. The rest can be anything it wants to be (so long as it's not sweet)—pita crumbs, pretzel crumbs, and the like—but matzo meal carries a specific type of bland nostalgia that speaks to me. And I do feel that a small amount of controlled everything bagel seasoning, garlic and all, is just quirky enough to be fun but not gross. When I say controlled, I mean don't buy the everything bagel chips; buy the plain chips and add only the amount of garlic and onion that I tell you to add.

Nonstick spray

½ cup (113 grams) unsalted butter or ½ cup (100 grams) coconut oil (refined or unrefined)

1½ cups (150 grams) matzo meal

1 cup (170 grams) semisweet chocolate chips

1 cup (170 grams) butterscotch chips

1½ cups (90 grams) plain bagel chips, coarsely crushed in a zip-top bag

2 tablespoons (20 grams) sesame seeds

1 tablespoon (10 grams) poppy seeds

¾ teaspoon dried minced onion

¾ teaspoon dried minced garlic

½ teaspoon kosher salt

One 14-ounce can sweetened condensed milk or sweetened condensed coconut milk

1 teaspoon pure vanilla extract

2 cups (90 grams) unsweetened coconut flakes

PREHEAT the oven to 350°F. Grease a 9 × 13-inch metal baking pan and line with enough parchment paper to allow for 1-inch wings on the long sides, making sure that the parchment is glued down by the grease as much as possible so the melted butter or coconut oil can't get underneath it. (If you only have a glass or ceramic pan, that's okay; just prepare to bake these a little longer!)

PLACE the butter or coconut oil in the pan and stick it in the oven for a few minutes until it melts. Swirl it around the bottom of the pan and scatter the matzo meal evenly all over. (You're not actually making a full-on crust; don't worry about packing it down or anything.) Sprinkle on the chocolate chips, butterscotch chips, bagel chips, sesame seeds, poppy seeds, dried minced onion, dried minced garlic, and salt, doing your best to get even coverage. Pour a little of the condensed milk on top to make some room in the can, then add the vanilla to the remaining condensed milk and mix it in. Pour the mixture all over the layers, making sure it's as evenly covered as possible. Sprinkle the coconut on top.

BAKE until the top is deep golden brown; begin checking for doneness at 20 minutes. Let cool completely (ideally overnight or for a few hours in the fridge) in the pan, then cut into 15 large bars (or smaller ones if you'd like). Get at 'em!

STORE in an airtight container in the fridge for up to a week.

MANDARIN ORANGE AND TOASTED SESAME BARS

Lemon bars have the bad luck of often being on a table next to brownies and blondies, and those options are usually more appealing. Not because lemon bars are objectively worse; they're just objectively louder and more demanding of your taste buds. You can have a bite of a blondie and then steal a bite of your child's brownie and a sip of your husband's beer or coffee without so much as a palate cleanser. But throw a lemon bar into the mix and, eh, you've kind of committed yourself. So I don't really eat lemon bars. What I do like, however, is a citrus bar that doesn't require you to pucker. One that actually allows the flavor of the egg in the custard to come through, providing some faint don tot (Chinese egg custard tart) energy. And one that's accompanied by the added interest of toasted sesame in the crust (which is good enough to be a stand-alone cookie). And a crust-to-goo ratio that is super heavy on that crust, always and forever.

MAKES 16 BARS

Crust

Nonstick spray

1 cup (130 grams) all-purpose flour

½ cup (80 grams) toasted sesame seeds, plus more for topping

6 tablespoons (75 grams) sugar

Zest of 1 mandarin orange

¼ teaspoon kosher salt

½ cup (113 grams) cold unsalted butter, cut into ½-inch cubes

1 large egg white

1 teaspoon toasted sesame oil

Filling

¾ cup (150 grams) sugar

1 tablespoon (8 grams) cornstarch

¼ teaspoon kosher salt

2 large eggs plus 3 large egg yolks

⅓ cup (80 grams) whole milk

1 tablespoon (6 grams) mandarin orange zest, plus ¾ cup (192 grams) mandarin orange juice (from 5 or 6 mandarins)

¾ teaspoon pure vanilla extract

½ cup (113 grams) cold unsalted butter, cut into ½-inch cubes

PREHEAT the oven to 350°F. Grease a 9-inch square metal baking pan and line with enough parchment paper to allow for 1-inch wings on opposite sides. (If you only have a glass or ceramic pan, that's okay; just prepare to bake these a little longer!)

IN a food processor, combine the flour, sesame seeds, sugar, orange zest, and salt and blend to combine and break up the seeds a bit. Scatter on the butter and pulse until it's pea size. Add the egg white and sesame oil and continue to pulse until the mixture starts to clump together. (You can also do this by hand in a big bowl. Use your fingers to incorporate the butter by smashing and rubbing it in with the dry ingredients until it's evenly dispersed and the butter is pea size. Add the egg white and toasted sesame oil and use a rubber spatula to gently mix into a shaggy mass.)

TRANSFER the dough to the prepared pan and press evenly all around the bottom. Bake until the crust is lightly golden; begin checking for doneness at 15 minutes.

REDUCE the oven temperature to 325°F.

TO make the filling, whisk together the sugar, cornstarch, and salt in a medium saucepan. Add the eggs and egg yolks and whisk until smooth. Whisk in the milk and orange juice and set over medium heat, whisking continuously, until the mixture begins to simmer and thicken and bubbles pop to the surface, 7 to 10 minutes. Remove from the heat and whisk in the orange zest and vanilla, then the butter, a little at a time, whisking until the butter has melted and the mixture is smooth.

POUR the filling mixture over the cookie crust (it's totally okay if the crust is still a little warm; you just don't want it to be piping hot) and bake until the edges are set but the center is just a tiny bit jiggly; begin checking for doneness at 25 minutes. Let cool completely in the pan. You can steal a taste now but to get the cleanest cuts, refrigerate for a few hours until cold.

SPRINKLE with toasted sesame seeds and then with a sharp knife, cut into 16 squares, wiping the blade after each cut.

STORE in an airtight container between layers of parchment in the refrigerator for up to 3 days.

RHUBARB ROSE BARS

For another variation on the theme of fruits-that-aren't-lemons-appropriating-the-form-of-lemon-bars, this one features the first sign of spring in the garden, rhubarb. Its natural aggressive sourness is softened by the warmth of coconut, rose, vanilla bean, and, well, just short of a literal pound of sugar. I suppose it's fitting that a rhubarb patch is thriving here on a sugar farm.

MAKES 16 BARS

Crust

Nonstick spray

1 cup (130 grams) all-purpose flour

½ cup (56 grams) fine almond flour

6 tablespoons (75 grams) granulated sugar

¼ teaspoon kosher salt

½ cup (113 grams) cold unsalted butter, cut into ½-inch cubes

1 large egg white

1 teaspoon rosewater

Filling and assembly

12 ounces (340 grams) fresh rhubarb, cut into 1-inch pieces

1½ cups (300 grams) granulated sugar, divided

1 vanilla bean, split, or 2 teaspoons vanilla bean paste

2 tablespoons (16 grams) cornstarch

¼ teaspoon kosher salt

2 large eggs plus 3 large egg yolks

Zest of 1 lemon, plus 2 tablespoons (30 grams) lemon juice

¼ cup (56 grams) unsalted butter, cut into ½-inch cubes

¼ cup (50 grams) unrefined coconut oil

Pink food coloring

Powdered sugar, for dusting

PREHEAT the oven to 350°F. Grease a 9-inch square metal baking pan and line with enough parchment paper to allow for 1-inch wings on opposite sides. (If you only have a glass or ceramic pan, that's okay; just prepare to bake these a little longer!)

IN a food processor, pulse together the all-purpose flour, almond flour, granulated sugar, and salt. Scatter on the butter and pulse until pea size. Add the egg white and rosewater and continue to pulse until the mixture starts to clump together. (You can also do this by hand in a big bowl. Use your fingers to incorporate the butter by smashing and rubbing it in with the dry ingredients until it's evenly dispersed and the butter is pea size. Add the egg white and rosewater and use a rubber spatula to gently mix into a shaggy mass.)

TRANSFER the dough to the prepared pan and press evenly all around the bottom. Bake until the crust is lightly golden; begin checking for doneness at 15 minutes.

REDUCE the oven temperature to 325°F.

TO make the filling, place the rhubarb in a medium saucepan and add water just to cover (about 1½ cups/360 grams) and ¼ cup (50 grams) of the granulated sugar. Scrape in the vanilla bean seeds and drop in the pod (or add the paste, if using). Simmer until the rhubarb is falling apart, about 10 minutes. Cool briefly, just so it's not hot, then strain and discard the solids.

IN a medium saucepan, whisk together the remaining 1¼ cups (250 grams) sugar, the cornstarch, and salt. Add the eggs and egg yolks and whisk until smooth. Whisk in the lemon juice and ¾ cup (180 grams) of the rhubarb juice. (Keep any extra rhubarb juice to sweeten iced tea or cocktails.) Cook over medium heat, whisking continuously, until the mixture begins to simmer and thicken and bubbles pop to the surface, 7 to 10 minutes. Remove from the heat and whisk in the lemon zest, then the butter and coconut oil a little at a time, whisking until melted and the mixture is smooth. Whisk in just enough food coloring to make the mixture a salmon-pink color, a couple of drops.

POUR the filling mixture over the cookie crust (it's totally okay if the crust is still a little warm; you just don't want it to be piping hot) and bake until the edges are set but the center is just a tiny bit jiggly; begin checking for doneness at 25 minutes. Let cool completely in the pan. You can steal a taste now but to get the cleanest cuts, refrigerate for a few hours until cold.

DUST with powdered sugar and then with a sharp knife, cut into 16 squares, wiping the blade after each cut.

STORE in an airtight container between layers of parchment in the refrigerator for up to 3 days.

ONE-BOWL ANY-BUTTER COOKIE BARS

File under: Things to bake on the weekend when you are totally scattered* but in need of something sweet.

These bars are great because they can be made using whatever nut or seed butter you have in your pantry and they don't require any fancy tools, just a bowl, a whisk, and a spatula. As is the case with all baking, but especially here, weighing your ingredients makes this recipe exponentially easier and more manageable while holding a child with one arm. You'll get so fast at making these that they'll probably come together before the oven is even done preheating, so plan an extra few minutes for that. Also, this recipe halves easily, so if you just have the scrapings of the bottom of a nut butter jar or don't want to have a whole batch lying around, go ahead and make a half batch in a loaf pan.

½ cup (about 120 grams) nut/seed/cookie butter (see Butters That Work!, opposite)

½ cup (113 grams) unsalted butter or ½ cup (100 grams) coconut oil (refined or unrefined)

1 cup (200 grams) sugar

2 large eggs

1 teaspoon pure vanilla extract

1½ cups (195 grams) all-purpose flour

¾ teaspoon kosher salt

1 teaspoon baking powder

2 tablespoons (21 grams) rainbow sprinkles, optional

PREHEAT the oven to 350°F. Grease an 8-inch square metal baking pan and line with enough parchment paper to allow for 1-inch wings on opposite sides. (If you only have a glass or ceramic pan, that's okay; just prepare to bake these a little longer!)

IN a large microwaveable bowl, combine the nut/seed/cookie butter and unsalted butter or coconut oil and microwave until the butter or coconut oil is melted, starting with 30 seconds and adding more time if needed. (You can also do this in a large saucepan over low heat.) Whisk together until

---

* *Causes of scatteredness may include:*
- *Needing to dress Barbies/hold babies with one hand and having only one hand to measure and mix*
- *Managing kids who want to help making these but don't yet share the kind of neuroticism about raw eggs and flour that you have*
- *Not quite knowing if the napping kids will wake up in one second or in one hour*
- *Needing to focus on whatever figure skating or other sports competition is on TV*

smooth, then whisk in the sugar. Confirm that the mixture is no longer hot to the touch, then whisk in the eggs, one at a time, followed by the vanilla. Sprinkle the flour evenly over the surface of the mixture, followed by the salt and baking powder. Give the dry ingredients a rough little whisk to combine, then incorporate them into the rest of the batter. (You may need to switch to a wooden spoon or rubber spatula here if the batter is too thick to whisk.) Fold in the sprinkles (if using) and then scrape the batter into the prepared pan, spreading it out evenly.

BAKE until golden around the edges and puffed on top; begin checking for doneness at 24 minutes, though some nut butters may take as long as 32 minutes to fully bake. Let cool completely in the pan. Dust with powdered sugar or frost if desired (see below) and slice into 16 squares.

STORE in an airtight container at room temperature or in the fridge for 4 or 5 days.

BUTTERS THAT WORK!

(Weights in grams will vary slightly depending on the butter you choose, but all work great!)

Speculoos
Nutella
Peanut butter
Almond butter
Cashew butter
Sunflower butter
Tahini

A RULE OF THUMB: *If your butter is sweetened, like speculoos or Nutella, know that these bars will be sweet enough to eat on their own. If it's unsweetened, like peanut butter or almond butter, consider dusting them postbake with powdered sugar or spreading on a frosting or glaze.*

S'MORES BARS

S'mores bars are the food equivalent to when the kids' naps all happen at the same time. A lot of things have to fall into place perfectly in order for all of it to work out, but when it does, it is so magical. I mean, five uninterrupted minutes in the middle of your day to sit on a recliner and read a cookbook? Heaven.

S'mores bars were my white whale for a while because it was a challenge to figure out the correct ratio and texture of each layer, to have them all sit nicely together, and to have them all look good. Things fell into place when I abandoned the idea of spreading actual marshmallow on top and instead went with a meringue frosting, which has a softer and silkier texture than marshmallow (sort of giving the illusion of a melted marshmallow). It is also pleasantly not cloying, way easier to make, and it looks so whimsical. I'm obsessed with the look of these just as much as I'm obsessed with the trifecta of crumbly crust, fluffy topping, and chewy chocolate brownie in the center. These took a while to perfect, but they were worth my excited scream when they got there.

MAKES 16 BARS

Crust

Nonstick spray

18 large rectangles (36 squares, or 2 full pouches, or just under 10 ounces/283 grams) graham crackers

Good pinch of kosher salt

10 tablespoons (141 grams) unsalted butter, melted

Brownie

¾ cup (170 grams) unsalted butter, melted and cooled slightly

1 cup (200 grams) sugar

⅔ cup (54 grams) Dutch-process or unsweetened cocoa powder

½ teaspoon instant espresso powder

4 large egg yolks (reserve the whites for the marshmallow layer)

1 teaspoon pure vanilla extract

¾ cup (98 grams) all-purpose flour

½ teaspoon kosher salt

¼ teaspoon baking powder

Marshmallow

4 large egg whites

1 cup (200 grams) sugar

¼ teaspoon cream of tartar

¼ teaspoon kosher salt

1 teaspoon pure vanilla extract

PREHEAT the oven to 350°F. Grease an 8-inch square metal baking pan and line with enough parchment paper to allow for 1-inch wings on all sides. (If you only have a glass or ceramic pan, that's okay; just prepare to bake these a little longer!)

TO make the crust, in a food processor, process the living daylights out of your graham crackers and salt. With the processor running, drizzle in the melted butter and process for a few more seconds, until the mixture clumps together. Pour the mixture into the prepared pan and press it down firmly and evenly.

BAKE until just set; begin checking for doneness at 10 minutes.

TO make the brownie layer, whisk together the butter, sugar, cocoa, and espresso powder in a large bowl. Whisk in the egg yolks one at a time, then add the vanilla. Sprinkle the flour, salt, and baking powder evenly over the surface of the batter. Give the dry ingredients a rough little whisk to combine, then incorporate them into the rest of the batter. Pour onto the graham crust (it's totally okay if the crust is still a little warm; you just don't want it to be piping hot), spread it out evenly, and bake until just set in the center; begin checking for doneness at 20 minutes. Let cool completely in the pan.

TO make the marshmallow layer, combine the egg whites, sugar, cream of tartar, and salt in the bowl of your stand mixer and set it over a pot of simmering water, making sure that the water doesn't touch the bottom of the bowl. Heat, whisking continuously, until the mixture reaches 175°F (you can either clip a candy thermometer on the side of the bowl or stick an instant-read thermometer in occasionally); it will be thin and frothy. Transfer the bowl to the stand mixer fitted with a whisk and beat on high until stiff and glossy, about 3 minutes, then mix in the vanilla. Spread over the brownies and then stick the pan under the broiler for a few minutes until it reaches your desired level of toastiness. Check it frequently because broilers work quickly! (You can also brown with a kitchen torch, but remove the bars from the pan and take off the parchment first.) Let cool completely in the pan, then cut into 16 squares using a moist sharp knife.

STORE in an airtight container in the fridge for up to 4 days.

JAM BARS, THREE WAYS

- RASPBERRY COCONUT CINNAMON
- PLUM HAZELNUT FIVE-SPICE
- APPLE MARZIPAN CARDAMOM

Efficiency is one of my favorite things in the world. Why carry one child upstairs when you could fill up your arms and also carry a load of laundry, four baby dolls, and two cups of really crumbly crackers? Why cook one meal for your family that half of them might hate when you could instead cook three that are tailored to various levels of pickiness using the same exact ingredients? A crust that doubles as a topping and somehow takes on unique textural qualities based on its relationship to the pan, filling, and oven heating element? Oh, heck yeah. Here, three variations on that very concept, to take you through the year as the seasons and your tastes change. (And have I mentioned that this is a one-bowl recipe?) Each version spotlights the star of the show, the fruit, and accessorizes to enhance it. Cardamom, almond paste, coconut, almond, hazelnuts, five-spice—yeehaw!

MAKES 16 BARS

1 cup (226 grams) unsalted butter, room temperature

⅔ cup (133 grams) sugar

½ teaspoon ground cinnamon OR five-spice OR cardamom

1 teaspoon pure vanilla extract

2 cups (260 grams) all-purpose flour

½ teaspoon kosher salt

½ cup (45 grams) toasted shredded sweetened coconut OR ½ cup (72 grams) chopped roasted hazelnuts OR ⅓ cup (37 grams) toasted sliced almonds and 4 ounces (113 grams) crumbled almond paste

½ cup (80 grams) raspberry jam OR plum jam OR apple butter

PREHEAT the oven to 350°F. Line an 8-inch square metal pan with enough parchment paper to allow for 1-inch wings on opposite sides. (If you only have a glass or ceramic pan, that's okay; just prepare to bake these a little longer!)

IN a stand mixer fitted with a paddle, combine the butter, sugar, spice, and vanilla and mix on medium until creamy and combined, 1 to 2 minutes. Reduce the speed to low, add the flour and salt, and mix until combined. Transfer about three-quarters of the mixture (totally okay to eyeball this) to the prepared pan and press it firmly and evenly.

BAKE until lightly browned around the edges; begin checking for doneness at 15 minutes. Cool briefly before adding the next layers.

TO make the topping, add the coconut, hazelnuts, or almonds and almond paste (depending on which jam you're using) to the reserved crust mixture, and combine with your hands into a coarse crumble.

SPREAD a thin layer of your jam of choice over the parbaked crust, leaving a ¼-inch border around the edges, and top with the crumble. Bake until browned on top; begin checking for doneness at 25 minutes. Let cool completely in the pan, then slice into 16 squares.

STORE in an airtight container at room temperature for 3 to 4 days.

MISO TOFFEE CRACKERS

Nothing quite says springtime like pouring a vat of boiling hot sugar over a tray of matzo and picking at it over the course of eight days as a soothing ritual for when you really miss bread. I usually feel strongly about maintaining close associations like this between specific foods and holidays, so I'm not one to promote, say, making stuffing when it's not Thanksgiving, but this cracker toffee is different enough from its unleavened brethren that it gets a pass(over). It's different enough because it takes advantage of the kitniyot (or, bean-centric group of foods that many people avoid on Passover) superstar miso paste, which brings funky depth to the toffee, as if you needed another reason to be powerless against this situation. If matzo toffee is a two-dimensional painting, this miso toffee is like a three-dimensional sculpture that you'll want to make room for in your kitchen immediately.

MAKES 48 CRACKERS

Nonstick spray

48 saltine crackers (a little more than 1 sleeve)

1 cup (226 grams) unsalted butter

1 cup (200 grams) packed light brown sugar

2 tablespoons (36 grams) white miso

12 ounces (340 grams) bittersweet chocolate, finely chopped, or 2 cups chips

Flaky salt

PREHEAT the oven to 350°F. Grease and line a rimmed sheet pan with parchment paper and then grease the top of the parchment as well. The grease under the parchment will help glue it down so that the toffee doesn't sneak underneath it, and the extra grease on top is because you're about to be in a sticky situation.

COVER the prepared sheet pan in a single layer of saltines.

IN a medium saucepan, melt the butter and brown sugar over medium heat, whisking to combine. Once it bubbles, stop whisking and allow it to bubble for about 3 minutes (reducing the heat if it becomes too spitty) until its color darkens slightly. Remove from the heat, whisk in the miso, and pour over the crackers in an even layer.

BAKE until splotchily browned; begin checking for doneness at 7 minutes.

CAREFULLY remove from the oven and immediately sprinkle the chocolate evenly all over. Let sit for 2 minutes so the chocolate melts, then use an offset spatula to spread the chocolate evenly over the crackers. Sprinkle with flaky salt and let set at room temperature or speed up the process in the fridge, about 20 minutes.

BREAK up into squares, and good luck limiting yourself to just one.

STORE in an airtight container at room temperature for up to 4 days or in the fridge for up to a week.

CHEWY NUTTY FRUITY GRANOLA BARS

Granola bars are great because they signal wholesomeness and some semblance of nutrition, even if all their ingredients are glued together by sugar. Which is why I get them anytime I see them behind a bakery case, and also why I spent so long developing these granola bars for the Bernie's bakery case in time for opening day. But then nobody, not one single person, bought them. We sold out of everything else, and the granola bars just sat there welling up with tears. This wouldn't be the first time my personal preference was in the vast minority (see: my '97 Buick LeSabre and my favorite Girl Scout cookie on page 42), but come on! These are so satisfyingly chewy and *good*! You could eat them every day! They've got fiber! And they're easily made gluten-free and vegan.

And, by the way, if you're in a nostalgic mood and looking to be more obvious about this being a dessert masquerading as nutrition, sub out the fruit and nuts for eight chopped Oreos.

MAKES 12 BARS

Nonstick spray

2 cups (180 grams) rolled oats

½ cup (about 90 grams) dried fruit (I like a mix of cherries and golden raisins)

½ cup (about 72 grams) roasted salted nuts (I like a mix of almonds and pistachios), coarsely chopped

½ cup (about 70 grams) seeds (I like a mix of sesame, millet, hemp, and pumpkin)

¼ cup (50 grams) packed light brown sugar

¼ cup (84 grams) honey or maple syrup

¼ cup (56 grams) unsalted butter or ¼ cup (50 grams) coconut oil (refined or unrefined)

½ teaspoon kosher salt

¼ cup (56 grams) tahini or ¼ cup (64 grams) unsweetened nut butter (choose a smooth versus grainy variety for best results)

1 teaspoon pure vanilla extract

PREHEAT the oven to 350°F. Grease a 9-inch square pan and line it with enough parchment paper to allow for 1-inch wings on opposite sides.

SPREAD the oats on a rimmed sheet pan and toast until fragrant and slightly darkened; begin checking for doneness at 10 minutes. Transfer to a large bowl and add the dried fruit, nuts, and seeds.

IN a medium saucepan, combine the sugar, honey or maple syrup, butter or coconut oil, and salt and set over medium heat, whisking to combine. Once it bubbles, stop whisking and allow it to cook for about 3 minutes (reducing the heat if it becomes too spitty), until its color darkens slightly. Remove from the heat and whisk in the tahini or nut butter and the vanilla. Add to the oat mixture and use a rubber spatula to fold together. Scrape into the prepared pan and press it down very firmly and evenly. (It's most efficient to place another piece of parchment over the mixture and press with your hands. If it's too hot for your hands, let it cool for a minute or two.) Refrigerate until just firm, 20 to 30 minutes, then transfer to a cutting board and cut into 12 bars.

STORE in an airtight container at room temperature for up to a week or for a little longer in the fridge.

STOLLEN BARS

Traditional stollen recipes make you work for it. And wait for it. And wait some more. But the last thing that a hungry pregnant lady wants to read in a recipe is a long rising time, let alone two long rising times and the need to hunt down candied orange peel. *We want stollen.* When do we want it? *Now.* The solution lies in these instant-satisfaction stollen bars, inspired by a recipe that I found years ago from the Australian chef Dan Lepard during a pregnancy craving–fueled stollen search. I haven't been able to go a holiday season since without making them. If cream cheese and stand mixers had existed in the 1400s, I believe this action-packed bar form of the traditional Christmas bread would have been the original.

I love how many variations of chewiness are shoved into one bite here: between the marzipan, the dried fruit, the nuts that soften slightly in the oven, and the buttery, orange-scented batter that glues it all together, they're chewy champions. Factor in a topping that must be applied while the bars are still hot, hightailing their journey into your mouth, and they are racking up some serious brownie (blondie?) points.

MAKES 12 LARGE BARS

Nonstick spray

½ cup (113 grams) unsalted butter, room temperature

4 ounces (113 grams) cream cheese, room temperature

1 cup (200 grams) sugar

Zest of 1 orange

1 large egg

½ teaspoon pure almond extract

2 cups (260 grams) all-purpose flour

⅔ cup (75 grams) fine almond flour

1 teaspoon baking powder

1 teaspoon ground cinnamon

¾ teaspoon kosher salt

¼ teaspoon ground cardamom

Pinch of ground cloves

Pinch of ground allspice

⅓ cup (53 grams) dried cherries

⅓ cup (53 grams) golden raisins

1 cup (128 grams) roasted unsalted pistachios

7 ounces (198 grams) marzipan, chopped into ¾-inch pieces

Topping
¼ cup (56 grams) unsalted butter, room temperature

⅓ cup (40 grams) powdered sugar

PREHEAT the oven to 350°F. Grease an 8-inch square metal baking pan and line with enough parchment paper to allow for 1-inch wings on all sides. (If you only have a glass or ceramic pan, that's okay; just prepare to bake these a little longer!)

IN a stand mixer fitted with a paddle, combine the butter, cream cheese, sugar, and orange zest and beat on medium high until pale and fluffy, 3 to 4 minutes. Add the egg and almond extract and beat to combine. Stop the mixer and sprinkle in the all-purpose flour and almond flour. Sprinkle the baking powder, cinnamon, salt, cardamom, cloves, and allspice evenly over the flours and give the dry ingredients a rough little whisk to combine, then turn the mixer on low to incorporate the dry ingredients into the wet ingredients, stopping when they're mostly combined. Add the cherries, raisins, and pistachios and mix until evenly distributed and you can no longer see any dry bits of flour. Stop the mixer and use a rubber spatula to fold in the marzipan pieces by hand. Scrape the mixture into the prepared pan and pat it out evenly with your hands or spatula.

BAKE until golden around the edges and lightly browned on top; begin checking for doneness at 30 minutes.

FOR the topping, spread the butter all over the bar while it's hot out of the oven so that it melts, then dust with powdered sugar, using the entire ⅓ cup (40 grams); it's excessive in the best way. Let cool completely in the pan (or dig out a corner to eat now while warm and then let the rest cool!), then cut into 12 bars (or smaller bars if desired).

STORE in an airtight container at room temperature for 4 to 5 days or in the refrigerator for up to a week.

YELLOW CAKE COOKIE BARS

On the spectrum of cake textures, from the airy egg-white-only low-fat angel food cake to the dense egg-yolk-heavy fatty yellow cake, these bars extend beyond the yellow cake pole—into territory that is so rich that these are better eaten in shorter, one-layer, three-bite squares. To get there, this batter utilizes almond flour for heft and then essentially forgoes liquid entirely and brings in the muscle, the cream cheese, to pull everything together. Conveniently, cream cheese also brings its signature sourness, providing balance to create a nostalgic powerhouse of a bar. For childhood in one square inch, look no further.

MAKES 24 BARS

Bars

Nonstick spray

1 cup (226 grams) unsalted butter

8 ounces (226 grams) cream cheese

1½ cups (300 grams) sugar

1 large egg plus 2 large egg yolks

1 tablespoon (13 grams) pure vanilla extract

1 cup (112 grams) fine almond flour

2 cups (260 grams) all-purpose flour

1 teaspoon kosher salt

Frosting and assembly

½ cup (113 grams) unsalted butter, room temperature

1½ cups (180 grams) powdered sugar

½ cup (40 grams) Dutch-process or unsweetened cocoa powder

⅛ teaspoon kosher salt

1 teaspoon pure vanilla extract

2 tablespoons (30 grams) milk, divided

2 ounces (57 grams) semisweet chocolate, finely chopped (or ⅓ cup chips) and then melted and cooled to room temperature

Sprinkles, optional

PREHEAT the oven to 350°F. Grease a 9 × 13-inch metal baking pan and line it with enough parchment paper to allow for 1-inch wings on the long sides. (If you only have a glass or ceramic pan, that's okay; just prepare to bake these a little longer!)

IN a large microwaveable bowl, melt the butter and cream cheese. Add the sugar. (The mixture will look broken to begin with; keep whisking until totally smooth.) Confirm that the mixture is no longer hot to the touch and then add the egg and yolks one at a time, whisking after each addition. Whisk in the vanilla and then the almond flour. Sprinkle the all-purpose flour and salt evenly over the surface and whisk until just combined.

SCRAPE it into the prepared pan, spread it out evenly, and bake until just set in the center and a toothpick comes out clean; begin checking for doneness at 22 minutes. Let cool completely in the pan.

TO make the frosting, in a stand mixer fitted with a paddle, combine the butter, powdered sugar, cocoa, and salt and mix on low until you're confident that sugar and cocoa won't fly everywhere, then increase the speed to medium and continue to mix until very smooth, scraping down the sides of the bowl with a rubber spatula as needed to ensure that everything combines evenly, 1 to 2 minutes. Add the vanilla and 1 tablespoon of the milk and, with the mixer running, drizzle in the chocolate. Beat on medium high until light and fluffy, 1 to 2 minutes, adding the remaining tablespoon of milk if it seems like it will be too stiff to spread.

SPREAD the frosting all over the cooled bars and top with sprinkles if desired. Cut into 24 squares.

STORE in an airtight container at room temperature for 4 to 5 days or in the fridge for up to a week.

SALADS

Come to a potluck in my neck of the woods and you will see the standard casseroles, potato salads, pies, and rolls. You will also see the quirkiest, most endearing genre of foods of all time, the sweet salads. If you're looking strictly at ingredients lists (fruit, cookies, candy bars, cream, Jell-O, pudding, and so on), they are desserts, but in practice there is a little more nuance. On the serving table, they will likely be set out closer to the Tater Tot hotdishes than the brownies, and on your plate, if you're doing things correctly, you will end up with a bite where the mayo-covered pasta meets the Cool Whip–covered Snickers bar. And that bite, dear friends, is the taste of an upper midwestern summer.

Church cookbooks are filled with variations of sweet salads. They are so ubiquitous in this area that if you're bringing a salad made of greens and vegetables to the party, it would behoove you to specify that you are bringing a *green* salad. The strengths of sweet salads include disarming charm and zero expectations for presentation (coincidentally also the top things I looked for in a husband??). They are easily transportable, prep-ahead-able, and capable of feeding large crowds. And, and! They are the absolute *best* catalysts for talking about your older family member who passed this recipe on to you, which, if we're lucky, turns into a conversation about your family's heritage and history. The Jew in me cannot overstate the excitement I get out of this style of storytelling; it's like talking about the deceased ancestor that you were named after, just with more gelatin.

If that's not enough to keep you from getting on your coastal high horse and trotting away from this section, let's break some of these salads down.

COOKIE SALAD: Cookies, cream, pudding, fruit. Commonly accepted desserts that are technically cookie salads: banana pudding, Eton mess, tiramisu.

JELL-O SALAD: Gelatin, other stuff. Commonly accepted desserts that are technically Jell-O salads: Bavarian cream, panna cotta.

CANDY BAR SALAD: Chopped candy bars, cream, pudding, apples. Commonly accepted desserts that are technically . . . no, never mind, this one might be on its own.

FLUFF: Pudding, whipped cream, other stuff. Commonly accepted desserts that are technically fluffs: ice cream is kind of just frozen fluff, I think?

Okay, I'm going to stop trying so hard. If you're still here, let's be friends. . . . Please enjoy my favorite chapter.

CLASSIC COOKIE SALAD

This isn't my recipe—it's a fleshed-out version of all the appearances this recipe makes in local church cookbooks—but I'm including it because it's a staple in the Hagen family and I want to show you the original before I have you make from-scratch pastry cream. That, and also because I make this regularly in this period of my life in which I am regularly pulled away from the kitchen to grab toddlers off the top of the piano they've just climbed on.

My mother-in-law, Roxanne, makes this for Easter with rainbow mini marshmallows, and she has also taught me all about the variations of toppings. You can do full cookies, halved cookies stuck on top to look like tombstones, crushed cookies, or any design that speaks to you. Accidentally buying the vanilla pudding that needs to be cooked, not the instant kind, and then pulling your hair out wondering how you just effed up the easiest recipe in the world is a rite of passage. I prefer cookie salad the day after it's made, when the cookies are softer and cake-like.

SERVES ABOUT 8

One 3.4-ounce package instant vanilla pudding

2 cups (480 grams) cold buttermilk

One 8-ounce container Cool Whip, thawed overnight in the fridge

One 11.5-ounce package Keebler Fudge Stripe cookies, coarsely crushed (reserve 5 to 7 whole cookies for the topping)

One 15-ounce can mandarin oranges, drained

Optional: One 8-ounce can crushed pineapple, drained, and/or 1 cup (45 grams) mini marshmallows

Optional, but don't ever feed this to me: sliced bananas

PREPARE the pudding in a large bowl according to the package directions using the buttermilk in place of milk. Chill in the refrigerator until soft set, about 10 minutes.

FOLD the Cool Whip, crushed cookies, most of the mandarins, and anything else you want into the pudding. Transfer to a serving bowl and refrigerate until ready to serve. Top with the reserved cookies and mandarins right before serving.

STORE in an airtight container in the refrigerator for up to 3 days.

OVERACHIEVER'S COOKIE SALAD

This Calculus BC of cookie salads is one you wouldn't think you needed in your life, until you actually taste it and decide that, even though the classic dump-and-stir recipe got the job done, you think you can clear your schedule this weekend to go the extra mile (er, maybe five miles) for your cousin-in-law's potluck. We make giant vats of this stuff at Bernie's and toss in all the day-old cookies when they are still lively but just dry enough that they've got some extra space in their bones to soak up a pudding bath. With that said, if you wanted to sub the fudge stripes here for Potato Chip Chocolate Chip Cookies (page 18), Thick Soft Cream Cheese Cutouts (page 15), Raspberry Jam Bars (page 70), or literally any other cookie or bar, I'd endorse this. (Measure out about 3 heaping cups of coarsely crushed cookies to get an equivalent amount.) Think of cookie salad as the French toast to your day-old cookie.

SERVES 8 TO 12

Pudding

6 tablespoons (75 grams) sugar

3 tablespoons (24 grams) all-purpose flour

¼ teaspoon kosher salt

3 large egg yolks

¾ cup (180 grams) heavy cream

¾ cup (180 grams) whole milk

1 teaspoon pure vanilla extract

¼ teaspoon pure almond extract

Cookies

1½ cups (195 grams) all-purpose flour, plus more for dusting

¾ cup (90 grams) powdered sugar

¾ teaspoon kosher salt

1½ teaspoons pure vanilla extract

¾ teaspoon pure almond extract

¾ cup (170 grams) cold unsalted butter, cut into ½-inch cubes

8 ounces (226 grams) semisweet chocolate, finely chopped, or 1⅓ cups chips

Assembly

2 cups (480 grams) cold heavy cream

8 ounces (226 grams) cream cheese, room temperature

½ cup (60 grams) powdered sugar

Two 11-ounce cans mandarin oranges, drained

One 8-ounce can crushed pineapple, drained

TO make the pudding, in a medium saucepan, whisk together the sugar, flour, and salt. Whisk in the egg yolks and a couple of splashes of the heavy cream until the mixture comes together into a smooth paste. Drizzle in the remaining heavy cream and milk while whisking until smooth. Set over medium heat and cook, whisking continuously, until the mixture is thickened enough to coat the back of a spoon, about 5 minutes. Add the vanilla and almond extracts. Pour into a heat-safe bowl and cover with plastic wrap so that the wrap touches the surface of the pudding. Refrigerate at least 1 hour or up to overnight.

TO make the cookies, whisk together the flour, powdered sugar, and salt in a stand mixer fitted with a paddle. With the mixer running on low, add the vanilla and almond extracts, then gradually add the butter. Mix until it comes together into a dough, slowly increasing the speed once you're confident that flour won't go flying everywhere. Divide the dough in half, press into disks, wrap in plastic, and refrigerate for at least 30 minutes or up to overnight.

ARRANGE oven racks in the upper middle and lower middle positions and preheat the oven to 350°F. Line two sheet pans with parchment paper.

WORKING with one dough disk at a time, roll out the dough on a floured surface to a scant ¼-inch thickness. Cut out 2-inch circles with a circle cookie cutter, then use a big piping tip to cut out ½-inch holes from the center. Reroll scraps and continue cutting out cookies, placing them on the prepared sheet pans an inch apart. Bake until they're just starting to brown around the edges; begin checking for doneness at 12 minutes. Let cool completely on the pans.

MEANWHILE, melt the chocolate in a double boiler or in a microwave in 30-second increments, stirring after each until smooth. Let cool slightly, then pour into a piping bag or a zip-top bag and snip off a corner. Pipe 4 thick chocolate stripes on each cookie and let set at room temperature or in the fridge.

TO assemble, in a stand mixer fitted with a whisk, beat the heavy cream, cream cheese, and powdered sugar on medium high to stiff peaks. Remove about one-third of the mixture and set it aside. Fold the cooled pudding into the remaining two-thirds of the whipped cream. Coarsely crush the cookies (reserving a few for the topping) and fold them in. Fold in the mandarins (reserve some of these for the topping, too) and pineapple. Transfer to a serving bowl, smooth out the top, and spread the reserved whipped cream on top. Refrigerate until you're ready to serve. (This can be made a day ahead. The cookies will soften as it sits.) Top with the reserved cookies and mandarins right before serving.

STORE in an airtight container in the fridge for up to 3 days.

CLASSIC CANDY BAR SALAD

In the sea of fluffy dessert salads, candy bar salad stands out because it provides the *most* satisfying chew of a cold Snickers bar, followed by the *most* refreshing crunch of a Granny Smith apple. I've seen church cookbook contributions with both peanuts and sunflower seeds as the topping. I like them both. This salad is like what would happen if the power couple apple and peanut butter left for a weekend away and their kids threw a rager.

SERVES 8 TO 12

One 3.4-ounce package instant vanilla pudding

⅔ cup (160 grams) whole milk

One 8-ounce container Cool Whip, thawed overnight in the fridge

4 medium (about 680 grams) Granny Smith apples, cored and chopped into bite-size pieces (no need to peel)

4 Snickers bars, chopped into bite-size pieces

Salted sunflower seeds or chopped salted peanuts, for topping

POUR the pudding mix into a large bowl. Whisk in the milk until smooth and thick. Fold in the Cool Whip in two additions. Fold in most of the apples and Snickers, reserving some of each for the top.

TRANSFER to a serving bowl and refrigerate until ready to serve. (Feel free to make this a day in advance; if you do, soak the reserved apples in lemon water to slow their browning.) Top with the reserved apples, Snickers, and seeds or nuts right before serving.

STORE in an airtight container in the fridge for up to 3 days.

OVERACHIEVER'S CANDY BAR SALAD

This from-scratch candy bar salad is here for one reason only: from-scratch candy bars. I am powerless against them and their cavity-causing stickiness. I've made them with every nut butter under the sun (and obviously tahini—omg they're so good with tahini). Aside from them tasting good, a big contribution to their addictive danger is how much easier they are to make than typical nougat-based candy bars because they use marshmallow crème as the base—no candy thermometers or boiling sugar is necessary. They can just live in your fridge for a while, and then, if you feel the need to pair them with something that has fiber and nutrition, toss them in with the apples in this salad and tell yourself it's fine . . . because it's salad . . .

SERVES 8 TO 12

Candy bars (see Note)

Nonstick spray

19 ounces (540 grams) dark chocolate, finely chopped, or 3 heaping cups chips, divided

1 tablespoon (13 grams) coconut oil (refined or unrefined), divided

3 cups (360 grams) powdered sugar

2 cups (192 grams) marshmallow crème

½ cup (128 grams) unsweetened unsalted peanut butter

⅛ teaspoon kosher salt

2 tablespoons (30 grams) milk

¾ cup (108 grams) roasted salted peanuts

9 ounces (255 grams) soft caramels

3 tablespoons (45 grams) heavy cream

Pudding

6 tablespoons (75 grams) sugar

3 tablespoons (24 grams) all-purpose flour

¼ teaspoon kosher salt

3 large egg yolks

¾ cup (180 grams) heavy cream

¾ cup (180 grams) whole milk

1 teaspoon pure vanilla extract

Assembly

3¾ cups (900 grams) cold heavy cream

¼ cup (30 grams) powdered sugar

4 medium (680 grams) Granny Smith apples, cored and chopped into bite-size pieces (no need to peel), soaked in lemon water for 10 minutes, and patted very dry

NOTE: *You'll be using only half of the candy bars here for the actual salad. They're easier to make in this larger quantity, and also I don't want you to go through all the sticky steps to make them and not have leftovers.*

TO make the candy bars, grease an 8-inch square pan and line with enough parchment paper to allow for 1-inch wings on all sides.

MELT 9.5 ounces (270 grams) of the chocolate and 1½ teaspoons of the coconut oil in a double boiler or in a microwave in 30-second increments, stirring after each until smooth. Pour into the prepared pan to cover the bottom. Freeze until set, 15 to 30 minutes. Keep your chocolate-melting vessel nearby since you'll be melting the other half of the chocolate in a bit.

IN a medium bowl, with a stiff rubber spatula, mix together the powdered sugar, marshmallow crème, peanut butter, salt, and milk until the mixture is soft and doughlike. (It will be incredibly sticky, and you may need to use your hands toward the end.) Remove the pan with the chocolate from the freezer, then wet your fingertips to prevent sticking and press the marshmallow filling over the chocolate in an even layer. Sprinkle the peanuts on top and press into the filling. Set aside.

PLACE the caramels and heavy cream in a small saucepan and set over low heat, stirring continuously, until the caramels are melted, 5 to 8 minutes. Spread the caramel over the marshmallow filling and refrigerate the pan for about 5 minutes to firm up slightly.

MEANWHILE, melt the remaining 9.5 ounces (270 grams) chocolate and 1½ teaspoons coconut oil. Pour the chocolate evenly over the caramel, then return the pan to the refrigerator until the chocolate is fully set, 1 to 2 hours.

USING the parchment, pull the candy out of the pan. Run a knife under warm water, wipe it dry, and cut the candy into 14 bars with 1 long cut and 6 cuts across. Cut 7 of the bars into small chunks to be used in the salad. (Refrigerate the remaining bars in an airtight container for another use, such as eating in the middle of the night. They'll be good for about 5 days.)

TO make the pudding, in a medium saucepan, whisk together the sugar, flour, and salt. Whisk in the egg yolks and a couple of splashes of the heavy cream until the mixture comes together into a smooth paste. Drizzle in the remaining heavy cream and milk while whisking until smooth. Set over medium heat and cook, whisking continuously, until the mixture is thickened enough to coat the back of a spoon, about 5 minutes. Add the vanilla and pour into a heat-safe bowl. Cover with plastic wrap so that the wrap touches the surface of the pudding so a skin doesn't form. Refrigerate until chilled, at least 1 hour or up to overnight.

TO assemble, in a stand mixer fitted with a whisk, beat the heavy cream and powdered sugar on medium high until stiff peaks form. Reserve 2 cups (480 grams) of the whipped cream in a separate bowl for the topping. Fold the pudding into the remaining whipped cream, then gently fold in most of the apples and most of the candy bar pieces, reserving some for the top. Serve the salad in individual glass bowls or one big bowl topped with the reserved whipped cream and the reserved apples and candy bars.

STORE in an airtight container in the refrigerator for up to 3 days.

ROASTED RHUBARB AND STRAWBERRIES WITH YOGURT WHIP, PRETZEL STREUSEL, AND SUMAC

OR STRAWBERRY PRETZEL SALAD, MINUS THE JELL-O, PLUS SOME SUMAC

Strawberry pretzel salad is one potluck standby that has always made sense to me in all ways. Points for a logical sweet-and-salty combo, points for beautiful bright layers, points for prep-ahead-ability, and points for a use of gelatin that is genuinely really good. The strawberry pretzel salad does not need improving. This is just a different format that, at one point in the early 2000s, restaurants might have called "deconstructed." All the components come together pretty quickly compared to its gelatinous counterpart, and while they should be plated right before serving, they can all be prepped a day ahead. This skews more intimate-dinner-party finale than potluck dessert (but if you're looking for the latter, flip to the next recipe for a variation on the classic layered version). Vinegary sumac and fresh mint are added flexes that taste good/look good/sound fancy/contribute brightness, but if they're not part of your current aesthetic, skip them.

SERVES ABOUT 6

Roasted rhubarb and strawberries

1 pound (454 grams) rhubarb, cut into 1-inch pieces

1 pound (454 grams) strawberries, quartered

½ cup (100 grams) sugar

Zest of 1 lemon

1 tablespoon (14 grams) vanilla bean paste, or seeds scraped from 1 vanilla bean pod

⅛ teaspoon kosher salt

2 teaspoons rosewater

Pretzel streusel

1 cup (83 grams) pretzel crumbs (from about 2 cups small salted pretzels)

½ cup (60 grams) powdered sugar

½ cup (113 grams) cold unsalted butter, cut into ½-inch cubes

Yogurt whip

½ cup (120 grams) cold whole milk Greek yogurt

1 cup (240 grams) cold heavy cream

2 tablespoons (15 grams) powdered sugar

½ teaspoon vanilla bean paste or extract

Assembly

Fresh basil and mint leaves

Sprinkle of sumac

TO roast the rhubarb and strawberries, preheat the oven to 325°F.

SPREAD the rhubarb and strawberries out on a rimmed sheet pan, top evenly with the sugar, lemon zest, vanilla, and salt and cover with foil. Roast for 20 minutes, then remove the foil and roast for another 15 minutes. Sprinkle the rosewater on top and then let cool completely. (If making this in advance, store in an airtight container in the fridge.)

TO make the pretzel streusel, preheat the oven to 350°F. Line a rimmed sheet pan with parchment paper.

COMBINE the pretzel crumbs and powdered sugar in a medium bowl. Add the butter and rub together with your fingers until the butter is thoroughly incorporated and the mixture is coarse and crumbly. Spread on the prepared sheet pan and bake for 10 minutes, until browned and crisp. It'll kinda melt together into one big, flat mass. Let cool completely on the pan and then break up into crumbles.

TO make the whip, in a stand mixer fitted with a whisk, combine the yogurt, heavy cream, powdered sugar, and vanilla and beat on medium high until medium-stiff peaks form.

TO assemble, add a plop of whip to individual serving plates or shallow bowls and top with the roasted fruit (cold or at room temperature), streusel, fresh herbs (torn if they're very big), and a small sprinkle of sumac.

STORE the components separately. The fruit and whip will keep, in separate airtight containers, in the fridge for up to 3 days. The streusel will keep, in an airtight container, at room temperature for up to a week.

BLUEBERRY CREAM CHEESE BAGEL CHIP SALAD

Where cream cheese goes, bagels will follow, and where bagels and cream cheese go, blueberries are, in most parts of the country, welcome. (New Yorkers, look away!) Which is why I believe this variation on the classic strawberry pretzel salad makes sense. Every time I've spread the cream cheese layer onto that crushed pretzel crust, I've thought, *This should really be going on a bagel crust,* so that is what I finally did, and here it is. Layer upon vibrant layer of summertime potluck mouthfeel: creamy, crunchy, sweet, salty, ~jiggly~.

SERVES 9 TO 12

Crust

3 heaping cups (165 grams) bagel chips (see Note)

⅓ cup (67 grams) sugar

½ cup (113 grams) unsalted butter, melted

Kosher salt, optional

Blueberry layer

1¼ cups (300 grams) water, divided

One 0.25-ounce packet plain gelatin

½ cup (100 grams) sugar

¼ teaspoon kosher salt

6 ounces (170 grams) frozen wild blueberries

¼ cup (80 grams) blueberry jam

Cream cheese layer

8 ounces (226 grams) cream cheese, room temperature

½ cup (100 grams) sugar

Zest of ½ lemon

1 cup (240 grams) cold heavy cream

1½ teaspoons pure vanilla extract

NOTE: *Salted, plain, or sesame bagel chips to play it safe. Everything bagel chips if you want to live on the edge. Roasted garlic is too weird; don't do that.*

TO make the crust, preheat the oven to 325°F.

IN a food processor, combine the bagel chips and sugar and blend into fine crumbs. Drizzle in the melted butter and pulse to combine. Taste and add salt if needed; your bagel chips might be salty enough on their own. Press the mixture into a clear glass 8- or 9-inch square baking dish. (The glass is really an aesthetic choice, so you can see the layers. Metal or ceramic will certainly work, too.)

BAKE until crisp and pulling away slightly from the sides of the pan; begin checking for doneness at 15 minutes. Let cool completely.

TO make the blueberry layer, add ½ cup (120 grams) of the water to a medium heat-safe bowl, sprinkle the gelatin on top, and set aside. In a medium saucepan, combine the sugar, salt, remaining ¾ cup (180 grams) water, and the blueberries and bring to a boil over medium-high heat, stirring to dissolve the sugar. Remove from the heat and stir in the jam. Pour the mixture over the bloomed gelatin and stir to completely dissolve the gelatin. Refrigerate until soft set, about 3 hours. (It should be thick and syrupy.)

MEANWHILE, to make the cream cheese layer, in a stand mixer fitted with a whisk, beat together the cream cheese, sugar, and lemon zest on medium high until smooth. Reduce the speed to medium and drizzle in the heavy cream and vanilla. Continue to beat until medium-stiff peaks form. Spread over the cooled crust and refrigerate until set, at least 2 hours.

WHEN the cream cheese layer is set and the blueberry mixture is soft set, spoon the blueberry mixture over the cream cheese layer and smooth the top. Refrigerate until completely set, at least 4 hours or overnight. To serve, grab a big spoon and dig in.

STORE, covered, in the refrigerator for up to 3 days.

PISTACHIO ROSE SHORTBREAD DELIGHT

An authentic pistachio delight is part of the subcategory of dessert salads called "fluffs" (see page 110), and is another name for Watergate salad. It typically contains pineapple, marshmallows, and no cookies, so believe me when I say this is a loose interpretation. I just couldn't pass up the opportunity to use "delight" in a recipe title, and, well, between the pistachio, rose, and yogurt up in here, this is my very definition of delight. You could categorize it as a cookie salad, but I believe this salad looks and tastes the best when the shortbread is mostly crumbs, so the eating experience differs slightly.

SERVES 8 TO 12

Pudding

6 tablespoons (75 grams) sugar

3 tablespoons (24 grams) all-purpose flour

¼ teaspoon kosher salt

3 large egg yolks

¾ cup (180 grams) heavy cream

¾ cup (180 grams) whole milk

1 teaspoon vanilla bean paste or extract

Cookies

¾ cup (170 grams) unsalted butter, room temperature

6 tablespoons (75 grams) sugar

1 large egg white

1½ teaspoons pure vanilla extract

½ teaspoon pure almond extract

Green food coloring

1½ cups (195 grams) all-purpose flour, plus more for dusting as needed

½ cup (60 grams) roasted salted pistachios, plus more for topping, coarsely chopped

¾ teaspoon kosher salt

½ teaspoon baking powder

Assembly

1½ cups (360 grams) cold heavy cream

¾ cup (180 grams) cold whole milk Greek yogurt

6 tablespoons (45 grams) powdered sugar

1 tablespoon (15 grams) rosewater

2 tablespoons (40 grams) raspberry jam

1 pint (about 283 grams) raspberries

Candied or dried rose petals, for topping, optional

TO make the pudding, in a medium saucepan, whisk together the sugar, flour, and salt. Whisk in the egg yolks and a couple of splashes of the heavy cream until the mixture comes together into a smooth paste. Drizzle in the remaining heavy cream and milk while whisking until smooth. Set over medium heat and cook, whisking continuously, until the mixture is thickened enough to coat the back of a spoon, about 5 minutes. Add the vanilla. Pour into a heat-safe bowl and cover with plastic wrap so that the wrap touches the surface of the pudding so a skin doesn't form. Refrigerate until chilled, at least 1 hour or up to overnight.

TO make the cookies, preheat the oven to 325°F. Line a sheet pan with parchment paper.

IN a stand mixer fitted with a paddle, combine the butter and sugar on medium high and beat until pale and fluffy, 2 to 3 minutes. Add the egg white, vanilla and almond extracts, and a couple of drops of green food coloring and beat to combine. Stop the mixer and add the flour and chopped pistachios, then sprinkle the salt and baking powder evenly over the dry ingredients. Give the dry ingredients a rough little whisk to combine and then turn the mixer on low and mix until just combined. Scrape down the sides of the bowl with a rubber spatula as needed to ensure that everything combines evenly.

SCRAPE the dough onto the prepared sheet pan and use your hands to flatten it out to a big ¼-inch-thick layer (it won't go all the way to the edges), dusting your hands or the top of the dough with flour if it's too sticky. Bake until barely browned around the edges; begin checking for doneness at 12 minutes. Let cool completely on the pan.

TO make the whip, in a stand mixer fitted with a whisk, combine the heavy cream, yogurt, powdered sugar, and rosewater and beat on medium high until medium-stiff peaks form. Remove about a third of the mixture and set aside. To the remaining whip, fold in the raspberry jam, chilled pudding, most of the raspberries, tearing them up as you add, and most of the cookie, crushing it with your hands as you add it.

TRANSFER to a serving bowl and smooth out the top. Spread on the reserved yogurt whip. Chill until ready to serve. (This tastes best after a few hours in the fridge, once the flavors have melded.) Crumble on the reserved cookie and top with the reserved raspberries, rose petals (if using), and chopped pistachios right before serving.

STORE in an airtight container in the refrigerator for up to 3 days.

GRAPE SALAD

What is there to say about grape salad that hasn't already been said by a small but passionate group of people on the internet during the *New York Times* Grapegate of 2014? That it doesn't represent Minnesota at all? That it actually does, but it's just old and out of fashion? That it really shouldn't matter because, well, it's good?? I'll hop on the train right there, because not only is it actually very good, striking a delicious balance of refreshing, sweet, and rich, but it also has my favorite type of ingredients list: one that is disarmingly simple and creates a sum exponentially better than its parts. But (!) if you put a bowl of sugar-coated choking hazards near my two tiny children, I will promptly move them and then rant about you behind your back to Nick later that night. So I present to you a child-safe, updated lewk that I hope will encourage Minnesotans to not be so sheepish about laying claim to grape salad.

SERVES 2 TO 4, EASILY DOUBLED TO SERVE MORE

1 heaping cup (150 grams) very thinly sliced seedless grapes (2 or 3 colors for a pretty variation)*

*For the prettiest aesthetic, don't use the ends of the grapes (reserve those for snacking).

1 tablespoon (13 grams) light brown sugar

⅛ teaspoon ground cinnamon

½ cup (120 grams) sour cream

Flaky salt

IN a medium bowl, toss the grapes with the brown sugar and cinnamon and let sit at room temperature for 10 minutes.

SPREAD the sour cream in a thin layer on a dinner plate (10-inch diameter or so; if doubling, use a larger serving plate), then scatter the grapes and their juices all over the sour cream. Sprinkle with flaky salt and serve.

BLACK-AND-WHITE COOKIE SALAD

New York City's classic black-and-white cookies do not exist in my town! So, when I get them through the mail or bring them back from a trip or make a whole huge batch of them, there is a safe chance that a fair amount of them will end up too dry for enjoyment on their own. Which makes them an ideal candidate to be tossed into a salad.

The base here is sort of a no-bake cheesecake situation and a nod to my favorite cheesecake in New York, which is the ricotta-based cheesecake at Piccolo Angolo. It's the kind of creamy, light dessert that you can eat after a large Italian meal and not feel like garbage. So while this is as dessert-y of a salad as they come, it has a pleasant refreshing aspect that makes it a good picnic option. Something you can handle eating when it's hot out and you wanna get on a bike afterward.

SERVES 8 TO 12

1 pound (454 grams) strawberries, thinly sliced

2 tablespoons (25 grams) granulated sugar

2 cups (480 grams) cold heavy cream

¾ cup (90 grams) powdered sugar, divided

One 15-ounce container whole milk ricotta, room temperature

One 8-ounce container mascarpone, room temperature

2 teaspoons vanilla bean paste, or seeds scraped from 1 vanilla bean pod

Zest of ½ lemon

¼ teaspoon kosher salt

12 ounces (340 grams) coarsely chopped black-and-white cookies (about 4 cups), plus more for topping (store-bought or homemade using the recipe on page 24)

IN a medium bowl, toss the strawberries with the granulated sugar and set aside.

IN a stand mixer fitted with a whisk, beat the heavy cream and ¼ cup (30 grams) of the powdered sugar on medium high until medium-stiff peaks form. Remove about a third of the whip and set aside. To the stand mixer, add the remaining ½ cup (60 grams) powdered sugar, the ricotta, mascarpone, vanilla, lemon zest, and salt and mix on medium until smooth. Stop the mixer and use a rubber spatula to fold in the chopped cookies and most of the strawberries.

TRANSFER to a serving dish and smooth out the top. Spread on the reserved whipped cream and refrigerate until ready to serve. Top with additional cookies and the remaining strawberries right before serving.

STORE in an airtight container in the refrigerator for up to 3 days.

POMEGRANATE COCONUT GELATIN MOLD

A bavarois* meets malabi† meets *I-told-you-I-was-bringing-a-salad-to-the-potluck-and-heck-yeah-this-is-what-I-meant-just-be-glad-there's-not-Mountain-Dew-and-peas-in-this-Jell-O-salad.*

MAKES ONE 6-CUP GELATIN MOLD (SERVES ABOUT 10)

Pomegranate layer

Nonstick spray

½ cup (120 grams) water

Pink food coloring

2 teaspoons plain gelatin

1 cup (240 grams) pomegranate juice

2 tablespoons (25 grams) sugar

1 teaspoon rosewater

Coconut layer

One 13.5-ounce can full-fat coconut milk, divided

One 0.25-ounce packet plain gelatin

5 large egg yolks

¼ cup (50 grams) sugar

¼ teaspoon kosher salt

Seeds scraped from 1 vanilla bean pod or 2 teaspoons vanilla bean paste

¾ cup (180 grams) heavy cream

Optional toppings

Toasted unsweetened shredded or flaked coconut

Coarsely chopped salted roasted peanuts or other nuts

GREASE a 6-cup gelatin mold and set aside.

TO make the pomegranate layer, in a medium heat-safe bowl, combine the water and a few drops of pink food coloring, then sprinkle the gelatin on top. Set aside.

IN a small saucepan, bring the pomegranate juice and sugar to a boil over high heat, whisking to dissolve the sugar. Remove from the heat and add the rosewater. Pour the mixture over the gelatin and whisk to completely

---

* *Bavarian cream, heavy on the eggs, super rich and luxurious*
† *Middle Eastern milk pudding traditionally topped with fruity rose syrup*

dissolve the gelatin. Pour into the prepared mold and let set completely in the refrigerator; begin checking at 2 hours, but it may need up to 4 hours.

TO make the coconut layer, add ½ cup (120 grams) of the coconut milk to a large heat-safe bowl, sprinkle the gelatin over the top, and set aside.

IN a medium saucepan, combine the egg yolks, sugar, salt, vanilla, and remaining coconut milk and whisk vigorously and thoroughly until smooth. Set over medium heat and cook, whisking continuously until the mixture is thickened enough to coat the back of a spoon, about 5 minutes. Pour it over the gelatin mixture and whisk until the gelatin is completely dissolved. Refrigerate until cool but still liquidy, about 2 hours.

IN a stand mixer fitted with a whisk, beat the heavy cream on medium high until stiff peaks form. Fold this into the coconut mixture, then pour into the gelatin mold on top of the pomegranate layer. Refrigerate until firm, about 2 hours.

UNMOLD onto a serving plate and top with toasted coconut and nuts, if desired. (To easily unmold, dip the mold in warm, not hot, water for a few seconds.)

STORE, covered, in the fridge for up to 4 days.

UBE FLUFF

The happiest section of our local grocery store is at the prepared foods counter: the fluffs. The fluffs sit piled high in big plastic tubs behind a pane of glass, with endless patience, perfectly content knowing that not everybody is going to purchase fluff that day, but the few who do will be brought so much unbridled joy. Fluffs stay fluffy forever because they are whipped cream folded with something stable like Jell-O or pudding or both. Their treasures inside might be canned or fresh fruit, marshmallows, cookies, or nuts.

My first face-to-face encounter with a fluff was at a Fourth of July potluck hosted by my sister-in-law's husband's dad's brother-in-law's sister, and it was her sister-in-law, Margarette, who brought a strawberry fluff that everyone raved about. (If this family connection sounds distant to you, you should hear where I got my lefse recipe . . .) Her special twist was that it contained tapioca pudding, a brilliant texture bonus. This tapioca element inspired me to experiment with my favorite childhood tapioca application, bubble tea, to create what might be a fluff that only a mother could love, but honestly I am just proud that it exists.

Ube (OO-bay) is purple yam that's sweet, earthy, and more subtle in flavor than its loud color suggests. It's a flavor commonly used in Asian, particularly Filipino, desserts and it is my go-to bubble tea flavor, tied only with its cousin, taro. Depending on where you live, tracking down ube halaya (jam) and extract might be a journey, but it's more likely you'll find those than fresh ube (and still have the energy to cook it down and make it usable). The tapioca pudding is another journey that takes kind of forever, and honestly, if you're still paying attention, I'm impressed.

SERVES 8 TO 12

Ube gelatin

2 cups (480 grams) water, divided

1 tablespoon (13 grams) ube extract

Two 0.25-ounce packets plain gelatin

6 tablespoons (75 grams) sugar

Ube tapioca pudding

One 13.5-ounce can light coconut milk

2 tablespoons (25 grams) sugar

¼ teaspoon kosher salt

¼ cup (50 grams) small pearl tapioca

1 large egg

½ teaspoon pure vanilla extract

¼ cup (72 grams) ube halaya (ube jam)

¼ teaspoon ube extract

Assembly

2 cups (480 grams) cold heavy cream

2 tablespoons (15 grams) powdered sugar

1 cup (45 grams) mini marshmallows

TO make the gelatin, in a medium heat-safe bowl, combine ½ cup (120 grams) of the water with the ube extract, then sprinkle the gelatin on top. Set aside. In a medium saucepan, bring the remaining 1½ cups (360 grams) water and the sugar to a boil over high heat, whisking to dissolve the sugar. Pour it over the gelatin mixture and whisk until the gelatin is completely dissolved. Refrigerate until completely set, about 2 hours or overnight.

TO make the pudding, in a medium saucepan, whisk together the coconut milk, sugar, and salt and bring to a simmer over medium-high heat. Stir in the tapioca, reduce the heat to low, and cook, uncovered, stirring often, until the tapioca is soft; begin checking for doneness at 35 minutes, though it could take 45 minutes or more depending on the brand.

IN a large heat-safe measuring cup, whisk the egg. Drizzle in a ladleful of the hot tapioca mixture while whisking very quickly, then slowly drizzle this into the pot while whisking. Keep whisking continuously over low heat until the mixture is thickened, about 5 minutes. Remove from the heat, stir in the vanilla and ube halaya, and transfer to a heat-safe bowl. Cover with plastic wrap so that it touches the surface of the pudding so a skin doesn't form. Refrigerate until chilled, at least 2 hours or overnight.

TO assemble, in a stand mixer fitted with a whisk, beat the heavy cream and powdered sugar on medium high until stiff peaks form. Use a fork to break up the ube gelatin into small pieces. Fold the gelatin, pudding, and most of the marshmallows into the whipped cream. Transfer to a serving bowl, top with the remaining marshmallows, and serve immediately or refrigerate until ready to serve.

STORE in an airtight container in the fridge for up to 3 days. Give it a stir before serving.

DESSERT FOR BREAKFAST

Only curmudgeons complain about dessert for breakfast. I know because I am that curmudgeon every single morning when my child asks for chocolate chips stirred into her oatmeal, but I've yet to find a better way of getting her to eat breakfast. For most of my life I've been a firm believer in setting my day up for success by scrambling an egg, blending up a green smoothie, or pounding some hummus. But around this town, if you invite people over to brunch and there isn't a mattress of carbohydrates dripping with caramelized sugar, your guests will look at you funny. I can't blame them, because dessert for breakfast tastes good. All the things in this chapter taste really *really* good; I just prefer to eat them during the armpit of the afternoon when everything is miserable and the world is ending. The health rules online say not to give in to your heightened craving for junk food at that hour—just eat fruit! But screw that! An afternoon snack of black sesame babka washed down with a matcha is a tried-and-true method of clawing your way to the evening. But "Dessert for Afternoon Snack" doesn't have the same ring to it. So while this chapter is marketed as things to make for the morning, know that you have full permission to eat them for elevenses, fika, after-school snack, tea, nosh, whatever nibbling practice you follow. Not that you needed my permission.

I have to get out in front of this and tell you that a majority of these are not easy breakfasts that you can throw together on a busy weekday. These recipes make you work, but they will reward you with complete and total buttery, pillowy, ooey, gooey, chocolaty, custardy bliss. The kind of goodness that will turn any protein-shake curmudgeon into a believer. The other good news is that for most of these, you can do a majority of the work the day before and bake the morning of, and that will actually yield a better, more flavorful result. So no, I'm not expecting you to wake up at four a.m. and see to it that your dough rises twice.

BUTTERED POTATO DOUGH

AN ALL-PURPOSE ENRICHED DOUGH

Enriched dough (dough that gets textural and flavor boosts from eggs, sugar, and fat) is what you need for swirly buns, babkas, raised doughnuts, and the like. It comes in many forms: some prefer the classic brioche route and shove a ton of butter into the dough; some use a tangzhong method and start with some flour cooked with liquid to coax the dough into holding more moisture; some use melted butter; others go with challah and brute-force the moisture with loads of oil and eggs; others go with heavy cream . . . it's a big doughy world out there. Here is my go-to enriched dough, which is the foundation for many of the recipes in this chapter. It strikes my ideal balance of richness, flavor, feel, and ease. Most of the secret lies in one ingredient: potato flour.

Potato flour gives you the same kind of texture and subtle flavor that you get from adding mashed potatoes and a big boost in moisture like the one that you would get from using a tangzhong or similar type of starter, but requires a fraction of the time and effort. That's because potato flour is essentially just dehydrated mashed potatoes, and it can hold on to so much more liquid than all-purpose flour. It's a delicious magic ingredient that I will preach about until the cows come home or until you just go out and buy some, which shouldn't be that hard because many bigger grocery stores carry it (typically in the natural or organic section). Other than potato, what makes this dough slay is lots of butter, a bit of oil as an insurance policy against dryness, buttermilk for sour depth, and a very good hydration level. It is on the stickier side, but trust me (and please please *pleeeease* weigh your ingredients); this will yield the fluffy bread cloud that you deserve. Some other things:

- This recipe halves very easily; some of the recipes in this book call for half of this batch. (Note: Half of ¼ cup is 2 tablespoons; half of ¾ cup is 6 tablespoons. But you don't actually need this information since you're weighing your ingredients. *Right?*)
- Do use a stand mixer. Kneading by hand would require you to dust your hands and work surface with too much flour, which will dry out the end result.
- Do take your time, and don't rush the butter additions and the kneading process. Kneading makes for strong gluten, which means the dough can hold more air, which means a fluffier result.

- An easy way to get more out of this dough is to slow down the rising process dramatically and give the flavor more time to develop. How do you do this? Put it in the fridge overnight. Since there are two rising periods, it's typically best to choose one to go overnight since too long in the fridge could reduce the effectiveness of the yeast. I usually opt to do the second rise overnight for ease of workflow (read: I can sleep in later and do less in the morning).

- Pay attention to temperatures. Not just oven temperatures but ingredient temperatures, atmosphere temperatures, and internal temperatures of the end product. A few degrees can make a big difference in rising time, bake time, and the end result. If the milk is too hot, it may kill the yeast. If your loaf looks done on the outside, it may still be undercooked on the inside. If your house is very warm, the dough will rise faster; if it is cool enough that you're wearing a sweater, you may wonder whether you did something wrong when your dough takes awhile to proof. So keep your instant-read thermometer nearby. And in general, be aware that timing is not the only element that you should pay attention to when determining whether your dough has risen or is done baking; the visual cues are just as important.

- To speed things up (or eliminate chance) during the rising and proofing stages, turn your oven into a proofer by sticking a pan of boiling water in your unheated oven along with the dough.

- You can use potato flakes in place of the potato flour, using the same amount by weight, which is about 1⅓ cups. Be sure to use a brand that contains only potatoes on the ingredients list. If you really can't be bothered to find potato flour or flakes, substitute ¾ cup (95 grams) bread flour for a less good but still good alternative.

Although this dough takes some time, it is quite user-friendly and well worth the effort.

4 cups (520 grams) bread flour, plus more for dusting

6 tablespoons (68 grams) potato flour

¼ cup (50 grams) sugar

2¼ teaspoons (1 packet) instant yeast

1½ teaspoons kosher salt

1 cup (240 grams) warm buttermilk (or whole milk /105° to 110°F)

2 tablespoons (25 grams) unrefined coconut oil, room temperature, or neutral oil

2 teaspoons vanilla bean paste or extract

4 large eggs

¾ cup (170 grams) unsalted butter, room temperature

Neutral oil, for the bowl

IN a stand mixer, whisk together the bread flour, potato flour, sugar, yeast, and salt. Add the buttermilk, oil, vanilla, and eggs and use the dough hook to combine into a stiff dough, starting off on low, and then increasing the speed to medium when you're confident that flour won't fly everywhere. This may take a couple of minutes and you may need to use a spatula to help incorporate everything, but you'll get there.

WITH the mixer running on medium, add the butter 1 tablespoon (14 grams) at a time, allowing it to incorporate between each addition. Once all the butter is incorporated, continue mixing on medium for 10 to 15 minutes, until smooth but still rather sticky. You can test to see if it's ready by pinching off a small ball of dough and stretching it between your fingers; if it gets thin enough to see light shining through without breaking, it's ready. If it tears quite easily, keep on mixing.

LIGHTLY oil a clean large bowl, then use oiled hands to stretch the dough into a ball with a smooth, taut surface. Place the dough in the oiled bowl with the smooth top down and turn it over to fully coat the dough in oil. Cover with plastic wrap and let rise in a draft-free place (or in an oven that's turned off with a pan of boiling water in it) until doubled in size, 1 to 2 hours.

MARZIPAN POPPY SEED BABKA MUFFINS

Marzipan and poppy seed was a flavor combination that I first got hooked on in Berlin, when I found marzipan poppy seed yogurt at a grocery store. It wasn't just almondy yogurt that required floss after eating; it actually had enough poppy seeds to benefit from their faint fruity flavor, as well as their nuttiness, which made sense as a pairing with the marzipan.

This muffin is a loose nod to lemon poppy seed muffins, which rule the grocery store muffin department, and my desire for marzipan babka. Since marzipan and babka dough are both white, you don't get the prettiest swirl, but poppy seeds bring in the drama and contribute striking crunchy pizzazz. And, yeah, a need for floss, but so what?

MAKES 12 JUMBO MUFFINS

Nonstick spray

Filling

1 cup (112 grams) fine almond flour

½ cup (70 grams) poppy seeds, finely ground in a spice grinder

¾ cup (150 grams) sugar

¼ cup (50 grams) unrefined coconut oil, melted

1 teaspoon pure almond extract

¼ teaspoon kosher salt

Zest of ½ orange

¼ cup (60 grams) milk

Crumble and assembly

All-purpose or bread flour, for dusting

1 batch Buttered Potato Dough (page 114)

¼ cup (33 grams) all-purpose flour

¼ cup (30 grams) powdered sugar

¼ cup (28 grams) sliced almonds

Big pinch of kosher salt

¼ cup (56 grams) cold unsalted butter, cut into ½-inch cubes

Egg wash: 1 egg beaten with a splash of water

GREASE 12 jumbo muffin wells.

TO make the filling, spread the almond flour in a small skillet and heat over low, stirring continuously, until lightly toasted, 3 to 4 minutes. Pour into a medium bowl and let cool for a few minutes. Add the ground poppy seeds, sugar, coconut oil, almond extract, salt, orange zest, and milk and mix with a stiff rubber spatula to combine.

ON a lightly floured surface, roll the dough out into a 16 × 22-inch rectangle. Dollop on two-thirds of the filling all over and spread it out. It's pretty sticky; don't worry about getting a perfectly even layer. Fold the top half of the dough down over the bottom half and dollop and spread on the remaining filling. Cut the dough vertically into 12 short strips, twist each several times, and coil and nestle each in a muffin well. Cover loosely with plastic wrap and let proof either in the fridge overnight (preferred!) or at room temperature, until puffy and risen by about half, about 45 minutes. (If you refrigerated them overnight, let them sit at room temperature for 45 minutes before baking.)

TO make the crumble (which you can do the day before or the day of baking), in a small bowl, combine the flour, powdered sugar, almonds, and salt. Add the butter and rub together with your fingers until the butter is thoroughly incorporated and the mixture is coarse and crumbly. Feel free to break up the almonds a bit. Keep in the fridge until ready to use.

PREHEAT the oven to 350°F.

GENTLY brush the top of the risen muffins with the egg wash and cover with the crumble. Bake until the tops are deep golden brown and the internal temperature is 190° to 195°F on an instant-read thermometer; begin checking for doneness at 28 minutes. Let cool for 15 minutes in the pan, then transfer to a wire rack. Eat them while they're warm!

STORE in an airtight container at room temperature for up to a couple of days (though they're best eaten the day they're made). You can also freeze these for up to 3 months; thaw at room temperature.

PUFFY POTATO DOUGHNUTS

Making a good doughnut is not hard. Fry anything at the proper temperature and it will be enjoyable. Challah dough, pizza dough, canned biscuit dough. Anyone can make doughnuts as long as they're of age to be responsible around hot oil. But making a great doughnut takes some extra consideration that isn't hiding in the obvious places, like the ingredients list. It's hiding in the few degrees of air temperature that fluctuate in our homes throughout the seasons, in the close attention you should pay to the visual rising cues, and in the annoying stop-in-your-tracks-and-flip-to-the-next-recipe direction that asks you to proof these overnight. Well, don't flip to the next recipe, because the little tricks I'm about to teach you are very easy and will take your doughnut game to the level you always hoped for.

Let's address the proofing. First, that annoying overnight stay in the fridge. There's only so much that sugar and good butter and vanilla bean can do for a dough. But let it sit in the fridge overnight and it will develop the kind of yeasty depth that hits you at the back of the mouth for a visceral groan of a reaction, the kind of thing that you just can't rush. Second, don't let the seasons or unattractive AC-blasting habits dictate your doughnut destiny. Unlike a pan of swirly buns all cozily nestled together, doughnuts are small and alone, and they get chilly easily, so they need all the help and warmth they can get to achieve maximum jiggliness. (This maximum jiggliness will ultimately yield a super-fluffy result that has that picturesque belly band around the equator.) Help comes in the form of a proofer: a small, temperature-controlled environment that will easily reach peak warm proofing temperature when you stick a pan of hot water in it. (I'm talking about your oven.) In an ideal world, you use your oven as a proofer every time you work with yeasted dough, but in the case of babkas and swirly buns and the like, your oven is probably busy preheating. As such, doughnuts are uniquely suited for this, since they're fried, not baked. How convenient! Last, don't rush this process. Let these babies double completely and get so super jiggly! Give them their time to bloom. It will all pay off, I promise.

You can fill your doughnuts with any jam or custard; I am a purist and love a simple sweet vanilla bean cream. Occasionally I go wild and opt for chocolate, though, so both options are here.

1 batch Buttered Potato Dough (page 114)

Vanilla bean filling

½ cup (65 grams) all-purpose flour

¾ cup (150 grams) sugar

½ teaspoon kosher salt

6 large egg yolks

1½ cups (360 grams) heavy cream

1½ cups (360 grams) whole milk

4 teaspoons (19 grams) vanilla bean paste, or seeds scraped from 2 vanilla bean pods

Frying and assembly

Neutral oil, for frying

About ½ cup (100 grams) sugar, for rolling

LINE two sheet pans with parchment paper. Divide the dough into 20 equal pieces and shape them into smooth, taut balls by stretching the ends under, pinching them, and rolling them around a few times so they're smooth. Place 2 inches apart on the prepared sheet pans. Cover with plastic wrap and refrigerate overnight (see Notes).

TO make the vanilla bean filling (which you can do the day before or the day of frying), combine the flour, sugar, and salt in a large saucepan. Whisk in the egg yolks and about ¼ cup (60 grams) of the heavy cream until the mixture comes together in a smooth paste, adding another drizzle of heavy cream if needed to bring it together. Drizzle in the remaining heavy cream and milk while whisking until smooth. Set over medium heat and cook, whisking continuously, until bubbles rise to the surface and pop, about 5 minutes. By this time the mixture will be very thick and pudding-like. You will likely need to pause whisking for a few brief moments to confirm that bubbles are rising, but this is an important sign that the pastry cream will be thick enough once it cools, so don't skip this step. Remove from the heat and continue to whisk for another minute or two so that the residual heat from the pot doesn't cause the mixture to curdle, then stir in the vanilla. Pour into a heat-safe bowl. Cover with plastic wrap so that it touches the surface of the pastry cream so a skin doesn't form. Refrigerate until chilled and thickened, at least 4 hours or overnight.

ON the day of frying, fill a loaf pan with boiling water and place it in the oven anywhere it will fit when the doughnuts are in there as well. Gently loosen the plastic wrap on the doughnuts so it's just sitting on top of them and stick the pans in the oven to proof until the doughnuts are completely doubled in size, 30 minutes to 1 hour.

FILL a large heavy-bottomed pot (ideally cast iron) with 2 inches of oil and clip on a candy thermometer. Heat to 350°F over medium-high heat. Gently, very gently, use an oiled spatula to lift the doughnuts from the pan to the oil and fry just a few at a time (you want there to be an inch or so of space between them as they're frying), for 1½ to 2½ minutes per side, until deep golden brown and with an internal temperature of around 150°F. (Their temperature will rise substantially right out of the oil, reaching about 180° to 190°F.) Transfer to a wire rack.

SPREAD the ½ cup (100 grams) sugar in a shallow bowl and, when the doughnuts are just cool enough to handle, roll the doughnuts in the sugar. Let cool completely, or if you're going to eat one immediately, fill only one with pastry cream and leave the rest until they're cooled.

TO fill the doughnuts, use a chopstick or skinny knife to poke a hole in a side of the doughnut without going all the way through. Fill a piping bag or large zip-top bag with the filling, snip off the end, and pipe a generous amount of filling into the doughnuts, tilting the piping bag in a couple of different directions to really fill it up and then releasing pressure as you near the top.

THESE are best eaten the day they're made.

NOTES

CHOCOLATE FILLING OPTION! This option is *very* good, but I personally prefer the vanilla: Add ⅔ cup (53 grams) Dutch-process or unsweetened cocoa powder and ½ teaspoon espresso powder when whisking together the dry ingredients. Instead of using expensive vanilla beans, add 2 teaspoons vanilla extract, since the chocolate will overpower the vanilla flavor anyway.

DON'T WANT TO WAIT OVERNIGHT? It's okay, I get it. You can fry these today. You'll lose some depth of flavor, but you'll still end up with great doughnuts. To do this, cover the dough balls loosely with plastic wrap and stick in the oven along with a loaf pan filled with boiling water. Close the door and proof until doubled, about 30 minutes.

CARDAMOM BUNS

The problem with some cardamom buns is the same as with any stand-alone bun: the risk of drying out too quickly is very high. But when they're nestled cozily in a pan, they smoosh together and keep each other moist. (Ew @ "keep each other moist," but what other option did I have?) Extra bonuses here are the soft edges from where they kiss in the oven and the sugar that caramelizes on the bottom of the pan, making a caramel roll comparison not terribly far off. When people come to Bernie's, they either flock to these or point at them and ask if they're caramel rolls. One of my favorite customer conversations is explaining that cardamom is like a woodsy, peppery cousin to cinnamon. These sweet sticky pillowy knots are one of our most popular breakfast items for good reason.

MAKES 12 BUNS

Nonstick spray

6 tablespoons (85 grams) unsalted butter, room temperature

2 tablespoons (25 grams) neutral oil

¾ cup (150 grams) packed light brown sugar

1½ teaspoons ground cardamom

⅛ teaspoon kosher salt

All-purpose or bread flour, for dusting

1 batch Buttered Potato Dough (page 114)

Egg wash: 1 egg beaten with a splash of water

2 tablespoons (24 grams) Swedish pearl sugar, for sprinkling (or substitute turbinado or granulated sugar)

GREASE a 9 × 13-inch metal pan. (If you have only a glass or ceramic pan, that's okay; just prepare to bake these a little longer!)

TO make the filling, combine the butter, oil, brown sugar, cardamom, and salt in a medium bowl and mix with a stiff rubber spatula until smooth.

ON a lightly floured surface, roll the dough out into a 16 × 22-inch rectangle. Spread three-quarters of the filling on the dough. Fold the top third of the dough down (as if you were folding a letter), spread the remaining filling on the bare dough, and then fold the bottom third up and over. Cut vertically into 12 short strips.

WORKING with one strip at a time, stretch it out gently, then twist it several times and coil it into a messy rustic knot. (It does not need to be perfect.)

Nestle into the pan in a 3 × 4 grid. Cover with plastic wrap and let proof either in the fridge overnight (preferred!) or at room temperature, until puffy and risen by about half, about 45 minutes. (If you refrigerated the buns overnight, let them sit at room temperature for 45 minutes before baking.)

PREHEAT the oven to 350°F.

GENTLY brush the buns with the egg wash and sprinkle with the pearl sugar. Bake until golden brown and the internal temperature is 190° to 195°F on an instant-read thermometer; begin checking for doneness at 30 minutes. Let cool slightly in the pan, then get at them while they're still warm.

STORE, covered, at room temperature for up to a couple of days (though these are best eaten the day they are made).

CHOCOLATE SWIRLY BUNS

Set your alarm for thirty minutes earlier than when you're pretty sure your least-morning-person kid will start stirring. Tiptoe downstairs, move the pan of chocolate-swirled dough that you shaped last night from the refrigerator to the counter, and preheat the oven. Make some coffee, do the crossword, and sit for a blissful few minutes of peace as the sun comes up. Nurse the baby, feed the dog, and get the buns in the oven, then unload the dishwasher as it becomes safer to make noise and disturb the toddler. Let the smell of the buns wash over you as you tend to the morning stretches and go through the princess dress wardrobe options for the day. And then, just when all hanger is about to let loose, unveil this pan of steamy, buttery, gooey, sweet, and chocolaty buns that hold the answers to every single one of life's questions except, perhaps, "Mama, where is wedding Barbie's left shoe?"

MAKES 12 BUNS

Nonstick spray

All-purpose or bread flour, for dusting

1 batch Buttered Potato Dough (page 114)

Filling

2 tablespoons (28 grams) unsalted butter, melted

1 tablespoon (13 grams) unrefined coconut oil, melted

⅔ cup (133 grams) sugar

6 tablespoons (30 grams) Dutch-process or unsweetened cocoa powder

½ teaspoon instant espresso powder

¼ teaspoon kosher salt

4 ounces (113 grams) semisweet chocolate, finely chopped

Egg wash: 1 egg beaten with a splash of water (see Note)

Syrup

½ cup (100 grams) sugar

½ cup (120 grams) water

½ teaspoon pure vanilla extract

½ teaspoon rosewater or almond extract or orange blossom water . . . you get the picture!

Glaze, optional (see Note), and assembly

1½ cup (180 grams) powdered sugar

¼ cup (60 grams) milk

Pinch of kosher salt

Flaky salt, optional

NOTE: *If using the glaze, feel free to omit the egg wash.*

GREASE a 9 × 13-inch metal pan. (If you have only a glass or ceramic pan, that's okay; just prepare to bake these a little longer!)

ON a lightly floured surface, roll the dough out into a 16 × 22-inch rectangle.

COMBINE the butter and oil in a small bowl and brush it all over the surface of the dough, leaving a ½-inch border at the top. In a separate small bowl, mix together the sugar, cocoa, espresso powder, and salt. Sprinkle it all over the dough, pressing it in with your hands. Scatter on the chopped chocolate. Working from the bottom, roll the dough into a tight log. Pinch the edges to seal and cut into 12 rolls. Arrange the rolls in the pan in a 3 × 4 grid, cut side up.

COVER with plastic wrap and let proof either in the fridge overnight (preferred!) or at room temperature, until puffy and risen by about half, about 45 minutes. (If you refrigerated the rolls overnight, let them sit at room temperature for 45 minutes before baking.)

PREHEAT the oven to 350°F.

GENTLY brush the rolls with the egg wash. Bake until golden and the internal temperature is 190° to 195°F on an instant-read thermometer; begin checking for doneness at 30 minutes.

WHILE the rolls are baking, make the syrup. Bring the sugar and water to a boil in a small saucepan over high heat, whisking to dissolve the sugar. Remove from the heat and whisk in the extracts.

IF using the glaze, combine the powdered sugar, milk, and salt in a medium bowl and whisk until smooth.

RIGHT when the buns come out of the oven, pour the syrup on top. Let cool for about 10 minutes, then glaze (if glazing), sprinkle with a little flaky salt (if using), and tear into them.

STORE, covered, at room temperature for up to a couple of days (though these are best eaten the day they are made).

BLACK SESAME BABKA

Welcome to one of my favorite recipes! Here are some reasons why it's one of my faves:

1. You know I'm a real sucker for any Asian Jewish mashup.
2. I am Team Backstreet Boys, forever and ever (a.k.a. the other BSB).
3. Its cross-section looks just like a sonogram picture, a discovery that I made in the exact moment that we got home with our sonogram picture of Ira. Let me tell you, a cross-section of babka is way more fun to post on Instagram than a picture of a dark blurry picture.
4. And, of course, it's delicious: I love the contrast between the dark, nutty sesame and the fluffy dough. It leaves no flavor stone unturned, because all black sesame's partners in crime are here: orange zest, almond, coconut, and crushed Oreos (which do double duty helping this thing stay together by absorbing some inner moisture and adding subtle Oreo flavor). I cannot imagine a better pairing for my afternoon matcha.

MAKES 1 LOAF

Nonstick spray

Filling

¼ cup (56 grams) unsalted butter, room temperature

1 tablespoon (13 grams) unrefined coconut oil, melted

⅓ cup (52 grams) black sesame seeds, finely ground in a spice grinder

⅓ cup (67 grams) sugar

⅛ teaspoon kosher salt

Zest of ½ orange

Crumble and assembly

All-purpose or bread flour, for dusting

½ batch Buttered Potato Dough (page 114), with the following additions (add these when you add the vanilla): zest of ½ orange and ½ teaspoon pure almond extract

4 Oreos, broken up and finely ground in a spice grinder

¼ cup (33 grams) all-purpose flour

¼ cup (30 grams) powdered sugar

1 tablespoon (10 grams) black sesame seeds

Big pinch of kosher salt

¼ cup (56 grams) cold unsalted butter, cut into ½-inch cubes

Egg wash: 1 egg beaten with a splash of water

GREASE a 5 × 9-inch metal loaf pan or 4 × 9-inch pullman loaf pan and line with enough parchment paper to allow for 1-inch wings on the long sides.

TO make the filling, combine the butter, oil, ground black sesame seeds, sugar, salt, and zest in a medium bowl and mix together with a stiff rubber spatula.

ON a lightly floured surface, roll the dough out into a 10 × 22-inch rectangle. Spread on the filling, leaving a ½-inch border at the top and reserving 2 tablespoons (28 grams) of the filling. Sprinkle with the cookie crumbs.

WORKING from the bottom, roll the dough into a tight log and pinch the edges to seal. Cut the log in half crosswise to make two shorter logs. Spread the top of one of the logs with the reserved filling and then twist the logs together. Transfer to the loaf pan, cover with plastic wrap, and let proof either in the fridge overnight (preferred!) or at room temperature, until puffy and risen by about half, about 45 minutes. (If you refrigerated it overnight, let it sit at room temperature for 1 hour before baking.)

TO make the crumble (which you can do the day before or the day of baking), combine the flour, powdered sugar, black sesame seeds, and salt in a small bowl. Add the butter and rub together with your fingers until the butter is thoroughly incorporated and the mixture is coarse and crumbly. Keep in the fridge until ready to use.

ARRANGE an oven rack in the lower middle position and preheat the oven to 350°F.

GENTLY brush the top of the risen babka with the egg wash and sprinkle the crumble all over the top. Bake until the top is deep golden brown and the internal temperature is 190° to 195°F; begin checking for doneness at 40 minutes.

LET cool for 20 minutes in the pan, then transfer to a wire rack. Enjoy warm or at room temperature. (It will slice cleaner if it's cooled completely, but warm babka is worth the extra sloppiness.)

STORE in an airtight container at room temperature for up to 4 days. If there's any left when it loses its moisture, make French toast! Or make babka chips by slicing it thinly and toasting in a 250°F oven until very crisp. Eat on their own or dip into a *fluff* (see page 110)!

STRAWBERRY, RASPBERRY, AND ELDERFLOWER JAM

One magical spring, Bonne Maman made a limited-edition jar of preserves that featured a gorgeous trio of strawberry, raspberry, and elderflower. I ate a *lot* of it but sadly didn't have a chance to get sick of it before the run was over. So this is my homemade version. It's a classic berry jam with a secret: it feels fancy, but you can't exactly pinpoint why. (It's the charm of the elderflower.) It's not flowery-perfume strong; it's very subtle, yet so enchanting.

MAKES ABOUT 2 CUPS

4 ounces (113 grams) raspberries

12 ounces (340 grams) strawberries, finely chopped

1¼ cups (250 grams) sugar

Large pinch of kosher salt (or omit it and eat your jam toast sprinkled with flaky salt)

Zest and juice of ½ lemon

Seeds scraped from 1 vanilla bean pod, or 2 teaspoons vanilla bean paste

2 tablespoons (30 grams) elderflower liqueur or cordial

IN a large heavy-bottomed pot (such as a soup pot or Dutch oven), toss the raspberries and strawberries with the sugar and salt and let sit covered for 1 to 2 hours to enhance the flavor.

WHEN you're ready to make the jam, stick a small plate in the freezer. Add the lemon zest and juice and vanilla to the pot (if using a vanilla bean, toss in the scraped bean, too, to infuse the jam) and bring to a boil over medium-high heat, stirring and scraping down the sides with a heat-safe spatula continuously so it doesn't burn. Cook until thickened and jam-like, 6 to 8 minutes, or longer if your berries are particularly juicy. To test if it's ready, remove the jam from the heat (continue to stir for another minute or two so the residual heat from the pot doesn't cause the jam to burn) and dollop a spot of jam on the frozen plate. Once it cools (which will be very quickly), check to see if it sets to a jam-like consistency. If so, it's ready. If it's still runny, return the jam to the heat and cook for another few minutes.

ONCE the jam is ready, stir in the elderflower, then transfer to a heat-safe container, discarding the vanilla bean (if using). Cool completely in the refrigerator (it will thicken as it cools) and slather it on toast.

STORE in an airtight container in the fridge for up to several weeks.

HALVA, WALNUT, AND CHOCOLATE CHUNK SCONE LOAF

The combination of halva, walnut, and chocolate was introduced to me in an Ottolenghi cookbook, and it instantly enchanted me. Obviously, chocolate and sweet sesame halva go together, and obviously walnuts contribute their crunchy, slightly chewy selves so brilliantly in chocolate chip cookies, so obviously a love triangle of the three is going to be a winner. This scone loaf has all the advantages of any scone baked in loaf form—that is, the opportunity for more moisture and thus a longer lifespan, as well as one additional advantage that specifically addresses halva's free-spirited nature: bake halva in a regular free-form scone and you run the risk of it melting out and escaping, but if you bake it in a scone with protective fences around the sides, it stays where it's supposed to be. Voilà! A loaf to love.

MAKES 1 LOAF

Nonstick spray

2 cups (260 grams) all-purpose flour, plus more for dusting

½ cup (100 grams) plus 1 tablespoon (13 grams) sugar, divided

1 tablespoon (14 grams) baking powder

¾ teaspoon kosher salt

¾ cup (170 grams) cold unsalted butter, cut into ½-inch cubes

8 ounces (226 grams) halva, any flavor, coarsely chopped

4 ounces (113 grams) semisweet chocolate, coarsely chopped

¾ cup (78 grams) roasted unsalted walnuts, coarsely chopped

2 large eggs

½ cup (120 grams) cold heavy cream

1 teaspoon pure vanilla extract

PREHEAT the oven to 400°F. Grease a 4 × 9-inch pullman loaf pan or 5 × 9-inch metal loaf pan and line with enough parchment paper to allow for 1-inch wings on the long sides.

IN a food processor, pulse together the flour, ½ cup (100 grams) of the sugar, the baking powder, and salt. Add the butter and pulse until the butter is roughly pea size, with a few bigger bits. (You can also do this by hand in a big bowl; use your fingers to incorporate the butter by smashing and rubbing it in with the dry ingredients until it's evenly dispersed and the butter is roughly pea size, with a few bigger bits.)

DUMP the mixture into a large bowl and toss in the halva, chocolate, and walnuts. In a separate medium bowl or large measuring cup, whisk together the eggs, heavy cream, and vanilla. Add the wet ingredients to the dry ingredients and mix with a rubber spatula or wooden spoon until just combined. Scrape the dough into the prepared pan and spread it out evenly. Sprinkle with the remaining 1 tablespoon (13 grams) of sugar.

BAKE until the loaf is browned on top and a toothpick inserted into the center comes out clean; begin checking for doneness at 50 minutes and tent with foil if the top browns too much for your liking before the center is done. Let cool for 20 minutes in the pan, then transfer to a wire rack. Cool for at least 10 more minutes before slicing and eating.

STORE in an airtight container at room temperature. This is best eaten within 3 days but will keep for up to 5 days.

JAM AND MOZZARELLA ENGLISH MUFFIN ROLLS

Just like pita, homemade English muffins are exponentially better than their store-bought counterparts, so much so that they should really be offended that they share the same name. Here is a swirly variation on English muffins, because making individual English muffins can get steppy and also because swirly buns are a fun prep-ahead for brunch. The mozzarella element contributes some bulk and protein that allows these the freedom to feel somewhat like a stand-alone breakfast; it also provides that creamy, savory quality so great with jam. Don't skimp on the cornmeal; that's the signature English muffin crunch.

MAKES 12 ROLLS

Dough

4 cups (520 grams) all-purpose or bread flour, plus more for dusting as needed

3 tablespoons (38 grams) sugar

2¼ teaspoons (1 packet) instant yeast

2 teaspoons kosher salt

1 cup (240 grams) warm whole milk (105° to 110°F)

½ cup (113 grams) unsalted butter, melted

1 cup (240 grams) Greek yogurt (2% or whole milk)

Neutral oil, for the bowl

Assembly

¼ cup (56 grams) unsalted butter, room temperature

About 6 tablespoons (60 grams) yellow cornmeal

1 cup (320 grams) jam (any kind; strawberry is particularly good)

8 ounces/226 grams sliced deli mozzarella (at room temperature so it's more flexible) or torn fresh mozzarella

Egg wash: 1 egg beaten with a splash of water (see Note)

Glaze, optional (see Note)

1 cup (120 grams) powdered sugar

3 tablespoons (45 grams) Greek yogurt (2% or whole milk)

Pinch of kosher salt

NOTE: *If using the glaze, feel free to omit the egg wash.*

IN a stand mixer, whisk together the flour, sugar, yeast, and salt. Add the milk, butter, and yogurt and use the dough hook to combine into a dough, starting off on low, and then increasing the speed to medium when you're confident that flour won't fly everywhere. Continue to mix for 12 to 15 minutes, until soft and smooth but still sticky. Transfer to a large oiled bowl, turning the dough to coat it fully in oil, cover with plastic wrap, and let rise in a draft-free place (or in an oven that's turned off with a pan of boiling water in it) until doubled, 1 to 2 hours.

COAT a 9 × 13-inch metal pan with the butter (Use the whole ¼ cup/ 56 grams of softened butter! It seems like a lot, but it'll taste good!) and dust all over with the cornmeal, tapping out any excess. (If you only have a glass or ceramic pan, that's okay; just prepare to bake these a little longer. You can also bake in a 3½-quart round braiser.)

DUST your work surface liberally with cornmeal and then roll the dough out into a 12 × 24-inch rectangle. With a small offset spatula, spread the dough with an even layer of the jam, then top evenly with the mozzarella, leaving a 1-inch border at the top. Working from the bottom, roll up the dough into a tight log and pinch the edges to seal. With a sharp knife, slice into 12 rolls.

PLACE the rolls in the prepared baking dish in a 3 × 4 grid and cover with plastic wrap. Let proof either in the fridge overnight (preferred!) or at room temperature, until puffy and risen by about half, about 45 minutes. (If you refrigerated the rolls overnight, let them sit at room temperature for 1 hour before baking.)

PREHEAT the oven to 375°F.

GENTLY brush the rolls with the egg wash, and bake until the rolls are golden brown; begin checking for doneness at 28 minutes. Let cool for 10 minutes.

IF using the glaze, combine the powdered sugar, yogurt, and salt in a medium bowl and whisk until smooth.

DRIZZLE the glaze over the warm rolls and serve.

STORE, covered, in the refrigerator for a couple of days (though these are best eaten the day they are made). Reheat in the microwave.

MANDEL BREAD CEREAL

A very long time ago, before recipes ever really went viral, a sweet blog reader named Zoe wrote to me and suggested I make homemade cereal. Not like granola, but actual cute sugary cereal. I loved that idea! I proceeded to spend a day stamping out millions of teeny-tiny raspberry-filled, glazed, sprinkled Pop Tart–style cookies, and thoroughly enjoying the one bowl of cereal that it made. This was clearly before kids.

Years later, when homemade pancake cereal went viral and spawned a bunch of variations, I felt that Zoe and I were personally seen. All the variations were so hilarious and exciting that I knew I wanted to keep the concept of homemade cereal alive, even if it's now many, many trend cycles ago. These days the thought of shaping all those tiny cookies is incomprehensible, but I can wrap my head around a slice-and-bake situation, which can yield lots of tiny slices in a short amount of time and is modeled on a crunchy cookie that's intended to get dunked in a liquid anyway.

Mandel bread is like Jewish biscotti; it usually contains almonds, since "mandel" means "almond" in Yiddish. I used oat flour here, so I can feel slightly less bad about giving my kids a bowl of cookies for breakfast, but the oat flour also contributes oaty flavor, so that's a bonus. The almonds in this case are tossed into the cereal mix, because mixing them into the dough would have disrupted the gracefulness of the tiny cookie slices. And dried fruit adds chewy contrast to the cookies. This is a great snack mix on its own, too, if it's not the morning and/or you ran out of milk.

MAKES ABOUT 6 CUPS

½ cup (100 grams) plus 2 teaspoons sugar, divided

½ cup (100 grams) extra virgin olive oil or neutral oil

1 large egg

1 teaspoon pure vanilla extract

¼ teaspoon pure almond extract

¾ cup (84 grams) oat flour

½ teaspoon kosher salt

1 cup (130 grams) all-purpose flour

½ teaspoon baking powder

½ cup (80 grams) semisweet mini chocolate chips

1 cup (112 grams) slivered, sliced, or coarsely chopped unsalted almonds

1 cup (120 grams) dried cranberries

Milk, for serving

ARRANGE oven racks in the upper middle and lower middle positions and preheat the oven to 350°F. Line two rimmed sheet pans with parchment paper.

IN a large bowl, whisk together ½ cup (100 grams) of the sugar and the oil until combined. Whisk in the egg, then the vanilla and almond extracts. Whisk in the oat flour and salt, then sprinkle the all-purpose flour and baking powder evenly over the surface of the batter and whisk to incorporate, switching to a rubber spatula when it gets too thick. Fold in the chocolate chips.

PULL off a handful of dough and shape it on a sheet pan into a ½-inch-thick snake. (It does not need to be perfect!) Continue shaping the dough into snakes, spacing them 2 inches apart on the prepared sheet pans. Sprinkle the tops with the remaining 2 teaspoons of sugar and bake until the bottoms are just set; begin checking for doneness at 12 minutes.

REMOVE from the oven and reduce the oven temperature to 250°F.

LET the snakes cool on the pans for 10 minutes, then carefully transfer to a cutting board (don't fret if any break in transit; they're about to get chopped up anyway) and use a sharp knife to cut each snake on a bias into roughly ¼-inch-thick slices. Transfer the slices back to the sheet pans, spreading them out evenly, and scatter on the almonds.

RETURN the sheet pans to the oven and toast until mandel bread and almonds are lightly browned and crisp; begin checking for doneness at 28 minutes. Switch each pan to the other rack and rotate the pans 180 degrees a little over halfway through the bake time.

LET cool completely on the pans, scatter on the cranberries, and then transfer to an airtight container. Eat in a bowl with milk!

STORE in an airtight container at room temperature for up to 2 weeks.

WILD RICE PANCAKES WITH POACHED RHUBARB

The most Minnesota pancake to ever exist makes use of our state grain, wild rice, to add quirky chewiness and pleasant nuttiness to an otherwise classic sweet pancake. Its appearance, flecked with black, seedy-looking things, is actually a lot bolder than it eats. This is a move inspired by the pancakes at the Minnesota Nice Cafe, in the lake town of Bemidji, where we go every summer to do as Minnesotans do and exist next to or within or on top of a lake all day. The poached rhubarb pairing solidifies this pancake's position as the most Minnesota pancake, because you are just not a Minnesotan if you have more than one degree of separation between you and a rhubarb patch. It will take no offense when you pair it with a secondary topping of maple syrup, because it knows exactly how sour it is. The secret to greatness here is no different from every other pancake's secret, which is three rounds of butter: once in the batter, once in the pan, and once out of the pan.

MAKES 8 TO 10 PANCAKES

Pancakes

⅓ cup (60 grams) wild rice, rinsed

3 cups (720 grams) water

1½ teaspoons kosher salt, divided

1 cup (130 grams) cake flour or all-purpose flour

½ cup (56 grams) fine almond flour

⅓ cup (67 grams) sugar

1 tablespoon baking powder

½ teaspoon ground cinnamon

⅛ teaspoon freshly grated nutmeg

2 large eggs

1 cup (240 grams) whole milk

1 teaspoon pure vanilla extract

¼ teaspoon pure almond extract

¼ cup (56 grams) unsalted butter, melted and cooled slightly, plus more for cooking and serving

Topping and assembly

½ cup (100 grams) sugar

½ cup (100 grams) water

Pinch of kosher salt

12 ounces (340 grams) rhubarb, cut into 1-inch pieces (fresh or frozen is okay)

Zest of ½ lemon

½ teaspoon vanilla bean paste or extract

Maple syrup, for serving

COMBINE the wild rice, water, and 1 teaspoon of the salt in a medium saucepan. Cover and bring to a boil over high heat, then reduce the heat to a simmer and cook until the rice is just tender but still has a little chew, 35 to 45 minutes. (The grains should have split but not totally burst.) Drain, rinse in cold water to cool, and set aside to drain well. You should have about 1 cup of cooked rice. (The rice can be cooked the night before and kept in the fridge.)

WHILE the rice is cooking, make the poached rhubarb. Combine the sugar, water, and salt in a medium saucepan and bring to a boil over high heat. Reduce the heat to low and add the rhubarb. Simmer gently until the rhubarb is just tender but still intact, 5 to 10 minutes. Be careful not to go much longer or the rhubarb will fall apart. Stir in the lemon zest and vanilla. (This can be made the night before and kept in the fridge.)

TO make the pancakes, in a large bowl, whisk together the flour, almond flour, sugar, baking powder, cinnamon, nutmeg, and the remaining ½ teaspoon salt. In a separate medium bowl or large measuring cup, whisk together the eggs, milk, and vanilla and almond extracts. Add the wet ingredients to the dry ingredients and whisk just a few times to moisten the dry ingredients. The mixture should still be quite lumpy. (This is the secret to a thick, fluffy pancake.) Stir in the melted butter, then fold in the wild rice to evenly distribute. Again, don't mix any more than necessary; keep that batter lumpy.

HEAT a large cast-iron or nonstick skillet or griddle over medium heat. When hot, drop in a pat of butter to grease the surface. Pour about ⅓ cup of the batter into the pan to make a nice big pancake. Cook until the edges are set, bubbles appear and pop, and the underside is golden brown, 2 to 3 minutes. Flip and cook the second side until golden and set, about 1 minute. Repeat with the remaining batter. If desired, rewarm the poached rhubarb in a saucepan or microwave. Serve the pancakes with more butter, rhubarb, and maple syrup.

STORE poached rhubarb in an airtight container in the refrigerator for 3 to 4 days. The pancakes are best eaten right away, but leftover pancakes can be kept in an airtight container in the refrigerator for up to 3 days. Rewarm in the microwave.

FAIRY FRENCH TOAST

On an effort scale from instant oatmeal to from-scratch pancakes, this falls right in the middle, and I love it for that. It packs some real oomph without requiring precise measurements,* which is usually what we need on weekends during the farming season when Nick abandons his pancake responsibilities to tend to the fields.

Taking a cue from Hong Kong–style French toast, sweetened condensed milk replaces maple syrup, providing creaminess and the underrated flavor of, well, milk. The chocolate sprinkles add whimsy, texture, and flavor and are inspired by the fairy toast found in Australia and New Zealand, which makes this one globe-trotting toast! Take your mouth to Hong Kong, Europe, and Australia/New Zealand in one bite of bread. I'll take those frequent flier miles.

MAKES 4 SANDWICHES

Eight ½-inch-thick slices day-old white bread

About ½ cup (128 grams) unsweetened hazelnut or almond butter

About ¼ cup (78 grams) sweetened condensed milk or sweetened condensed coconut milk

¼ teaspoon kosher salt, plus more if the nut butter is unsalted

4 large eggs

½ cup (120 grams) milk

1½ teaspoons pure vanilla extract

Unsalted butter, for cooking

About ¼ cup (42 grams) chocolate sprinkles

Flaky salt

---

* I'm giving precise measurements here, but I don't expect you to follow them. Consider them loose guidelines.

SPREAD 4 slices of the bread with the nut butter and drizzle with about half of the sweetened condensed milk. If the nut butter is unsalted, better sprinkle each with a pinch of salt, too. Sandwich the other slices of bread on top.

IN a wide shallow bowl or baking dish, whisk together the eggs, milk, vanilla, and salt. Soak each sandwich for 1 to 2 minutes per side.

HEAT a skillet over medium heat. Drop in a pat of butter and swirl it around. Add the sandwiches (you may need to do this in batches), cover, and cook until golden, 1 to 2 minutes per side.

DRIZZLE the tops of each with additional sweetened condensed milk and sprinkle liberally with chocolate sprinkles and a pinch of flaky salt. Eat immediately!

ORANGE CHOCOLATE PISTACHIO SCONE MUFFINS

One of our staples in the Bernie's bakery case is the scone muffin (lovingly called "scuffin" by some of our regulars) with a rotating selection of mix-ins. Just as with the scone loaf (page 134), baking scones in jumbo muffin tins allows you to bake up a pretty wet dough, thus avoiding the most common and terrifying flaw of scones—dryness. As a bonus, the increased contact of scone surface area with the metal muffin tin makes for a great crisp outer shell that creates a satisfying contrast with the soft, buttery insides. My favorite scuffin variation was created by our first bakery manager, Elisa, when we had a surplus of candied orange peel after making panettones at Christmastime. The bright peel cut through the richness of the scone like a star (or Santa Claus?) shooting across the night sky. And of course the pistachio and chocolate fell naturally into place, creating a color palette and flavor profile that hints at Christmas but doesn't whack you over the head with holiday energy, so if you want to make these any other time of year, they won't feel out of place.

MAKES 6 SCUFFINS

Muffins

Nonstick spray

2 cups (260 grams) all-purpose flour, plus more for dusting

½ cup (100 grams) plus 1 tablespoon (13 grams) sugar, divided

1 tablespoon (14 grams) baking powder

¾ teaspoon kosher salt

Zest of 1 orange

¾ cup (170 grams) cold unsalted butter, cut into ½-inch cubes

6 ounces (170 grams) bittersweet chocolate, coarsely chopped

1 cup (128 grams) roasted pistachios, coarsely chopped (salted or unsalted)

¼ cup (42 grams) finely chopped candied orange peel

2 large eggs

½ cup (120 grams) cold heavy cream

1 teaspoon pure vanilla extract

½ teaspoon pure almond extract

Glaze, optional

1 cup (120 grams) powdered sugar

2 tablespoons (30 grams) orange juice

PREHEAT the oven to 400°F. Grease 6 jumbo muffin wells.

IN a food processor, pulse together the flour, ½ cup (100 grams) of the sugar, the baking powder, salt, and orange zest. Scatter on the butter cubes and pulse until the butter is roughly pea size, with a few bigger bits. (You can also do this by hand in a big bowl, using your fingers to incorporate the butter by smashing and rubbing it in with the dry ingredients until it's evenly dispersed and the butter is roughly pea size, with a few bigger bits.)

DUMP into a large bowl and toss in the chocolate, pistachios, and candied orange peel. In a separate medium bowl or large measuring cup, whisk together the eggs, heavy cream, and vanilla and almond extracts. Add the wet ingredients to the dry ingredients and mix with a rubber spatula or wooden spoon until just combined. Scoop into the prepared muffin tin, filling the wells most of the way. Sprinkle with the remaining tablespoon (13 grams) of sugar.

BAKE until browned on top and a toothpick inserted into the center comes out clean; begin checking for doneness at 20 minutes. Let cool in the pans. Carefully twist and remove. (If you'd like to serve these warm, you can also remove and glaze after about 15 minutes.)

IF using the glaze, combine the powdered sugar and orange juice in a small bowl and whisk until smooth. Drizzle on the scones and enjoy.

STORE in an airtight container at room temperature. These are best eaten within a day or two.

PINEAPPLE BUNS

Chicken-fried steak, egg creams, and pineapple buns have all bonded over having things in their names that they don't actually contain. (I have a soft spot for this set because "Molly" means "sea of bitterness." Come on!) I have nothing against pineapple as a fruit, but I'm not at all mad that there's no pineapple in pineapple buns, because they are so gosh-darn lovable just the way they are.

Classic Chinese bakery fare, pineapple buns are pillowy soft, slightly sweet yeasted buns with a crackly cookie hat that sorta looks like a pineapple, hence the name. Their pillowy soft qualities are the result of using a tangzhong, or water roux, in the dough. It's an extra step of cooking some liquid with a little flour before mixing it in with the rest of the ingredients. This lets the dough hold way more moisture, and more moisture = softer texture and better shelf life. (If you didn't do the cooking step and just tossed all these ingredients into the mixture, your dough would be way too wet.) I was resistant to try out this method for the longest time because I am an impatient person, but my sister, who helped me devise this recipe, finally strong-armed me into it, and I was convinced after the first bite. Not all pineapple buns have custard bellies, but I think the custard gives these buns the oomph that they deserve. The custard and the dough are made with coconut milk, so you get that nice subtle flavor, added richness, and a nondairy treat for the large percentage of Chinese people with lactose intolerance. My favorite way of making these is baking them close to each other so they kiss and give you more fluffy edges and some height.

Custard

One 13.5-ounce can full-fat coconut milk

⅓ cup (50 grams) custard powder (such as Bird's brand)*

3 tablespoons (38 grams) sugar

¼ teaspoon pure almond extract

¼ teaspoon kosher salt

or ⅓ cup (42 grams) cornstarch, adding 1 teaspoon pure vanilla extract when you add the almond extract

Dough

One 13.5-ounce can full-fat coconut milk, divided

4½ cups (585 grams) bread flour, divided, plus more for dusting

¼ cup (50 grams) sugar

2¼ teaspoons (1 packet) instant yeast

1 teaspoon kosher salt

2 large eggs

2 tablespoons (26 grams) unrefined coconut oil, room temperature

Neutral oil, for the bowl

Topping and assembly

¼ cup (50 grams) unrefined coconut oil, room temperature

¼ cup (50 grams) sugar

1 large egg

¼ teaspoon pure almond extract

¾ cup (98 grams) all-purpose flour

½ teaspoon baking powder

¼ teaspoon kosher salt

Nonstick spray

Egg wash: 1 egg beaten with a splash of water

TO make the custard, whisk together the coconut milk, custard powder, and sugar in a small saucepan. Cook over medium-low heat, whisking continuously, until thick and pudding-like, a few minutes. Remove from the heat and add the almond extract and salt. Pour into a heat-safe bowl and cover with plastic wrap so that the wrap touches the surface of the pudding so a skin doesn't form. Refrigerate until chilled, at least 1 hour or up to overnight.

TO make the tangzhong, combine ¾ cup (160 grams) of the coconut milk and ¼ cup (33 grams) of the flour in a small saucepan and whisk until smooth. Cook over medium-low heat, whisking continuously until thickened and pasty, a few minutes. Remove from the heat and whisk in the remaining coconut milk to cool the tangzhong until it's just warm. (If it's still hot, let it cool for a few minutes more.)

IN a stand mixer fitted with a dough hook, whisk together the remaining 4¼ cups (552 grams) flour, the sugar, yeast, and salt and then add the eggs, coconut oil, and tangzhong mixture and mix on low until everything is combined. (You may need to use a spatula to help incorporate everything.) Increase the speed to medium high and knead until the dough is smooth and still a little sticky, 12 to 15 minutes.

LIGHTLY oil a clean large bowl, then use oiled hands to stretch the dough into a ball with a smooth, taut surface. Place the dough in the oiled bowl with the smooth top down and turn it over to fully coat the dough in oil. Cover with plastic wrap and let rise in a draft-free place (or in an oven that's turned off with a pan of boiling water) until doubled in size, 1 to 2 hours.

TO make the cookie top, combine the coconut oil and sugar in a medium bowl and smush together with a stiff rubber spatula or wooden spoon until the mixture is lightened and homogeneous (or do this in a stand mixer with a paddle). Add the egg and mix vigorously until combined, then add the almond extract. Add the flour, baking powder, and salt, then mix together to form a dough. Turn out onto a piece of plastic wrap, form into a small log that is 2 to 3 inches wide, wrap tightly, and refrigerate until firm, at least 1 hour.

GREASE a 9 × 13-inch metal baking pan. (You can also make these in a rimmed half sheet pan; they will spread a bit more, but they'll be just as tasty!) On a lightly floured surface, pat the dough out into a 12 × 16-inch rectangle and cut into 12 squares (3 rows of 4). Using an ice cream scoop, divide the custard among the squares, adding about 2 tablespoons (32 grams) to each. Form each into a bun by folding the edges into the center and pinching well to seal. Place the buns pinched side down in the prepared pan, then cover with plastic wrap and let proof either in the fridge overnight (preferred!) or at room temperature, until puffed up and jiggly, about 45 minutes. (If you refrigerated the rolls overnight, let them sit at room temperature for 45 minutes before topping and baking.)

PREHEAT the oven to 350°F.

SLICE the cookie dough log into 12 slices. Gently flatten each slice with your hands, lightly flouring your work surface or hands if needed, then place one on top of each bun. Gently brush the cookie dough and exposed tops of the buns with the egg wash, then bake until the tops are crackly and golden brown; begin checking for doneness at 45 minutes. Cool for 10 minutes in the pan and then carefully transfer to a wire rack. Enjoy warm or at room temperature.

STORE in an airtight container at room temperature for up to 2 days.

CHALLAH HOTTEOK

A yeasted self-syruping pancake! A doughnut for when you don't want to deep-fry! An inside-out caramel roll bun thing! I was introduced to hotteok (HO-tock) when Nick and I went to the 2018 Olympics in Pyeongchang. The vision of all these pleasingly plump dough balls being fried side by side at a food stall at the opening ceremony will always be burned in my memory as one of the more perfect visions of food there ever was. I love that these yeasted pancakes are like doughnuts but a little greasier in a good way, and easier to eat while hot, since you don't need to wait for them to cool to fill them. Because—spoiler alert—they're prefilled with sugar that melts down into syrup within the pancake.

Classic Korean hotteok dough is a sticky enriched dough that occasionally contains rice flour for added softness. I like to use a version of my go-to challah dough, because its soft texture and subtle sweetness is ideal for this application, and, of course, I'm a sucker for the imperfect alliteration in "challah hotteok."

MAKES 12 PANCAKES

2⅔ cups (347 grams) bread flour, plus more for dusting

⅓ cup (60 grams) potato flour

2 tablespoons (25 grams) granulated sugar

2¼ teaspoons (1 packet) instant yeast

1½ teaspoons kosher salt

1 cup (240 grams) warm water (105° to 110°F)

2 large eggs

½ cup (100 grams) neutral oil, plus more for the bowl and cooking

1 cup plus 2 tablespoons (225 grams) packed light brown sugar

¼ cup (35 grams) toasted pine nuts, optional

IN a stand mixer, whisk together the bread flour, potato flour, granulated sugar, yeast, and salt. Add the water, eggs, and oil and use the dough hook to combine into a dough, starting off on low, and then increasing the speed to medium when you're confident that flour won't fly everywhere. (You may need to use a spatula to help incorporate everything.) Knead until the dough is smooth but still quite sticky, 10 to 15 minutes.

LIGHTLY oil a clean large bowl, then use oiled hands to stretch the dough into a ball, pinching the ends under to form a taut surface. Place the dough in the oiled bowl with the smooth top down and turn it over to fully coat the dough in oil. Cover with plastic wrap and let rise in a draft-free place until doubled in size, 1 to 2 hours, or in the refrigerator overnight (preferred!).

LINE two sheet pans with parchment paper. On a floured surface, divide the dough into 12 equal parts. Flatten a piece with your hands to about 4 inches in diameter (dusting your hands with a little flour to prevent sticking) and place 1½ tablespoons (18 grams) of brown sugar (flattening it so it's not a big ball) and a sprinkle of pine nuts (if using) in the center of each. Pinch the edges of the dough shut very well to form a little dumpling. Roll the ball so it's smooth, then flatten into a pancake that's about ¾ inch thick. Place seam side down on the prepared sheet pans, 2 inches apart, and cover loosely with plastic wrap.

STICK a loaf pan of boiling water in your oven (that's turned off) and stick the pans of dough balls in there, too. Proof until puffy and slightly risen, 15 to 20 minutes.

HEAT a large skillet over medium-low heat and pour in enough oil to fully and generously coat the bottom. When the oil is hot, gently add a pancake—it should sizzle immediately but quietly. If it sizzles vigorously and loudly, turn the temperature down. If it doesn't sizzle, remove the pancake and wait a few more minutes for the oil to heat up. Cook the pancakes in batches (spacing about 1 inch apart), covered, until deep golden brown and cooked through, 1½ to 2½ minutes per side. Add more oil to the pan if needed. If some sugar leaks out of the pancakes and starts to collect at the bottom of the pan and burn, turn off the heat and allow the oil to cool for a few minutes, then use a dry paper towel to carefully remove the sugar. (It will kind of be attracted to the towel as you dab it into the oil.) Reheat the pan, add more oil if needed, and continue on.

TRANSFER the pancakes to a wire rack and let cool for a good few minutes before tearing into them. I like to eat these with my hands, leaning over the sink to catch any syrup drips, but feel free to be civilized and use a plate.

STORE in an airtight container at room temperature for up to a couple of days; reheat in the microwave so the sugar gets melty again. (Though these are definitely best eaten as soon as they are made.)

SPRINKLE CAKE DOUGHNUTS

Waking up before sunrise to go to five thirty a.m. synchronized ice skating practice, stopping at Dunkin' Donuts on the way for sprinkle-crusted Munchkins and picking off the sprinkle crust to eat all by itself before eating the rest of the doughnut, then strapping on my skates and zooming around in circles a hundred times was one very specific joy of my childhood. How do kids do it???? These days I feel nauseous after one second on the swings at the park.

I figure I've got at least four years before Bernie's of age for early-morning ice skating practice, and we don't even have a Dunkin' in town, so . . . here are sprinkle-crusted doughnuts!! They are the gold standard of old-fashioned cake doughnuts, with their rich, sour creamed qualities, hints of almond and vanilla, crisp fried exterior that melts in your mouth, and crunchy shell of sprinkles that will temporarily tattoo your lips and tell the outside world that you are actually capable of being a fun parent.

Their signature craggly crunchy shell and soft innards are the result of a very soft dough, or perhaps more accurately, a very thick batter, and having that dough go into the fryer cold. A big piping bag and some arm muscle are key.

Dough

¼ cup (56 grams) unsalted butter, melted and cooled slightly

⅔ cup (133 grams) sugar

3 large egg yolks

2 teaspoons pure vanilla extract

1 teaspoon pure almond extract

Zest of ½ lemon

¾ cup (180 grams) sour cream, room temperature

2¾ cups (358 grams) cake flour

2 teaspoons baking powder

1 teaspoon kosher salt

Glaze and assembly

3¾ cups (450 grams) powdered sugar

5 tablespoons (75 grams) water, plus a little more as needed

¼ teaspoon kosher salt

1½ teaspoons lemon juice

½ teaspoon pure vanilla extract

¼ teaspoon pure almond extract

Neutral oil, for frying

Lots of rainbow nonpareils

LINE a sheet pan with parchment paper (or two quarter sheet pans if that will fit better in your freezer).

TO make the dough, in a stand mixer fitted with a paddle, combine the butter and sugar and beat on medium high until fully combined and light, about 1 minute. Add the egg yolks, one at a time, mixing well after each addition. Beat in the vanilla and almond extracts and lemon zest. Add the sour cream and beat until smooth. Stop the mixer and sprinkle in the flour. Sprinkle the baking powder and salt evenly over the flour and give the dry ingredients a rough little whisk to combine, then turn the mixer to low to incorporate the dry ingredients into the wet ingredients. Scrape down the sides of the bowl as needed with a rubber spatula to ensure that all the ingredients combine evenly.

SCRAPE the dough into a large piping bag or large zip-top bag and snip off a 1-inch opening. Pipe 3-inch rings onto the prepared sheet pan, joining the ends together. These will look fairly rustic, and that's how they're supposed to be. If the dough is difficult to pipe, knead the piping bag in your hands a bit to warm it slightly. You can pipe the doughnuts pretty close to each other since you don't have to worry about spreading. Freeze them for at least 30 minutes or overnight (or cover and freeze for up to 3 months). They should be very cold when they go into the fryer, so keep them in the freezer until the oil is hot enough to receive them.

TO make the glaze, in a medium bowl, whisk together the powdered sugar, water, salt, lemon juice, and vanilla and almond extracts until smooth. The glaze should be pourable and on the thicker side, but if it's pasty or so thick that you think a delicate doughnut would break when dunked into it, add more water little by little until you get there.

FILL a large heavy-bottomed pot (ideally cast iron) with 2 inches of oil and clip on a candy thermometer. Heat to 350°F over medium-high heat. Set a cooling rack over a rimmed sheet pan.

PEEL the frozen dough rings off the parchment paper and carefully lower them into the oil. Fry them in batches of 3 or 4 until puffed and evenly deep golden brown, about 2 minutes per side. Using a fish spatula or slotted spoon, transfer the doughnuts to the wire rack to drain and cool until safe to handle. If the oil temperature lowers, make sure it comes back up to 350°F in between batches.

DIP each doughnut into the glaze to fully coat and return it to the wire rack. Sprinkle liberally with nonpareils, then let the glaze dry completely.

STORE in an airtight container at room temperature for up to a day or two (though these are best eaten the day they're made).

EVERYTHING I CAN TELL YOU ABOUT SUGAR BEETS

Without having to cite Nick as a coauthor
because he is busy right now tending the beets

Sugar beets are big white root vegetables related to red beets, and their primary purpose is to get processed into sugar: granulated sugar, brown sugar, powdered sugar, molasses, sugar syrups destined to go into soda, candy bars, and the like. Chemically and functionally, it's pretty much the same sugar that comes from its more famous sibling, cane sugar, and it makes up about half of the sugar processed in the United States. While sugarcane grows best in hot, wet climates like Florida and Louisiana, beet sugar does better in the cozy sweater weather of Michigan, Montana, some parts of Colorado and the Pacific Northwest, and, of course, Minnesota and North Dakota. Northern and eastern European countries also grow lots of sugar beets (and historically, a lot of Jewish farmers were involved in the sugar industry, so I like to imagine that some of my distant Hungarian and Polish ancestors were also sugar farmers, not that I have anything to base that on). When I walk the grocery aisles and get a sack of sugar, I'm buying sugar beet sugar. Depending on where you live, you're also getting sugar beet sugar, or you're getting cane sugar, or a mixture of the two.

The life of a sugar beet in this region begins as early as March, when suddenly every single social interaction involves cursing the snow and wishing for warmer weather. By the end of the month I don't know what I want more: for this repetitive conversation cycle about the weather (which I am fully guilty of perpetuating) to end or for a very antsy Nick to stop putzing around the house and just get outside in the sun where he belongs. The middle to end of March is our cutoff point for when we can safely schedule an out-of-state trip because once the snow melts and the ground dries, it's a full-on race to get into the fields to plant the seeds. The reality is that Nick spends most Aprils snowblowing, and I have now gotten accustomed to making plans without him for my birthday (really good plans, out of spite, like to Miami with my girlfriends or Culver's with the kids), which is at the end of May, assuming there's a medium-to-large chance that he'll be planting then. Planting days are longer days, but they're predictable and Nick can usually get at least five hours of sleep.

To plant sugar beets, the seeds go into a tractor and then get pooped out of a lot of different holes from a machine that shoves them in at exactly the right depth, an equal distance apart.

After planting, which can take a couple of weeks, it's a short matter of time before all the flat, dark brown fields start showing the most satisfying stripes of bright-green baby leaves. Even though the real magic happens underground (since they're root vegetables and all), it's really important to keep the leaves looking nice, and to prevent them from being overtaken by weeds (which will shield them from the sunlight and steal their nutrients) or nibbled on by bugs or affected by fungus or bacteria. Heat waves, cold snaps, rain, hail, droughts, or high winds may also cause major issues that need to be managed. So that's what Nick spends the bulk of his summer doing: hoping for rain at just the right time, scouting the fields to see if there was too much rain, checking his weather app to see if there will be rain again, acquiring the very definition of a farmer's tan, and . . . watching the Tour de France. His long workdays come in fits and spurts during the summer, but he also gets some full days of downtime that we can spend anywhere within a few hours' driving distance, preferably somewhere with a forgiving cancellation policy in case there's a sudden downpour and the fields have to be drained immediately. Late June and early to mid-July are when we can take our weekend trips to various lakes in the area, and it's also when farmers and anyone associated with farmers know that they have permission to get married (if they *must* have a summer wedding).

On rare occasions, freak weather events like a late-season frost, or the apocalyptic sandstorm of 2022, have actually killed some beets, requiring farmers to replant the lost crop. But assuming all goes well and Nick does his job of pulling weeds and keeping the beets healthy, by August he begins to get his equipment ready for harvest. He spends a lot of time in the workshop, fixing this and that; he warms up his fleet of trucks; and he does a lot of shuffling of tractors and things, so I start to have a tighter leash on the girls when they're outside scooting and Cozy Couping.

September is what's called Sugar Beet Pre-Haul, which is a dress rehearsal for harvest. Each farmer has one week during the month to take their harvesters out to the fields and flip the first pancake, so to speak. They pull a few beets from the ground and make sure their equipment is functioning smoothly without the time crunch of actual harvest, which happens in October.

Okay, now to October! The big show! Or as they call it in the biz, the Main Campaign. By this time, the beets are about the size of basketballs if basketballs were squished into a cone shape, and their leaves as long as an Ariana Grande ponytail. Ideally it is full-on pumpkin spice latte temperature outside, because sugar beets love sweater weather even more than I do. In fact, farmers let them leave their soil cocoons only if it's sweater weather. Any warmer and they might spoil after they're picked; any colder and they could frost, which could also cause spoilage. So, assuming the air is crisp and it's appropriate Sufjan Stevens–listening weather, midnight on October 1 is go time.

Here's how beets are harvested:

John or Tom, veteran harvest helpers, drive something called a rotobeater, a tool that chops all those Ariana Grande ponytails right off onto the ground. The leaves stay in the field to later get worked back into the soil. Right after their haircuts, Nick or brother-in-law Jason swoops in with a gigantic Go-Go-

Power-Rangers-style piece of machinery that digs the bald beets out of the ground and carries them up on a chain that deposits them right into the bucket of a semitruck that is driving right next to the harvester at just about the exact same speed. It occasionally has to speed up or slow down to allow the beets to layer themselves evenly in the truck. When one truck is filled up, it speeds up to get ahead of the harvester and leave the field to take the load to the sugar beet plant in town, and another truck swoops in right behind it to be filled up. So the harvester keeps on rolling at a walking pace while trucks rotate through, collecting the beets, driving them to the plant, emptying them out, and then driving back to the field for more beets.

Now's an appropriate time to have you Google "Sesame Street Sugar Beet song" for a visual on this. Turn the volume *off* unless you want the song stuck in your head all week.

Harvest time has great energy, because the whole town rallies around it. Beet trucks are everywhere, stray beets dot the roads, and there's a whole team of people helping out at each farm, beyond the year-round farmers. Harvest goes twenty-four hours a day as long as the weather allows, with harvesters and trucks running all through the night. Because there's such a short window of time between when the beets have reached maturity and when the ground freezes, it's important to get the beets out of the ground fast. In the morning when I bring out the day's treats to the workshop, I catch the drivers either coming in from a shift or leaving for the day.

When the beets get dropped off at the plant, they are put into great big piles, which are the closest thing we have to mountains in this area, and when winter rolls in, cool air is pumped into the middle of the piles to lower the temperature so they can be stored safely until the spring. Throughout the fall, winter, and spring, beets will be plucked from those mountains and turned into sugar. To do that, the beets basically get chopped up and boiled until the pulp is fully separated from the sugars. The sugars get turned into our favorite baking ingredients, and the pulp gets fed to livestock. Processing sugar sends a distinct funky smell throughout town, which is rather jarring, kinda like toots, but I'm used to it now.

Meanwhile, back at the farm, when Nick finishes harvest, his sleep schedule is completely nonexistent and he's somehow skinnier despite all my hearty lunches and daily treats. But there's always this bright glow of satisfaction radiating from within, because this is the end of his marathon and he deserves a medal and an uninterrupted viewing of *Star Wars: Andor*. He has just enough time to sit back and relax at our end-of-harvest feast with all the other farmers before he (1) gets sick and is bedridden for a few days, and (2) goes back into the field to prepare the ground for next year's crop before the snow falls. Luckily those days don't last too long, so he can also go back to being the fun parent.

CHOCOLATE (SUGAR) BEET MUFFINS

The most accurate way to describe the taste of a sugar beet is how my brother-in-law, Jason, puts it: "Like a white potato sprinkled with sugar." And as someone who dislikes red beets and thus is hypersensitive to the flavor, I would also add that a faint beet-y dirt quality is present. So it's like a much sweeter, blander red beet, which is why it makes sense that its main purpose is to be processed into flavor-neutral table sugar, and why you can't find them raw in a grocery store.

My first harvest here I asked Nick to bring a couple of sugar beets in from the field so I could play around with them in the kitchen. I made some latkes. I really liked them, and their flavor will always bring me back to that first wild, muddy harvest when I didn't see Nick for weeks on end except for when he'd come in zombie-ish from his shift in the middle of the night, just as I was getting ready to leave for my bakery shift. Another harvest, when my dad was visiting, he yanked one right out of the ground, bit into it like an apple, and decided we should grate it and put it in a carrot cake instead of the carrots. My dad loved it, but he loves literally every food that's not goat cheese, so you have to take his enthusiasm with a grain of salt.

As my taste buds have matured, I've grown an appreciation for the pairing of chocolate and beets (see the Beet Red-ish Velvet Cake on page 191), because the dirt quality of the beets enhances chocolate in a uniquely cool way. So here is a chocolate-heavy, harvest-ready ode to beets that's hearty and handheld, and thus perfect to send with a farmer as they head out to the field. Since there's a 99 percent chance you don't have access to sugar beets, I've made sure these are also great (*whispers: they're better*) with red beets, so you have the option. As with any muffin ever, the best part is the top, which gets crunchy from a liberal sprinkling of sugar and overflows sloppily and with glee onto the edges of the pan.

Nonstick spray

1½ cups (196 grams) all-purpose flour

½ cup (56 grams) fine almond flour

¾ cup (60 grams) Dutch-process cocoa powder

2 teaspoons baking powder

1 teaspoon kosher salt

½ cup (113 grams) unsalted butter, room temperature

2 tablespoons (25 grams) coconut oil (refined or unrefined), room temperature, or neutral oil

1 cup (200 grams) plus 3 tablespoons (38 grams) sugar, divided

Zest of ½ orange

2 large eggs

1 tablespoon (13 grams) pure vanilla extract

¾ cup (180 grams) whole milk

2½ cups (206 grams) loosely packed grated beets, from about 2 medium red beets or 1 sugar beet

8 ounces (226 grams) semisweet chocolate, coarsely chopped, divided

PREHEAT the oven to 400°F. Line 12 standard (not jumbo) muffin wells with muffin liners and generously grease the spaces between the muffin wells, since the batter may overflow a little.

IN a medium bowl, whisk together the all-purpose flour, almond flour, cocoa, baking powder, and salt. In a stand mixer fitted with a paddle, combine the butter, oil, 1 cup (200 grams) of the sugar, and zest and beat on medium high until pale and fluffy, 2 to 3 minutes. Add the eggs one at a time, mixing well after each addition, followed by the vanilla. Reduce the speed to low and add the milk and dry ingredients and mix until mostly combined. (You'll finish up combining everything by hand when you fold in the beets and chocolate.) Remove the bowl from the stand mixer and use a rubber spatula to fold in the beets and 1 cup (6 ounces/170 grams) of the chopped chocolate.

DIVIDE the batter evenly between the prepared muffin wells. They will seem pretty full, but they're supposed to be that way. Sprinkle on the remaining 2 ounces (56 grams) chocolate chunks and 3 tablespoons (38 grams) sugar.

BAKE until domed and a toothpick inserted into the center comes out clean; begin checking for doneness at 18 minutes. Let cool in the pans, then use a small offset spatula to loosen the edges and remove.

STORE in an airtight container at room temperature. These are best eaten within a day or two.

{ CAKES }

I have always been and always will be a loyal member of Team Cake. Cake recipes speak to me like captivating mysteries to solve, and I have happily (well, obsessively) spent countless sleepless nights wondering what I can do to push the envelope to make them better, moister, and more flavorful. Decorating cakes with frosting, marzipan, flowers, and sprinkles is my artistic medium of choice. And until kids entered the picture, my ideal way to spend an entire free day was to sit at my kitchen counter with all my food coloring and a vat of frosting, turn on *BoJack Horseman* in the background, and unleash on a turntable of cake. Nick could be in the fields harvesting until midnight and I wouldn't care; I'd have buttercream to keep me company.

The cakes I like to eat are very hearty and moist. They're bulked up for a Midwest winter and know no diets. I won't stop at anything—or for anyone, even the voices in my head telling me to stop using the word "moist" so much—to get there. I am always tinkering with recipes to find the ratio of fat to flour that is going to yield the most luxurious texture possible without making the whole thing cave (too much fat will do that). I love playing with different flours to fine-tune the texture and taste and incorporating vegetables, fresh herbs, and anything else that will lend an unexpected flavor or natural color. And I typically lean away from fancy elements, like brittles or meringue frostings, and instead opt for thick layers of cake and American buttercream or cream cheese frosting for a very homespun bite. The same goes for decor—I find a rustic coating of frosting and amateur-looking marzipan cutouts more inviting than a polished poured ganache (although I could be biased, since my skill level tops out at amateur marzipan cutouts).

In this chapter you'll find cakes for any situation: a big blowout birthday, an after-school snack, a harvest celebration, or a breakfast bite, and some solid candidates for a dinner-party dessert. Cakes are, hands down, the most creatively satisfying form of food to me, so if this whole book represents my happy place, this chapter is the heart of it.

A FEW GENERAL NOTES ON CAKES

DO NOT OVERMIX AND DO NOT OVERBAKE. Overmixing batter will develop the glutens in the flour, which could create a gummy texture. Gluten development is great for bread, not for cake. If you're using a mixer, the best way to prevent overmixing is by stopping the mixer just before the ingredients are fully incorporated, then using your rubber spatula to complete mixing by hand. Overbaking could dry out your cake. Prevent overbaking by keeping a close eye on your cake in the oven. As it gets closer to being done, check on it frequently but quickly so that you don't let the heat escape from the oven.

STORAGE. Unless otherwise noted, cakes are generally best eaten within a day or two, though they will typically keep for up to about 4 days (cupcakes and mini cakes may dry out by then). Unless my cakes are topped with whipped cream, I keep them covered at room temperature since they're best eaten at that temperature. A cold cake will not only have a stiff texture that can read as dry, but its flavor will be dampened, since cooler temperatures make things taste less sweet. Unfortunately, the FDA doesn't approve of room temperature storage if cream cheese is involved in the frosting (and while sugar in cream cheese frosting acts as a preservative, the FDA hasn't officially commented on this). If you choose to store any cake in the fridge, make sure it's covered well or in an airtight container, and please *pleeeease* bring it to room temperature before serving.

CAKES FREEZE WELL! This is the most convenient thing about cakes. I love baking in advance so I can devote more time to decorating the day of or the day before the party. Bake your layers, let them cool, level them (trust me, don't try leveling a frozen cake), wrap them in plastic wrap, and freeze them for up to a few weeks. If you're planning to freeze layers for longer than a few weeks, add an extra level of protection against freezer smells with a layer of foil, and they will be good for a few months. Or, if you have a deep freezer (an appliance that gets much colder than the average freezer and is, ironically, very common around the upper Midwest), your wedding cake will taste like new after a year. When it comes time to frost, let your layers soften slightly at room temperature for 20 or 30 minutes, still wrapped to catch the condensation, then unwrap and cover in frosting. This way, when the layers settle, the frosting coats won't buckle or bubble. Frosting cold cake is particularly helpful when working with cream cheese frosting, which is by design much floppier than buttercream and tends to droop. The cold temperature helps it firm up. But again, please let your cake come to room temperature before eating.

A GENERAL ANSWER TO THE QUESTION "CAN I BAKE THIS CAKE AS CUPCAKES?" Sure, you can bake pretty much any batter-based cake in a cupcake tin. But for all these cakes, I have tested and tested and lain awake at night and obsessed over the proper shape for each cake, and I've assigned each cake a first-choice shape (or shapes) for various reasons. Either it tastes best that way, or the fillings work only in that format, or the frosting needs to be applied with specificity. (It may be too droopy for a layer cake but just perfect on a sheet cake.) If there are any second-choice shape options, they will be found within the recipe.

In general, my preferred cake shape is layers, because you get a very good distribution of cake and frosting, the frosting moistens the cake, the cake stays lively, each bite has a great ratio of each, and your shelf life is better. Sheet cakes are nice because they're more user-friendly and easier to prepare, and the fact that it's a big cake means that it can hold on to moisture better. The experience of eating one thick layer of cake and one thick layer of frosting is not as good as if it were layered, but the perks of a sheet cake typically make up for this.

Now, cupcakes. Cupcakes have the same issue as sheet cakes in that they lack that layered experience—*and they also* are small—so they can dry out more easily and that scares me. Cakes with moisture that won't quit, generally oil-based cakes, such as the Almond Butter Mini Cakes (page 234) and Roasted Squash Cake (page 220), do well as cupcakes. The Vanilla Cupcakes (page 172) are an anomaly that just feel right as cupcakes; call it the *Sex and the City* Magnolia Bakery effect of 2000. For other cakes, you're allowed to bake them in smaller sizes, but just please watch them like a hawk in the oven so they don't overbake, and please plan to serve them that day.

FOR A LAYER-CAKE FROSTING TUTORIAL, flip to page 178.

VANILLA CUPCAKES WITH VANILLA FROSTING

MY GO-TO BUTTER-BASED CAKE

If you were to paint a white egg in its shell sitting on a white table, you wouldn't just take white paint to white paper, would you? (Assuming you are at least pretending to be a good painter.) You'd look closely and see that the shadows and light reflecting onto the egg aren't just white: they're various shades of gray—perhaps there's some blue or a few tints of orange from the light reflecting—and you'd pull out those colors accordingly to create dimension and beauty.

Guess what? Vanilla cake becomes transcendent when it receives that same sort of attention. Don't just dump in the bottle of vanilla extract and hope for the best; consider what potions bring out her glowing natural beauty, and go forth with vengeance against all of those people who have ever used "vanilla" as an insult. Coconut oil to enhance the butter and protect against a dry result, sour cream and heavy cream to enrich beyond belief, a tantalizing combination of just the right amount of almond and smidgen of lemon to elevate. As my mom always says, proper accessorizing should make people say "Wow, you look great!" and not "Hey, cool necklace." And that is exactly what is happening here to help a seemingly basic creation become the absolute best version of itself. The coconut, almond, and lemon don't stand out; they are simply all a part of the mission to help vanilla shine.

This recipe is the foundation for many of my go-to butter-based cakes, and it is quite versatile. See the Note on page 175 for directions for baking this as a big cake, or swap flavorings, flours, and liquids to take it to an entirely different flavor world (see Beet Red-ish Velvet Cake, page 191; Big Buttery Chocolate Cake, page 246; Coconut Raspberry Rose Pistachio Cake, page 176; Rose Rose Cake, page 225; Sprinkle Cake 2.0, page 186; and Marzipan Cake, page 203).

Cupcakes

1¾ cups (228 grams) all-purpose flour

1½ teaspoons baking powder

¾ teaspoon kosher salt

6 tablespoons (90 grams) sour cream, room temperature

¾ cup (180 grams) heavy cream, room temperature

2 teaspoons vanilla bean paste, or seeds scraped from 1 vanilla bean pod

½ teaspoon pure almond extract

½ cup (113 grams) unsalted butter, room temperature

¼ cup (50 grams) unrefined coconut oil, room temperature

1 cup (200 grams) sugar

2 large eggs, room temperature

Frosting and assembly

1 cup (226 grams) unsalted butter, room temperature

4 cups (480 grams) powdered sugar

¼ teaspoon kosher salt

1½ teaspoons lemon juice

1½ teaspoons vanilla bean paste, or seeds scraped from a little less than 1 vanilla bean pod

¼ teaspoon almond extract

¼ cup (60 grams) heavy cream

Sprinkles, optional

ARRANGE oven racks in the upper middle and lower middle positions and preheat the oven to 350°F. Line two 12-cavity cupcake pans with 14 cupcake liners, spacing them out evenly between the two pans.

IN a medium bowl, sift together the flour and baking powder, then lightly stir in the salt and set aside. In a separate medium bowl or large measuring cup, whisk together the sour cream, heavy cream, vanilla, and almond extract and set aside.

IN a stand mixer fitted with a paddle, combine the butter, coconut oil, and sugar and beat on medium high until pale and fluffy, 3 to 4 minutes. Add the eggs one at a time, mixing well after each addition and scraping down the sides of the bowl with a rubber spatula as needed to ensure that everything combines evenly. Reduce the speed to low and add the flour mixture and cream mixture in three alternating additions, mixing until mostly combined. Turn off the mixer and use your spatula to finish up the mixing by hand, making sure to combine thoroughly without overmixing.

USING an ice cream scoop, divide the batter evenly among the 14 cupcake liners, filling them a little more than three-quarters of the way (they won't rise a ton).

BAKE for 10 minutes, then switch each pan to the other rack and rotate the pans 180 degrees. Continue to bake until the cupcakes are thinking about starting to turn brown, the tops are springy, and a toothpick inserted into the center comes out clean or with just a few crumbs on it; begin checking for doneness after another 6 minutes. If they need more time, continue to bake and check them frequently (like every minute or so). Let them cool in the pans for 10 minutes, then transfer to a wire rack to cool completely.

TO make the frosting, in a stand mixer fitted with a paddle, combine the butter, powdered sugar, and salt and mix on low until you're confident that sugar won't fly everywhere, then gradually increase the speed to medium and continue to mix until smooth. Add the lemon juice, vanilla, almond extract, and heavy cream, increase the speed to medium high, and continue to mix until light and fluffy, about 2 minutes. Scrape down the sides of the bowl with a rubber spatula as needed to ensure that everything combines evenly.

FROST the cupcakes as desired, top with sprinkles (if using), and pretend you're Carrie Bradshaw.

FOR notes on storing leftover cake, see page 170.

NOTE: *You can double this recipe and bake it in a 9 × 13-inch pan or three 8-inch round pans for a big party cake. Begin checking 9 × 13-inch cakes at 35 minutes and 8-inch layers at 30 minutes. If making a layer cake, make an additional half batch of frosting.*

COCONUT RASPBERRY ROSE PISTACHIO CAKE

My quest for the perfect pink frosted layer cake began in 1992, while watching an episode of *Barney & Friends* when the friends made a giant pink frosted layer cake for Barney's two-hundred-millionth birthday. The pale-pink fluffy frosting was applied in such appealing fashion, I wanted to dive right into the TV and frost alongside those kids so badly. (A quick Google of "Barney and Friends pink frosted cake" will show you what I mean.) I think of that scene every time I have the chance to frost a big pink cake.

This grown-up big pink cake is officially as perfect on the inside as it is on the outside because it strings together one of my all-time favorite flavor combinations: coconut, rose, pistachio, and raspberry. Between the coziness of the coconut, the bright fruitiness of raspberry jam, the natural beauty of freeze-dried raspberries in the frosting, the nuttiness of the pistachio, and the floral fanciness of rose, it is one fantasy cake.

MAKES ONE 3-LAYER 8-INCH CAKE

Cake

Nonstick spray

3⅓ cups (433 grams) all-purpose flour

4 teaspoons (19 grams) baking powder

1½ teaspoons kosher salt

1 cup (226 grams) unsalted butter, room temperature

½ cup (100 grams) unrefined coconut oil, room temperature

2 cups (400 grams) sugar

4 large eggs, room temperature

2 teaspoons vanilla bean paste or extract

½ teaspoon pure almond extract

½ teaspoon coconut extract

One 13.5-ounce can full-fat coconut milk

Frosting

1 cup (226 grams) unsalted butter, room temperature

4 cups (480 grams) powdered sugar

⅛ teaspoon kosher salt

2 teaspoons rosewater

8 ounces (226 grams) cream cheese, room temperature

2 tablespoons (6 grams) freeze-dried raspberries, very finely ground in a spice grinder and sifted to remove the seeds

Filling and assembly

½ cup (64 grams) roasted salted pistachios, finely ground in a spice grinder, plus more for decor (if you only have unsalted pistachios, add a pinch of kosher salt to the filling)

Zest of ¼ lemon

¼ teaspoon pure almond extract

½ cup (160 grams) raspberry jam

Dried or candied rose petals, for decor, optional

PREHEAT the oven to 350°F. Grease three 8-inch round cake pans and line the bottoms with parchment paper.

IN a medium bowl, sift together the flour and baking powder, then lightly stir in the salt and set aside. In a stand mixer fitted with a paddle, combine the butter, coconut oil, and sugar and beat on medium high until pale and fluffy, 3 to 4 minutes. Add the eggs one at a time, mixing well after each addition and scraping down the sides of the bowl with a rubber spatula as needed to ensure that everything combines evenly. Add the vanilla, almond, and coconut extracts and reduce the speed to low. Add the flour mixture and coconut milk in three alternating additions, mixing until mostly combined. Turn off the mixer and use your spatula to finish up the mixing by hand, making sure to combine thoroughly without overmixing.

DIVIDE the batter among the prepared pans, spreading it out evenly. Bake until the tops are springy and a toothpick inserted into the centers comes out with just a few crumbs; begin checking for doneness at 30 minutes. Let cool in the pans for 10 minutes, then transfer to a wire rack to cool completely.

TO make the frosting, in a stand mixer fitted with a paddle, combine the butter, powdered sugar, and salt and mix on low until you're confident that sugar won't fly everywhere, then gradually increase the speed to medium high and continue to mix until smooth and fluffy, about 2 minutes. Lower the speed to medium, add the rosewater and cream cheese, and mix until just combined. Transfer 1 cup (240 grams) of the frosting to a medium bowl for the filling and set aside. To the stand mixer, add the freeze-dried raspberry powder and mix to combine.

TO make the filling, add the ground pistachios, lemon zest, and almond extract to the reserved frosting and use a rubber spatula to combine.

TO assemble, level the cake layers and stack them with a layer of pistachio filling, then a layer of jam in between each. Frost all over with the pink frosting (see page 178) and sprinkle with pistachios and rose petals (if using).

FOR notes on storing leftover cake, see page 170.

HOW TO FROST A CAKE

When cakes taste this good, I don't believe you need over-the-top, intricate decor. Of course it's fun sometimes, but the true star of the show is the taste. I'll take an ugly cake that tastes good over a dry pretty cake any day. With a turntable and an offset spatula, achieving a rustic, lovable layer cake is within anyone's reach. Cardboard cake circles that are 2 inches larger in diameter than your cake are also helpful for transferring the cake from turntable to serving plate to storage vessel. A bench scraper is nice if you like smooth sides, and if you're looking to bring your decor game to the next level, dip your toes into piping bags and tips, a flower nail, food coloring, and fondant tools if you're into that. (I'm not, yet!) There is a world of fancy frosting techniques out there, so once you become comfortable with the basics, go ahead and look up online videos, check out more books, or take a decorating class and go to town with the frosting.

There are many ways to frost a cake. Here's how I do it.

1. If your layers are domed, level them. Skim off the top using a very gentle sawing motion with a large serrated knife. These scraps make great snacks and can also be used to taste test your frosting if you're looking for the full effect.

2. Tape a cardboard cake board onto a cake wheel and then "glue" the first layer to the cake board with a dollop of frosting. (A)

3. If the frosting and filling are one and the same, use an offset spatula to spread a thick layer of frosting all the way to the edges. Top with another cake layer and repeat. (B)

   If the filling is something else, like jam, pipe a border of the outside frosting around the edges as a dam and then fill it with filling. Top with another cake layer and repeat. (C)

4. Stick on the top layer upside down so that you have a smooth, less crumbly surface on top. (D)

5. Get a big plop of frosting on top and spread it all the way to the edge, allowing the excess to fall down the sides. (E)

6. Spread the excess frosting smoothly on the sides (F) and level off the top corners by smoothing them down your spatula. To do this, start at the far side of the cake and drag your spatula toward you, skimming it across the top evenly to get smooth corners. (This part takes practice.) (G) If at this point you notice that some of the crumbs from the cake are loosening and showing up in the frosting, you can stick the cake in the fridge or freezer for about 20 minutes so the frosting can firm up and lock in those crumbs before adding more frosting for the final layer. If not, go ahead and add more frosting around the sides and top, and style to your heart's content.

7. You can use a bench scraper to gently scrape down the sides for crisp, clean edges, or you can continue using the offset spatula for rustic swoops (H) or spin the cake wheel with one hand while you make cool grooves with your spatula with the other hand.

8. Unleash your creativity and go wild. Add sprinkles, frosting flowers, fresh flowers, frosting borders, marzipan decor (see page 249), nuts and seeds, cake toppers—the world is your cake oyster! (I)

HAWAIJ CARROT CAKE WITH ORANGE BLOSSOM CREAM CHEESE FROSTING

Okay, here's my favorite Nick story of all time. It was a very long day of testing carrot cake recipes; I was trying to create the most perfect carrot cake for my dad's upcoming birthday, because the guy loves carrot cake. I made many, many carrot cakes that day, trying some with brown butter, softened butter, various mix-ins, and so on. On days like this when I absolutely need to taste test dozens of cakes but I don't want to feel like complete garbage, I do what any sommelier does when they don't want to get drunk: I have a spit cup. (Gross, I know.) My spit cup sat in the spot where I typically keep the bowl of cake scraps collected from leveling the layers, which are some of Nick's favorite snacks. Do you know where this is going? I turned my back for a few seconds to get some frosting going in the mixer, and the next thing I knew, Nick was standing there in the kitchen, talking with a very full mouth about how good and *soooo* moist this carrot cake was. You know why he thought it was soooo moist, right?

Lol. (Good thing he was standing over a spit cup?)

This cake is the winner from that fateful day, with a few additional improvements that I've made in the years since. The Yemeni spice blend hawaij for coffee (not to be confused with its savory sibling, hawaij for soup) is a nontraditional but seamless addition to carrot cake that takes the classic cinnamon profile and adds more depth by way of cardamom and ginger. Think of hawaij as pumpkin spice that took a dive in cardamom. Chopped dates snuggle perfectly into the world of the sesame and hawaij, and were a suggestion from one of our Bernie's bakers, Max, who used them when we were out of raisins one day. And orange blossom water in the frosting adds a bright sense of maturity that is utterly transformative.

MAKES ONE 3-LAYER 8-INCH CAKE

Cake

Nonstick spray

¾ cup (150 grams) granulated sugar

1 cup (200 grams) packed light brown sugar

1½ cups (300 grams) neutral oil

1 teaspoon hawaij for coffee (or sub ½ teaspoon ground ginger, ½ teaspoon ground cardamom, and a pinch each of ground nutmeg and ground cloves)

2 teaspoons ground cinnamon

4 large eggs, room temperature

1 tablespoon (13 grams) pure vanilla extract

2½ cups (325 grams) all-purpose flour

1½ teaspoons kosher salt

1½ teaspoons baking powder

1 teaspoon baking soda

2 cups (200 grams) freshly grated carrots

2 tablespoons (20 grams) sesame seeds

¾ cup (96 grams) roasted pistachios, coarsely chopped (salted or unsalted)

½ cup (40 grams) golden raisins or chopped pitted dates, optional

Frosting and assembly

1 cup (226 grams) unsalted butter, room temperature

4 cups (480 grams) powdered sugar

⅛ teaspoon kosher salt

1½ teaspoons orange blossom water

8 ounces (226 grams) cream cheese, room temperature

Homemade marzipan carrots, for decor, optional (see page 249)

PREHEAT the oven to 350°F. Grease three 8-inch round cake pans and line the bottoms with parchment paper.

IN a large bowl, whisk together the granulated sugar, brown sugar, oil, hawaij, and cinnamon. Add the eggs one at a time, whisking well after each addition, then whisk in the vanilla. Sprinkle the flour evenly over the top of the batter, then sprinkle the salt, baking powder, and baking soda evenly over the flour. Give the dry ingredients a rough little whisk to combine and then whisk them into the rest of the batter. When the dry ingredients are mostly incorporated, switch to a rubber spatula and fold in the carrots, sesame seeds, pistachios, and raisins (if using).

DIVIDE the batter evenly among the prepared pans and bake until the tops are springy and a toothpick inserted into the center comes out clean; begin checking for doneness at 26 minutes. Let cool in the pans for 10 minutes, then transfer to a wire rack to cool completely.

TO make the frosting, in a stand mixer fitted with a paddle, combine the butter, powdered sugar, and salt and mix on low until you're confident that sugar won't fly everywhere, then gradually increase the speed to medium high and continue to mix until smooth and fluffy, about 2 minutes. Lower the speed to medium, add the orange blossom water and cream cheese, and mix until just combined. Scrape down the sides of the bowl with a rubber spatula as needed to ensure that everything combines evenly.

TO assemble, level the cake layers and stack them up with a layer of frosting in between them. Frost the cake all over (see page 178) and decorate with marzipan carrots (if using).

FOR notes on storing leftover cake, see page 170.

NOTE: *You can also make this into 20 cupcakes or a 9 × 13-inch cake. To bake, begin checking for doneness at 22 minutes for cupcakes and 40 minutes for a 9 x 13-inch cake.*

LAVENDER LEMON LOAF

If you use too much lavender in a baked good, you feel like you're eating a bath bomb. But when used correctly, it will transport you to a picnic on a sunny seventy-degree day where the birds are chirping, your hair looks great, and the bugs got the memo to stay the heck away from your cake. One way to use lavender correctly in baking is to pair it with lemon and lots of sugar, which is exactly what's happening here. Lemon and lavender are a highly functional couple because they make each other the best version of themselves and work in tandem to create Not Just Another Lemon Loaf. The loaf itself has a velvety, rich texture thanks to almond flour and sour cream, making it a perfect snack cake that will hang out on your counter staying great for a good few days.

MAKES 1 LOAF

Cake

Nonstick spray

⅔ cup (133 grams) extra virgin olive oil

1 cup (200 grams) sugar

Zest of 1 small lemon

3 large eggs, room temperature

1 teaspoon pure almond extract

¼ cup (64 grams) lemon juice (from 1 to 2 lemons)

¾ cup (180 grams) sour cream, room temperature

½ cup (56 grams) fine almond flour

1½ cups (195 grams) all-purpose flour

1 teaspoon kosher salt

1 teaspoon baking powder

¼ teaspoon baking soda

Glaze

3 tablespoons (45 grams) milk, plus a little more as needed

1 tablespoon dried lavender buds (see Note)

1½ cups (180 grams) powdered sugar

Pinch of kosher salt

Purple food coloring, optional

NOTE: *Dried lavender buds can be found in health food sections or online. Make sure to purchase buds that are specifically labeled for consumption/culinary use, as opposed to those intended for craft use, which may be treated with chemicals.*

PREHEAT the oven to 350°F. Grease a 4 × 9-inch pullman loaf pan or a 5 × 9-inch metal loaf pan and line with enough parchment paper to allow for 1-inch wings on the long sides.

IN a large bowl, whisk together the olive oil, sugar, and lemon zest. Add the eggs one at a time, whisking well after each addition, then whisk in the almond extract. Add the lemon juice, sour cream, and almond flour and whisk to combine. Sprinkle the all-purpose flour evenly over the top of the batter, then sprinkle on the salt, baking powder, and baking soda evenly over the flour. Give the dry ingredients a rough little whisk to combine and then incorporate them into the rest of batter, whisking until just combined.

TRANSFER the batter to the prepared pan and bake until a toothpick inserted in the center comes out clean; begin checking for doneness at 55 minutes.

LET cool in the pan for 10 minutes, then use the parchment wings to lift the loaf out of the pan and transfer it to a wire rack to cool completely.

MEANWHILE, make the glaze. Combine the milk and lavender in a small saucepan. Bring to a simmer over medium heat, then remove from the heat and let steep and cool for 20 minutes. Pour the milk through a fine-mesh sieve into a medium bowl and discard the lavender. Add the powdered sugar, salt, and a drop or two of purple food coloring (if using) to the infused milk and whisk until smooth. If the mixture is too thick to pour, add a little water or more milk bit by bit until it becomes pourable, but you still want it fairly thick so that the drips hold their shape down the sides of the cake. Spread or pour the glaze over the cooled cake.

FOR notes on storing leftover cake, see page 170.

SPRINKLE CAKE 2.0

No one:
Me: I made a new sprinkle cake!

One of my biggest achievements as a baker was when my friend and expert baker Jesse Szewczyk conducted a blind test at The Kitchn with all the best sprinkle cakes on the internet and crowned mine the queen. This was a recipe that I had spent months and months on, but I still felt like there was more to explore in the world of sprinkle cakes. Because as my college timpani teacher Joe used to say, "If it ain't broke, fix it anyway."

To review, sprinkle cake is not just a vanilla cake with sprinkles. It is:

+ A white cake, hence all of the eight (8!) egg whites, so that the sprinkles can pop against a stark background.
+ Made with clear imitation vanilla. Because *nostalgia*. This is a Christina Tosi tip. I also believe that a little almond extract belongs.
+ Made with bright sprinkles that are suspended evenly throughout.

This one is better than my first because:

+ The frosting has a hint of tanginess from a plop of cream cheese. It's not a full-on cream cheese frosting; it just has cream cheese tendencies.
+ It's bigger and fluffier.
+ It has a good ratio of cake flour to all-purpose flour that edges closer to the tender texture of a nostalgic cake but still has the kind of textural substance that I need out of life.
+ It gives you the option to use homemade sprinkles and homemade rainbow chips in the frosting to fully customize your aesthetic.

But here's your warning:

It's a project. This is not a quick and easy cake: it takes no shortcuts, and it dirties all the dishes. This cake is a better-than-the-original sequel (#pitchperfect #mightyducks) because it has a bigger budget and timeline, and the box office proceeds will reflect that. (You can, however, spread out the work and make your sprinkles and rainbow chips in advance.)

The first cease and desist I received in my life was from the Funfetti people kindly asking that I call my homemade Funfetti cake by another name. It is one of my proudest career accomplishments, and now this 2.0 cake is right up there with it.

Cake

Nonstick spray

2 cups (260 grams) cake flour

1½ cups (195 grams) all-purpose flour

1 tablespoon (14 grams) baking powder

½ teaspoon baking soda

1½ teaspoons kosher salt

¾ cup (180 grams) sour cream, room temperature

1½ cups (360 grams) heavy cream, room temperature

4 teaspoons (17 grams) clear imitation vanilla extract

1 teaspoon pure almond extract

1 cup (226 grams) unsalted butter, room temperature

½ cup (100 grams) unrefined coconut oil, room temperature

2 cups (400 grams) sugar

8 egg whites, room temperature

1 cup (135 grams) Rainbow Sprinkles (recipe follows, or store-bought)

Frosting

1½ cups (340 grams) unsalted butter, room temperature

4 cups (480 grams) powdered sugar

⅛ teaspoon kosher salt

1½ teaspoons pure vanilla extract

½ teaspoon pure almond extract

4 ounces (113 grams) cream cheese, room temperature

1 cup (about 190 grams) Rainbow Chips (recipe follows, or store-bought)

PREHEAT the oven to 350°F. Grease three 8-inch round cake pans and line the bottoms with parchment paper.

IN a medium bowl, sift together the cake flour, all-purpose flour, baking powder, and baking soda, then lightly stir in the salt and set aside. In a medium bowl or large measuring cup, whisk together the sour cream, heavy cream, and vanilla and almond extracts and set aside.

IN a stand mixer fitted with a paddle, combine the butter, coconut oil, and sugar and beat on medium high until pale and fluffy, 3 to 4 minutes. Add the egg whites one at a time, mixing well after each addition and scraping down the sides of the bowl with a rubber spatula as needed to ensure that everything combines evenly. Reduce the speed to low and add the flour mixture and cream mixture in three alternating additions, mixing until mostly combined. Turn off the mixer, add the sprinkles, and use your spatula to finish up the mixing by hand, making sure to combine thoroughly without overmixing.

DIVIDE the batter evenly among the prepared pans, spreading the batter out evenly with the back of a spoon or an offset spatula. Bake until the tops are springy and a toothpick inserted into the centers comes out clean or with just a few crumbs on it; begin checking for doneness at 28 minutes. If they're not yet done, check frequently until they are because you want to avoid overbaking at all costs. Let cool in the pans for 10 minutes, then transfer to a wire rack to cool completely.

TO make the frosting, in a stand mixer fitted with a paddle, combine the butter, powdered sugar, and salt and mix on low until you're confident that sugar won't fly everywhere, then gradually increase the speed to medium high and continue to mix until smooth and fluffy, about 2 minutes. Lower the speed to medium, add the vanilla and almond extracts and cream cheese, and mix until just combined, then mix in the rainbow chips. Scrape down the sides of the bowl with a rubber spatula as needed to ensure that everything combines evenly.

TO assemble, level the cake layers and stack them up with a layer of frosting in between them. Frost the cake all over (see page 178).

FOR notes on storing leftover cake, see page 170.

NOTE: *You can also make this into 32 cupcakes or a 9 × 13-inch cake. To bake, begin checking for doneness at 18 minutes for cupcakes and 50 minutes for a 9 x 13-inch cake. The frosting amount will yield enough for a 9 x 13-inch cake and just enough for a thin layer on each cupcake. (If you're a big frosting person, make an additional half batch of frosting.)*

RAINBOW SPRINKLES

MAKES 1½ CUPS (ENOUGH FOR ONE SPRINKLE CAKE 2.0, PLUS SOME EXTRAS FOR DECORATION)

2 large pasteurized egg whites

2½ cups (300 grams) powdered sugar, plus more as needed

Food coloring

LINE 4 sheet pans with parchment paper.

IN a small bowl, whisk together the egg whites and powdered sugar. The consistency should be slightly thicker than Elmer's glue. Add a bit of water or more powdered sugar if it is too thick or thin. Divide into as many bowls as you want colors (I'd recommend 4 or 5) and add the food coloring as desired, making the colors nice and bright so they pop against the background of the cake. (If the food coloring thins out the consistency too much, add a bit more powdered sugar.)

TRANSFER each batch of sprinkle mixture to a piping bag or small zip-top bag, snip off a tiny hole (or fit the piping bag with a very small tip) and pipe lines or small dollops onto the parchment paper.

LET dry completely at room temperature for 4 hours or overnight. Use a bench scraper to scrape the sprinkles off the paper; if you piped lines, chop them up into small sprinkles.

STORE in an airtight container at room temperature for up to several weeks.

RAINBOW CHIPS

MAKES 2 CUPS

12 ounces (340 grams) white chocolate, finely chopped, or 2 cups chips

Gel food coloring

Melted coconut oil (refined or unrefined), as needed

LINE a sheet pan (or quarter sheet pan, if that fits better in your fridge or freezer) with parchment paper.

MELT the chocolate in a double boiler or in a bowl in the microwave in 30-second increments, stirring after each, until smooth. Divide into as many bowls as you want colors (I'd recommend 4 or 5) and stir food coloring into each. (White chocolate is a little finicky; if you find it seizes up when you add the food coloring, stir in melted coconut oil a little at a time until it smooths out again.)

SPREAD on the parchment in blobs and place in the fridge or freezer until firm, about 10 minutes. Chop into little bits.

STORE in an airtight container at room temperature for up to several weeks.

NOTE: *This recipe makes twice what you need for this cake. It's fun to have leftovers for decor or other uses, but if you'd like to avoid leftovers, then simply make a half batch.*

BEET RED-ISH VELVET CAKE

When I was growing up, my birthday tradition with my dad, whose birthday is the day after mine, was to sit at the Pope's table at Buca Di Beppo, eat our weight in garlic bread and meatballs, and then somehow find room for their big red velvet birthday cake with fluffy white frosting, red gel icing, and bright-green pistachios around the sides. It was probably made using enough food coloring to shave like five minutes off my life. I ate a giant slice on my birthday and then had leftovers for breakfast every morning for a week.

These days my love of natural food coloring and my life on a beet farm have brought me back to a love of red velvet cake, only this time made with beets (not the kind of beet that Nick grows, but still, same family). They lend a beautiful dark red color to this cake batter, then stay red through baking thanks to a splash of vinegar in the batter (for further reading on this, Google "betalains").

Conveniently, the beets also add value in the flavor department—and that's coming from someone who does not like eating beets. For when beets are paired with cocoa, their gross funkiness is erased and what's left is a super-cool, earthy quality of cocoa that'd be tough to mimic otherwise. This is a lovely, tender cake that's got great personality and inspires a good dose of nostalgia.

MAKES ONE 3-LAYER 8-INCH CAKE

Cake

Nonstick spray

2 cups (260 grams) cake flour

1½ cups (195 grams) all-purpose flour

4 teaspoons (19 grams) unsweetened cocoa powder

4 teaspoons (19 grams) baking powder

1½ teaspoons kosher salt

¾ cup (180 grams) heavy cream, room temperature

¾ cup (180 grams) sour cream, room temperature

¾ cup (180 grams) beet juice, shaken, room temperature (see Notes)

1 tablespoon (15 grams) distilled white vinegar

1 tablespoon (13 grams) pure vanilla extract

1 cup (226 grams) unsalted butter, room temperature

½ cup (100 grams) unrefined coconut oil, room temperature

2 cups (400 grams) sugar

4 large eggs, room temperature

Frosting and assembly

1 cup (226 grams) unsalted butter, room temperature

4 cups (480 grams) powdered sugar

⅛ teaspoon kosher salt

1 teaspoon pure vanilla extract

8 ounces (226 grams) cream cheese, room temperature

Finely chopped raw or roasted salted or unsalted pistachios, for decor, optional

PREHEAT the oven to 350°F. Grease three 8-inch round cake pans and line the bottoms with parchment paper.

IN a medium bowl, sift together the cake flour, all-purpose flour, cocoa, and baking powder, then lightly stir in the salt and set aside. In a separate medium bowl or large measuring cup, whisk together the heavy cream, sour cream, beet juice, vinegar, and vanilla.

IN a stand mixer fitted with a paddle, combine the butter, coconut oil, and sugar and beat on medium high until pale and fluffy, 3 to 4 minutes. Add the eggs one at a time, mixing well after each addition and scraping down the sides of the bowl with a rubber spatula as needed to ensure that everything combines evenly. Reduce the speed to low and add the flour mixture and cream mixture in three alternating additions, mixing until mostly combined. Turn off the mixer and use your spatula to finish up the mixing by hand, making sure to combine thoroughly without overmixing.

DIVIDE the batter among the prepared pans, spreading it out evenly with the back of a spoon or an offset spatula. Bake until the tops are springy and a toothpick inserted into the centers comes out clean or with just a few crumbs on it; begin checking for doneness at 30 minutes. Let cool in the pans for 10 minutes, then transfer to a wire rack to cool completely.

TO make the frosting, in a stand mixer fitted with a paddle, combine the butter, powdered sugar, and salt and mix on low until you're confident that sugar won't fly everywhere, then gradually increase the speed to medium high and continue to mix until smooth and fluffy, about 2 minutes. Lower the speed to medium, add the vanilla and cream cheese, and mix until just combined. Scrape down the sides of the bowl with a rubber spatula as needed to ensure that everything combines evenly.

TO assemble, level the cake layers and stack them up with a layer of frosting between them. Frost the cake all over (see page 178) and decorate with pistachios (if using).

FOR notes on storing leftover cake, see page 170.

NOTES: *You can also make this into 28 cupcakes or a 9 × 13-inch cake. To bake, begin checking for doneness at 20 minutes for cupcakes and 45 minutes for a 9 x 13-inch cake. The frosting amount will yield enough for a 9 x 13-inch cake and just enough for a thin layer on each cupcake. (If you're a big frosting person, make an additional half batch of frosting.)*

Freshly made beet juice will give you the brightest color, but store-bought is okay. Store-bought sometimes has added lemon juice in it, which is totally fine.

PISTACHIO BASBOUSA

Basbousa is a syrup-soaked semolina cake that originated in the Ottoman Empire. It is the ideal snacking cake because it doesn't require any bells and whistles like frosting or decor, it retains its moisture for a while, and it is a true explosion of flavor. It just hangs out on the counter waiting patiently for you to realize that it's been a couple of hours since your last bite of cake. Pistachios are my nut of choice here because, in the absence of a frosting or glaze, the green color they give the cake can shine, and the flavor pairs nicely with the traditional coconut and rosewater.

MAKES ONE 8-INCH SQUARE CAKE

Nonstick spray

¾ cup (96 grams) roasted unsalted pistachios, plus more for topping (if you only have salted, decrease the added salt to ½ teaspoon)

½ cup (28 grams) unsweetened coconut flakes (or ¼ cup shredded unsweetened coconut)

⅔ cup (84 grams) all-purpose flour

⅔ cup (120 grams) semolina flour

2 teaspoons baking powder

¾ teaspoon kosher salt

6 tablespoons (75 grams) extra virgin olive oil

One 13.5-ounce can full-fat coconut milk, divided

3 large eggs

1½ cups (300 grams) sugar, divided

½ teaspoon pure almond extract

1 teaspoon rosewater, optional

PREHEAT the oven to 350°F. Grease an 8-inch square metal pan and line with enough parchment paper to allow for 1-inch wings on opposite sides.

IN a food processor, blend the pistachios until they're very finely ground, almost the consistency of a coarse cornmeal. You may need to get in there a couple of times with a spatula to scrape down the sides and bottom to ensure that everything is blending evenly. Remove ¼ cup (28 grams) of the ground pistachios and set aside for the topping. To the food processor, add the coconut, all-purpose flour, semolina flour, baking powder, and salt and pulse a few times to combine. Add the olive oil and ¾ cup (180 grams) of the coconut milk and pulse until just combined and no more.

IN a stand mixer fitted with a whisk, combine the eggs, ¾ cup (150 grams) of the sugar, and the almond extract and beat on high until pale and fluffy, about

5 minutes. Remove the bowl from the stand mixer and use a spatula to fold in the pistachio mixture.

POUR the batter into the prepared pan and bake until golden on top and a toothpick inserted into the center comes out clean or with just a few crumbs; begin checking for doneness at 30 minutes.

WHILE the cake bakes, make the syrup. Combine the remaining coconut milk and remaining ¾ cup (150 grams) sugar in a small saucepan and whisk until smooth. Bring to a boil over medium-high heat while whisking to dissolve the sugar, then remove from the heat. Whisk in the rosewater (if using).

WHEN the cake comes out of the oven, pour the syrup over the hot cake and let cool completely in the pan. (You may need to pour it over in several additions, giving it a moment to soak in before adding the rest.) I think this cake is best at room temperature. (When it's still warm, it tends to taste a little too sweet.) Top with reserved pistachios, slice into squares, and enjoy.

FOR notes on storing leftover cake, see page 170.

STONE FRUIT STREUSEL CAKE

Peak-season stone fruit doesn't need anything, and it knows it. It's one of those beautiful people who can get into the club with the most basic jeans and T-shirt on, and who need only one attempt to take the perfect selfie. Here it is in the metaphorical jeans and T-shirt, plain Jane dough and plain Jane streusel, shining so bright like the Julia Roberts of fruit that it is. I love the way the juices soak down into the dough and expand the reaches of its flavor and how the streusel and cornmeal add sweetness and crunch without stealing any stardom from the fruit.

Think of this cake when it's August, or whenever stone fruit season for you is, and eat it for breakfast in the bright early sun or as an afternoon snack with iced coffee. If you haven't yet reached peak stone fruit season but still need this cake, toss your fruit with a little extra sugar.

MAKES ONE 11 × 15-INCH CAKE

Unsalted butter, room temperature, for the pan

Yellow cornmeal, for the pan

½ batch Buttered Potato Dough (page 114)*

To enhance the flavor of this dramatically, do this one change: let the dough rise in the fridge overnight instead of at room temperature as written.

1½ pounds (680 grams) mix of different stone fruit, like peaches, plums, nectarines, and cherries, pitted and cut into ¼-inch slices (or halved if cherries)

¼ cup (50 grams) packed light brown sugar, plus more as needed

Streusel

½ cup (113 grams) unsalted butter, room temperature

⅓ cup (67 grams) sugar

¼ teaspoon ground cinnamon

½ teaspoon pure vanilla extract

1 cup (130 grams) all-purpose flour

¼ teaspoon kosher salt

½ cup (72 grams) roasted unsalted hazelnuts or almonds, coarsely chopped, optional

GENEROUSLY butter a rimmed sheet pan and dust it with cornmeal. Pat or roll out the dough to about an 11 × 15-inch rectangle; it will go almost to the edge of the pan but not quite. In a large bowl, toss the stone fruit with the brown sugar and give it a taste. If you'd like it sweeter, feel free to add a little

SWEET FARM!

more sugar. Scatter the stone fruit evenly over the dough. Cover loosely with plastic wrap and let proof until puffy, about 30 minutes.

PREHEAT the oven to 375°F.

TO make the streusel, in a stand mixer fitted with a paddle, combine the butter, sugar, cinnamon, and vanilla and mix on medium until creamy and combined. Reduce the speed to low, add the flour and salt, and mix to combine. Add the nuts (if using). Stop the mixer and and break up the mixture with your fingers into a crumbly consistency.

SCATTER the streusel over the cake and bake until golden brown around the edges and the streusel is lightly browned; begin checking for doneness at 30 minutes.

LET cool slightly, slice into rectangles, and eat warm.

STORE, covered, in the fridge for up to a couple of days. Bring to room temperature or rewarm before serving.

CHOCOLATE TAHINI FUDGE CAKE WITH TAHINI WHIP AND HALVA

This is . . . I think . . . the best dessert I've ever made on *Girl Meets Farm*. Which I can't take all the credit for because my sister, Stoop, helped me develop it. It's the nicest thing she's ever done for me other than give me her driver's license when I was nineteen so I could order White Russians in college. It was originally supposed to be a lava cake, but a happy accident (the wrong size pan? a forgotten cake in the oven?) led to this brownie-type thing that is a chewy, dense, chocolaty vehicle for the best whipped cream on the planet. An extra-sweet crumble of halva on top brings it all home while also making you feel like you're out at a restaurant that is too fancy for my usual buttercream-frosted layer cakes. Really, the fact that I'm obsessing this much over a cake that isn't covered in marzipan sprinkly bells and whistles should tell you something.

MAKES ONE 9-INCH CAKE

Cake

Nonstick spray

1 cup (226 grams) unsalted butter

½ cup (112 grams) tahini

4 ounces (113 grams) semisweet chocolate, finely chopped, or ⅔ cup chips

1¾ cups (350 grams) sugar

4 large eggs, room temperature

1 teaspoon pure vanilla extract

½ teaspoon kosher salt

1 cup (130 grams) all-purpose flour

Whipped cream and assembly

1 cup (240 grams) cold heavy cream

¼ cup (30 grams) powdered sugar

Pinch of kosher salt

¼ cup (56 grams) tahini

Halva, any flavor, crumbled

PREHEAT the oven to 300°F. Grease a 9-inch round cake pan and line the bottom with parchment paper.

IN a large heat-safe bowl, combine the butter, tahini, and chocolate. Set the bowl over a saucepan of barely simmering water and cook, stirring, until just melted and smooth. Add the sugar and whisk to combine. Remove from the heat. Add the eggs one at a time, whisking well after each addition, then whisk in the vanilla and salt. Add the flour and whisk until just combined.

POUR the batter into the prepared pan. Bake until a toothpick inserted into the center comes out with a few fudgy crumbs and the sides pull slightly away from the pan; begin checking for doneness at 55 minutes. Let cool completely in the pan.

TO make the tahini whipped cream, in a stand mixer fitted with a whisk, combine the heavy cream, powdered sugar, and salt. Beat on medium until medium peaks form, about 1 minute, then add the tahini. Beat until smooth and just shy of stiff peaks, about 30 seconds more.

REMOVE the cooled cake from the pan. Cut into wedges and serve with a dollop of tahini whipped cream and some crumbled halva on top.

STORE the cake, covered, at room temperature for up to 4 days. Whipped cream can be stored in an airtight container in the fridge for up to a couple of days.

MARZIPAN CAKE

This cake is a celebration of my pure and endless love for marzipan, which I have had ever since I collected marzipan pigs that my dad would bring back from work trips when I was little. Its sweet, almondy chewiness has always had me under a spell. Every time I see it on a menu, in a recipe, or in some special form at a store, I get tunnel vision and fixate on it until it gets in my mouth. A lot of my core memories are centered on marzipan: eating marzipan-filled chocolate bars from Anderson's chocolate shop in Richmond, Illinois, on the way to our family vacations in Wisconsin; dragging Nick across Berlin to track down a shop that sold only marzipan; waiting all year for Chicago's Christkindlmarket so I could stock up on marzipan-flavored tea and hot cocoa; making my friend Alanna's marzipan crumble every Rosh Hashanah; staying up late during slumber parties to watch *Homestar Runner* episodes featuring the best character, Marzipan, during the dawn of viral internet videos; and lining up those tiny pink pigs from my dad on my desk and occasionally cutting into one of them to nibble on a snout or belly. I'm still holding on to Marzipan as a baby name if we have another kid.

In this recipe, marzipan is found in both the cake batter and in sheets between the layers, so you get tasty little chewy almond bits throughout the cake, and even more chewy interest between the layers for the ultimate combination of cakey and chewy. Technically you're using almond paste, which is just a less-sweet version of marzipan (since you're also adding sugar in the cake and frosting)—an annoying technicality in the world of marzipan, but "almond paste cake" sounds less cute than "marzipan cake." A layer of plum jam balances nicely with this whole situation and will get you humming themes from *The Nutcracker*.

Cake

Nonstick spray

3½ cups (450 grams) all-purpose flour

1 tablespoon (14 grams) baking powder

1½ teaspoons kosher salt

¾ cup (180 grams) sour cream, room temperature

1½ cups (360 grams) heavy cream, room temperature

1 tablespoon (14 grams) vanilla bean paste or extract

½ teaspoon almond extract

1 cup (226 grams) unsalted butter, room temperature

⅔ cup (134 grams) unrefined coconut oil, room temperature

7 to 8 ounces (198 to 226 grams) almond paste*, broken into roughly 1-inch pieces

1½ cups (300 grams) sugar

Zest of ½ lemon

4 large eggs, room temperature

Frosting

1½ cups (340 grams) unsalted butter, room temperature

6 cups (720 grams) powdered sugar

½ teaspoon kosher salt

1 tablespoon (15 grams) lemon juice

2¼ teaspoons pure vanilla extract

½ teaspoon pure almond extract

6 tablespoons (90 grams) heavy cream

Food coloring, optional

Assembly

7 to 8 ounces (198 to 226 grams) almond paste*

Powdered sugar, as needed for dusting

⅓ cup (107 grams) plum jam (raspberry jam would also be good!)

Almond paste typically comes in packages of either 7 or 8 ounces. Use whichever size package you have access to; either will work.

PREHEAT the oven to 350°F. Grease three 8-inch round cake pans and line the bottoms with parchment paper.

IN a medium bowl, sift together the flour and baking powder, then lightly stir in the salt and set aside. In a separate medium bowl or large measuring cup, whisk together the sour cream, heavy cream, vanilla, and almond extract and set aside.

IN a stand mixer fitted with a paddle, combine the butter, coconut oil, almond paste, sugar, and lemon zest and beat on medium high until pale and fluffy, 3 to 4 minutes. Add the eggs one at a time, mixing well after each addition and scraping down the sides of the bowl with a rubber spatula as needed to ensure that everything combines evenly. Reduce the speed to low and add the flour mixture and cream mixture in three alternating additions, mixing until mostly combined. Turn off the mixer and use your spatula to finish up the mixing by hand, making sure to combine thoroughly without overmixing.

DIVIDE the batter among the prepared pans, spreading it out evenly with the back of a spoon or an offset spatula. Bake until the tops are springy and a toothpick inserted into the centers comes out clean or with just a few crumbs on it; begin checking for doneness at 28 minutes. If they're not yet done, check frequently until they are because you want to avoid overbaking at all costs. Let cool in the pans for 10 minutes, then transfer to a wire rack to cool completely.

TO make the frosting, in a stand mixer fitted with a paddle, combine the butter, powdered sugar, and salt and mix on low until you're confident that sugar won't fly everywhere, then gradually increase the speed to medium and continue to mix until smooth. Add the lemon juice, vanilla and almond extracts, heavy cream, and food coloring (if using) and increase the speed to medium high and continue to mix until light and fluffy, about 2 minutes. Scrape down the sides of the bowl with a rubber spatula as needed to ensure that everything combines evenly.

TO assemble, divide the almond paste in half and roll each half into a ball. Use a rolling pin to roll out each ball into a 7-inch circle. (If it's too sticky to work with, dust with a little powdered sugar.)

LEVEL the cake layers and stack them up with a thin layer of frosting, a circle of almond paste, and a layer of jam in between each. Frost the cake all over with decor as desired (see page 178).

FOR notes on storing leftover cake, see page 170.

NATURALLY COLORED RAINBOW CAKE

When Bernie turned six months old, I did what should be considered perfectly normal for any first-time parent and started planning her first birthday party. I spent hours online finding the perfect decor, splurged on a bespoke knitted birthday crown, put together four different wardrobe options, used the typewriter to manually type up invitations, and developed her very first birthday cake, this naturally colored rainbow cake. Only after I had crafted tiny cake toppers out of clay did I do multiple test runs to ensure that her first-ever cake and frosting experience would be perfect. Some of those test runs are still in the back of our freezer because I'm sentimental. I was so happy with the natural colors and the fact that the flavors were very subtle and yielded just a delightfully sweet, festive birthday cake. Anyway, her first birthday party was scheduled for the end of March 2020, so you know what ended up happening . . . but she devoured that cake.

MAKES ONE 4-LAYER 6-INCH CAKE

Cake

Nonstick spray

3½ cups (455 grams) all-purpose flour

3½ teaspoons (16 grams) baking powder

1½ teaspoons kosher salt

1 cup (226 grams) unsalted butter, room temperature

½ cup (100 grams) unrefined coconut oil, room temperature

2¼ cups (450 grams) sugar

4 large eggs, room temperature

1 tablespoon (13 grams) vanilla bean paste or extract

½ cup (120 grams) sour cream, room temperature

1 cup (240 grams) whole milk, divided

¼ cup (60 grams) carrot juice, shaken

¼ cup (60 grams) beet juice, shaken

2 teaspoons lemon juice

½ cup (12 grams) lightly packed fresh mint leaves

¼ cup (35 grams) frozen wild blueberries, thawed, juices reserved

Frosting

¾ cup (170 grams) unsalted butter, room temperature

3 cups (360 grams) powdered sugar

⅛ teaspoon kosher salt

1 teaspoon vanilla bean paste or extract

6 ounces (170 grams) cream cheese, room temperature

PREHEAT the oven to 350°F. Grease four 6-inch round cake pans and line the bottoms with parchment paper. (You can bake in batches if you don't have four pans.)

IN a medium bowl, sift together the flour and baking powder, then lightly stir in the salt and set aside.

IN a stand mixer fitted with a paddle, combine the butter, coconut oil, and sugar and beat on medium high until pale and fluffy, 3 to 4 minutes. Add the eggs one at a time, mixing well after each addition and scraping down the sides of the bowl with a rubber spatula as needed to ensure that everything combines evenly. Add the vanilla and sour cream and mix to combine. Reduce the speed to low, add the flour mixture, and mix until about 80 percent combined. (You're going to continue to mix once you add the coloring, so mixing partially at this stage prevents overmixing the batter.) Divide the batter evenly into 4 bowls. (Using a scale helps with this! You should have around 1500 grams of batter; divide by 4 for about 375 grams per layer.)

TO the first bowl, add ¼ cup (60 grams) of the milk and the carrot juice and fold into the batter until smooth and just combined. To the second bowl, add ¼ cup (60 grams) of the milk, the beet juice, and lemon juice and fold in until smooth and just combined. In a high-speed blender, blend the mint leaves with ¼ cup (60 grams) of the milk until very smooth. (If your blender isn't full enough to blend, add a spoonful or two of batter from the third bowl and try again; try not to add more batter than necessary.) Add this mixture to the third bowl and fold in until smooth and just combined. Rinse out the blender and repeat the process with the remaining ¼ cup (60 grams) milk and the blueberries and their juices for the final bowl.

TRANSFER the batters to the prepared pans, spreading them out evenly with the back of a spoon or an offset spatula. Bake until the tops are springy and a toothpick inserted into the centers comes out clean or with just a few crumbs on it; begin checking for doneness at 30 minutes. (Some of the cakes may be done before the others; try your darnedest not to let them overbake.) Let cool in the pans for 10 minutes, then transfer to a wire rack to cool completely.

TO make the frosting, in a stand mixer fitted with a paddle, combine the butter, powdered sugar, and salt and mix on low until you're confident that sugar won't fly everywhere, then gradually increase the speed to medium high and continue to mix until smooth and fluffy, about 2 minutes. Lower the speed to medium, add the vanilla and cream cheese, and mix until just combined. Scrape down the sides of the bowl with a rubber spatula as needed to ensure that everything combines evenly.

TO assemble, level the cake layers and stack them up with a layer of frosting between them. Frost the cake all over (see page 178). Slice and reveal the pretty colors!

FOR notes on storing leftover cake, see page 170.

COFFEE CAKE WITH FRESH MINT FROSTING

Nearly every morning after we've all eaten breakfast and read a few morning books or hosted a couple of doll weddings, and it's time for us to go our separate ways, to work and preschool and the like, I zip back upstairs to put my face on and take in one of life's great pleasures: I brush my teeth for a second time to get the breakfast out, then immediately take my last few sips of coffee. It's a janky way of mimicking the magic of the fresh mint iced coffee at Philz Coffee on the West Coast. Fresh mint and coffee aren't paired as often as they should be, because the combination of bitter and fresh is so uniquely satisfying. This is a super-simple coffee-flavored layer cake that's enhanced with chocolate just so, without going full-on mocha.

The exterior demonstrates one of my favorite ways to employ fresh herbs in a cake: by infusing them into the butter that's used in the buttercream. It's an extra step that takes some planning ahead, but it is well worth it for the flavor. I'd also recommend trying out this method with basil or rosemary on a lemon or chocolate cake—it's very fun.

MAKES ONE 3-LAYER 8-INCH CAKE

Frosting

4 leafy stalks (10 grams) fresh mint (no need to pull the leaves from the stems)

1½ cups (340 grams) unsalted butter

4 cups (480 grams) powdered sugar

¼ teaspoon kosher salt

3 tablespoons (45 grams) whole milk

Cake

Nonstick spray

3⅓ cups (433 grams) all-purpose flour

2½ cups (500 grams) sugar

6 tablespoons (30 grams) unsweetened cocoa powder

2 tablespoons (8 grams) instant espresso powder

1½ teaspoons kosher salt

2¼ teaspoons baking powder

1¼ teaspoons baking soda

3 large eggs

1½ cups (360 grams) whole milk

¾ cup (150 grams) neutral oil

1 tablespoon (15 grams) pure vanilla extract

1 cup (240 grams) strong hot coffee

GET started on the frosting first, since the minty butter will take a bit of time. Place the fresh mint stalks in a saucepan and use a stiff rubber spatula to smash them a bit to release some flavor. Add the butter and melt over medium-low heat, then continue to heat for 10 minutes, stirring occasionally. Don't let the butter bubble at all; if it starts to, reduce the heat. Pour the butter through a fine-mesh sieve into the bowl of a stand mixer, smashing the leaves to make sure they release as much flavor as possible. Discard the mint, then set the butter aside to cool until it reaches room temperature and is opaque and firm on top, around 3 hours depending on the temperature of your kitchen. (If your kitchen is warm and the butter doesn't firm back up, place in the fridge for 10 to 15 minutes. You can also place the bowl in an ice bath and stir.) Now bake the cake!

PREHEAT the oven to 350°F. Grease three 8-inch round cake pans and line the bottoms with parchment paper.

IN a large bowl, whisk together the flour, sugar, cocoa, espresso powder, salt, baking powder, and baking soda. In a separate medium bowl or large measuring cup, whisk together the eggs, milk, oil, and vanilla. Whisk this mixture into the dry ingredients, then add the coffee and whisk until just combined

DIVIDE the batter evenly among the prepared pans and bake until the tops are springy and a toothpick inserted into the centers comes out clean; begin checking for doneness at 28 minutes.

LET cool in the pans for 10 minutes, then transfer to a wire rack to cool completely.

TO continue on with the frosting, give the butter a stir. Don't be alarmed if there's some liquid on the bottom; just stir it in until the butter is smooth and thickened. Add the powdered sugar and salt and beat with the paddle on low. When you're confident that sugar won't fly everywhere, gradually increase the speed to medium and continue to mix until smooth. Add the milk, increase the speed to medium high, and continue to mix until light and fluffy, about 2 minutes. If the frosting seems too soft, stick it in the fridge for 5 to 10 minutes, then beat it again until fluffy.

TO assemble, level the cake layers and stack them up with a layer of frosting between them. Frost the cake all over (see page 178).

FOR notes on storing leftover cake, see page 170.

NOTE: *You can also make this into 32 cupcakes. To bake, begin checking for doneness at 18 minutes. The frosting amount will yield enough for a thin layer on each cupcake. (If you're a big frosting person, make an additional half batch of frosting.)*

ROSEMARY POTATO LOAF CAKE

It's true that the butteriest, creamiest mashed potatoes of your life will morph into an otherworldly soft, velvety cake when you sprinkle in some pantry basics. Potato enhances a crumb in a similar way that pumpkin sets the table for mega moisture, but what's nice about potato is that its mild manners don't come with the expectations of pumpkin spice, so you can go on painting whatever flavors you want on this cake canvas. Here I've chosen rosemary and chocolate for a winter kind of cozy.

MAKES 1 LOAF

Cake

Nonstick spray

1 large (13- to 15-ounce/368- to 425-gram) russet potato

½ cup (113 grams) unsalted butter, sliced into pats

½ teaspoon finely chopped fresh rosemary leaves

½ cup (120 grams) heavy cream

1¼ cups (250 grams) sugar

2 large eggs

½ teaspoon pure vanilla extract

1¾ cups (228 grams) all-purpose flour

2 teaspoons baking powder

¾ teaspoon kosher salt

Chocolate ganache and assembly

3 ounces (85 grams) bittersweet chocolate, finely chopped, or ½ cup chips

3 tablespoons (45 grams) heavy cream

Flaky salt

PREHEAT the oven to 350°F. Grease a 4 × 8-inch metal loaf pan, a 4 × 9-inch pullman loaf pan, or a 5 × 9-inch metal loaf pan and line with enough parchment paper to allow for 1-inch wings on the long sides.

POKE the potato all over with a fork and microwave until a fork pokes easily through the center; begin checking for doneness at 5 minutes. (You can also bake the potato at 350°F for about an hour.) Let cool for a few minutes, until it's just cool enough to handle but still rather hot.

SCATTER the butter and rosemary in a large bowl. Scoop out the innards of the potato to get 1⅓ cups (226 grams), add to the bowl, and let the hot potato melt the butter as you mash with a fork or potato masher. Whisk in the heavy cream until creamy and mostly smooth (a few lumps are okay). Whisk in the sugar, eggs, and vanilla, then sprinkle the flour, baking powder, and salt evenly over the surface of the batter. Give the dry ingredients a rough little whisk to combine, then mix them into the rest of the batter, switching to a rubber spatula when the batter gets too thick.

TRANSFER the batter to the prepared pan, spreading it out evenly, and bake until puffed and golden on top and a toothpick inserted into the center comes out clean; begin checking for doneness at 1 hour. Let cool in the pan for 10 minutes, then use the parchment paper wings to help you lift it out and transfer to a wire rack to cool completely.

TO make the ganache, combine the chocolate and heavy cream in a bowl and microwave for a few seconds *just* until the heavy cream begins to bubble. Stir together until smooth and pour over the cake. Top with flaky salt and let the ganache set (or get kind of sloppy and slice immediately).

FOR notes on storing leftover cake, see page 170.

RAINBOW CHIP FINANCIERS

It's as if Entenmann's Little Bites grew up, studied abroad in France, and came back with a slammin' texture and epic stories to tell. Don't let their small size fool you—these tiny nuggets have nutty, caramelized substance.

MAKES 24 MINI MUFFINS

Nonstick spray

½ cup (56 grams) all-purpose flour, plus more for dusting the pan

½ cup (113 grams) unsalted butter, cut into pieces

1¼ cups (150 grams) powdered sugar

¾ cup (90 grams) fine almond flour

¾ teaspoon kosher salt

3 large egg whites

½ teaspoon pure almond extract

½ cup (100 grams) rainbow candy-coated chips

PREHEAT the oven to 350°F. Grease 24 nonstick mini muffin wells very well and lightly flour them, tapping out the excess.

PLACE the butter in a small skillet (use a light-colored or stainless steel skillet so you can see the butter brown) and set it over medium-low heat. When the butter melts, let it cook, swirling occasionally, until it begins to foam. When it starts foaming, watch carefully and swirl the pan every 10 seconds or so until the butter develops dark brown specks, smells nutty, and the sizzle popping sounds subside, about 5 minutes. (Watch it closely!) Immediately remove it from the heat, pour it into a heat-safe bowl, and let it cool completely.

IN a medium bowl, whisk together the powdered sugar, almond flour, all-purpose flour, and salt. Add the egg whites, cooled browned butter, and almond extract and whisk well until fully combined and smooth. Switch to a rubber spatula and fold in the rainbow chips.

SCOOP into the prepared pan and bake until puffed up and lightly golden; begin checking for doneness at 14 minutes (these overbake very easily). Let cool for 5 minutes in the pan, then use a small offset spatula or butter knife to help you transfer to a wire rack to cool completely. These are best once they're fully cooled.

FOR notes on storing leftover cake, see page 170.

CHOCOLATE PEANUT BUTTER CAKE

One of the first times I colored outside the recipe lines, so to speak, was when I made my friend Rob's birthday cake in college and departed from the typical addition of milk, using coconut milk instead. It contributed beautiful richness and the flavor was very subtle yet complementary. It was a fantastic, wildly moist cake.

The problem was that no one at Rob's party cared about my cake revelation. Everybody went about mindlessly eating that perfect cake while chatting about paradiddles or cymbals or whatever—which I guess is what you get for going to music school and treating it like culinary school.

Another problem is that once you open up a can of coconut milk, you've gotta find a use for the rest of it. Fourteen years later, I've found the best use! The thick creamy solids at the top of the can make for the silkiest, glossiest, easiest, most ethereal frosting; it falls somewhere between buttercream and whipped cream. And peanut butter is here because often when I'm eating chocolate cake, I ask myself . . . why isn't this a chocolate peanut butter cake?

MAKES ONE 9 × 13-INCH CAKE

Cake

Nonstick spray

2 cups (400 grams) sugar

1¾ cups (228 grams) all-purpose flour

¾ cup (60 grams) unsweetened cocoa powder

1½ teaspoons kosher salt

1½ teaspoons baking powder

1½ teaspoons baking soda

One 13.5-ounce can full-fat coconut milk, divided

2 large eggs, room temperature

½ cup (100 grams) unrefined coconut oil, melted and cooled slightly

1 tablespoon (13 grams) pure vanilla extract

1 cup (240 grams) hot coffee

Frosting and assembly

¾ cup (170 grams) unsalted butter, room temperature

½ cup (128 grams) unsweetened unsalted peanut butter

¼ teaspoon kosher salt

3 cups (360 grams) powdered sugar

Sprinkles make sense

PREHEAT the oven to 350°F. Grease a 9 × 13-inch metal pan. (I like to serve this right out of the pan, but if you plan to remove it from the pan before decorating and serving, line the bottom with parchment, too.)

IN a large bowl, whisk together the sugar, flour, cocoa, salt, baking powder, and baking soda.

OPEN the can of coconut milk and scoop out ⅔ cup (160 grams) of the creamy solids on top. If the solids come up short of ⅔ cup, it's okay to supplement with the thicker milk toward the top of the can. Set aside for the frosting.

POUR the remaining coconut milk (about 1 cup/240 grams) into a medium bowl, add the eggs, coconut oil, and vanilla and whisk to combine. Add the mixture to the dry ingredients and whisk to mostly combine (it'll be pretty thick), then add in the coffee and whisk until just combined.

POUR the batter into the prepared pan and bake until the top is springy and a toothpick inserted into the center comes out clean; begin checking for doneness at 32 minutes. Let cool completely in the pan.

TO make the frosting, in a stand mixer fitted with a whisk, combine the butter, peanut butter, and salt and beat on medium high until creamy. Reduce the speed to low, add the powdered sugar, and beat until combined and the consistency of a very thick, pasty frosting. (It will look like there's too much powdered sugar at first, but keep mixing and increase the speed to medium once you're confident sugar won't fly everywhere.) Add the reserved coconut cream, increase the speed to medium high, and beat until the mixture is smooth, glossy, fluffy, and thick enough to hold medium peaks, 3 to 4 minutes.

SPREAD the frosting generously all over the top of the cake, add sprinkles, and get at it.

FOR notes on storing leftover cake, see page 170.

NOTE: *You can also make this into 24 cupcakes. To bake, begin checking for doneness at 20 minutes.*

ROASTED SQUASH CAKE WITH BROWN SUGAR FROSTING

Ira's first favorite food was squash, so naturally her first birthday was squash themed. We ate squash hummus, squash soup, and this squash cake, and Auntie Elaine crocheted her a squishy squash. I felt accomplished for sneaking a vegetable into the baby via cake. This is sort of like pumpkin bread lite in that it has a similar spiced feel of a pumpkin bread, but it doesn't sock you in the face with autumn vibes—which was by design, since Ira's birthday is in February. It leans more heavily on the caramelized squash and brown sugar flavor in the frosting. And its moisture is at a level 10, which makes it ideal for cupcakes (or a baby smash cake!).

MAKES ONE 3-LAYER 8-INCH CAKE OR 24 CUPCAKES

Cake

1 medium (2½-pound/1.1-kilogram) butternut squash, halved and seeded

1 cup (200 grams) neutral oil, plus a little more for the squash

1 teaspoon ground cinnamon

1 teaspoon freshly grated nutmeg

½ teaspoon ground cloves

Nonstick spray

⅔ cup (160 grams) buttermilk

2½ cups (500 grams) sugar

4 large eggs

3 cups (390 grams) all-purpose flour

1 tablespoon (14 grams) baking powder

1½ teaspoons kosher salt

1½ teaspoons baking soda

Frosting and assembly

1 cup (226 grams) unsalted butter, room temperature

1½ cups (300 grams) packed light brown sugar

½ teaspoon ground cinnamon

Pinch of kosher salt

8 ounces (226 grams) cream cheese, room temperature

Optional decor: fresh herb sprigs, candied citrus, a dusting of cinnamon, a sprinkling of seeds or nuts

PREHEAT the oven to 400°F.

PLACE the squash halves cut side up on a sheet pan, coat with a thin layer of oil and sprinkle evenly with the cinnamon, nutmeg, and cloves. Roast until a fork pokes easily into the center; begin checking for doneness at 40 minutes. Let sit until cool enough to handle, about 10 minutes.

WHILE the squash is cooling, grease three 8-inch cake pans and line the bottoms with parchment paper, or line 24 cupcake wells with cupcake liners. Lower the oven temperature to 350°F.

MEASURE out 3 cups (about 624 grams) of the squash flesh into a large bowl. Reserve any remaining squash for another use. To the bowl, add the buttermilk and mash with a fork until mostly smooth (a few lumps are okay). Add the 1 cup (200 grams) oil, the sugar, and eggs and whisk until smooth. Sprinkle the flour evenly over the top of the batter, then sprinkle on the baking powder, salt, and baking soda. Give the dry ingredients a rough little whisk to combine, then incorporate them into the rest of the batter, whisking until just combined.

DISTRIBUTE the batter evenly among the prepared pans or cupcake liners, filling each liner about three-quarters of the way. Bake until the tops are springy and a toothpick inserted into the centers comes out clean; begin checking for doneness at 30 minutes for cakes and 20 minutes for cupcakes. Let cool in the pans for 10 minutes, then transfer to a wire rack to cool completely.

TO make the frosting, in a stand mixer fitted with a paddle, combine the butter, brown sugar, cinnamon, and salt and beat on medium high until creamy, about 2 minutes. Reduce the speed to medium, add the cream cheese, and beat until just combined. Scrape down the sides of the bowl with a rubber spatula as needed to ensure that everything combines evenly.

TO assemble, level the cake layers and stack them up with a layer of frosting between them. Spread the remaining frosting on the top. (I like to keep the sides naked.) Or pipe on top of the cupcakes in swirls. Top with desired decor.

FOR notes on storing leftover cake, see page 170.

NOTE: *You can also make this into ten 4-inch cakes or two 4 × 9-inch pullman loafs. To bake, begin checking for doneness at 24 minutes for 4-inch cakes and 55 minutes for loaf cakes.*

FRESH MINT OLIVE OIL CAKE WITH PRESERVED LEMON YOGURT WHIP

You might think that pulverizing your entire herb garden and shoving it into a cake would be overpowering, too vegetal, and just gross, but it's in fact subtle, uniquely refreshing, and equally appropriate for both a fancy adult dinner-party dessert and a Kermit-the-Frog-themed child's birthday party. The inspiration for this cake came from a dessert I had at the Exchange restaurant in LA that was as tasty as it was visually intriguing. The cake was broken up to look almost like moss in an edible terrarium, and it was nestled with some lemon and yogurt elements that played so nicely together. When I got home, I instantly got to work on this cake, and it's become one of my favorites because it makes all your friends go, *Whoaaaa, what's going on with that cake?* but it eats very smoothly. Baking the mint mutes it so that you get its herbal flavor without the toothpaste-style burn. The crumb is bouncy, and the fluffy whip on top enhances with a hint of preserved lemon funk. Also! Bonus: The cake batter comes together entirely in a blender.

MAKES ONE 9-INCH CAKE

Cake

Nonstick spray

1¼ cups (250 grams) sugar

1 cup (40 grams) firmly packed fresh mint leaves

¾ cup (150 grams) extra virgin olive oil

½ cup (120 grams) cold milk (see Note)

3 large cold eggs (see Note)

½ teaspoon pure vanilla extract

Zest of 1 lemon

½ cup (56 grams) fine almond flour

1 teaspoon kosher salt

1 teaspoon baking powder

¼ teaspoon baking soda

1½ cups (195 grams) all-purpose flour

Yogurt whip

½ cup (120 grams) cold whole milk Greek yogurt

1 cup (240 grams) cold heavy cream

½ cup (60 grams) powdered sugar

2 tablespoons (32 grams) preserved lemon paste (or very finely chopped rinsed preserved lemon rinds)

NOTE: *Cold milk and cold eggs in the batter help the green mint color stay bright!*

TO make the cake, preheat the oven to 350°F. Grease a 9-inch round cake pan and line the bottom with parchment paper.

IN a high-speed blender, blend the sugar, mint, olive oil, milk, eggs, vanilla, and lemon zest on high for 1 full minute, until very smooth with no visible flecks of mint. Add the almond flour, salt, baking powder, and baking soda and blend until just combined. Add the all-purpose flour and pulse a few times until *just* combined; be extra careful not to blend any longer than you need.

POUR the batter into the prepared pan and bake until the top is springy and a toothpick inserted in the center comes out clean; begin checking for doneness at 36 minutes. Let cool in the pan for 10 minutes, then transfer to a wire rack to cool completely.

TO make the yogurt whip, in a stand mixer fitted with a whisk, combine the yogurt, heavy cream, and powdered sugar and beat on medium high until medium peaks form, about 1 minute. Add the preserved lemon paste and mix until just combined.

YOU can spread the yogurt whip over the whole cake and serve immediately, but if you don't plan to eat the whole cake at once, dollop each naked slice with whip as you eat it.

STORE the untopped cake, covered, at room temperature for up to 4 days. Whipped cream can be stored in an airtight container in the fridge for up to a couple of days. Leftover cake that's topped with whip can go in the fridge for up to a couple of days.

ROSE ROSE CAKE

Years ago, when my sister-in-law, Anna, got engaged, I immediately volunteered to make the wedding cakes for her low-key, intimate wedding reception of just 350 people. The thought of taking on something like this by myself didn't feel so masochistic before kids; back then, it was a chance to hone my skills and learn new things.

Anna's one request was to incorporate florals, so I spent the months leading up to the wedding developing floral-forward cake flavors and brushing up on the buttercream rose technique I'd learned when I worked at the town bakery. With a new set of petal tips and food coloring, I hunkered down and got to work, creating a series of flower-covered sheet cakes that I posted to my blog. It was one of my all-time favorite projects. For the wedding reception, I made five towering round cakes with bouquets of buttercream flowers on top of each (plus a million cupcakes, because did I mention the wedding was 350 people?). I was way too sleepy to dance at the party, but I was a proud mama to those cakes.

Today I'm a little rusty with the roses, but I still love breaking out the petal tips from time to time, and when I do, I love to make sheet cakes like this one that look like flower planters. Since they're buttercream roses, I figured we should lean all the way in and scent the cake and frosting with rosewater. The combination of the floral notes with almond and lemon as support makes this cake feel almost like a big petit four. The crumb is *so* buttery and extra dense thanks to the almond flour, and the frosting, while sweet, is balanced by the lemon.

The frosting amount here will yield enough to generously spread all over the cake. If you're fixing to plant a whole rose garden on top, go ahead and make an extra half batch of frosting, since you'll be using a considerable amount of it in the flowers.

If you came here to learn how to pipe roses, I'll be real with you and say that no series of photos with my clumsy fingers will stack up to the education that you'll get by watching videos online, so please YouTube "buttercream rose" and be prepared to *practice practice practice.*

Cake

Nonstick spray

3 cups (390 grams) all-purpose flour

1 tablespoon (14 grams) baking powder

1 cup (112 grams) fine almond flour

1½ teaspoons kosher salt

¾ cup (180 grams) sour cream, room temperature

1½ cups (360 grams) heavy cream, room temperature

1 cup (226 grams) unsalted butter, room temperature

½ cup (100 grams) unrefined coconut oil, room temperature

2 cups (400 grams) sugar

Zest of 1 lemon

4 large eggs, room temperature

1 tablespoon (14 grams) vanilla bean paste or extract

¼ cup (60 grams) rosewater

½ teaspoon pure almond extract

Frosting

1 cup (226 grams) unsalted butter, room temperature

4 cups (480 grams) powdered sugar

¼ teaspoon kosher salt

1 tablespoon (15 grams) rosewater

1 teaspoon vanilla bean paste or extract

1 teaspoon lemon juice

¼ teaspoon pure almond extract

¼ cup (60 grams) heavy cream

PREHEAT the oven to 350°F. Grease a 9 × 13-inch metal pan and line with enough parchment to allow for 1-inch wings on the long sides. (If you plan to serve the cake right out of the pan, you can forego the parchment.)

IN a medium bowl, sift together the all-purpose flour and baking powder, then lightly stir in the almond flour and salt and set aside. In a medium bowl or large measuring cup, whisk together the sour cream and heavy cream and set aside.

IN a stand mixer fitted with a paddle, combine the butter, coconut oil, sugar, and lemon zest and beat on medium high until pale and fluffy, 3 to 4 minutes. Add the eggs one at a time, mixing well after each addition and scraping down the sides of the bowl with a rubber spatula as needed to ensure that everything combines evenly. Beat in the vanilla, rosewater, and almond extract. Reduce the speed to low and add the flour mixture and cream mixture in three alternating additions, mixing until mostly combined. Turn off the mixer and use your spatula to finish up the mixing by hand, making sure to combine thoroughly without overmixing.

TRANSFER the batter to the prepared pan, spreading it out evenly, and bake until the top is springy and a toothpick inserted into the center comes out clean or with just a few crumbs; begin checking for doneness at 35 minutes. Let cool completely in the pan.

TO make the frosting, in a stand mixer fitted with a paddle, combine the butter, powdered sugar, and salt and mix on low until you're confident that sugar won't fly everywhere, then gradually increase the speed to medium and continue to mix until smooth. Add the rosewater, vanilla, lemon juice, almond extract, and heavy cream, increase the speed to medium high, and continue to mix until light and fluffy, about 2 minutes. Scrape down the sides of the bowl with a rubber spatula as needed to ensure that everything combines evenly.

TRANSFER the cake to a big serving platter or keep it in the pan to serve, and frost as desired.

FOR notes on storing leftover cake, see page 170.

NOTE: *You can also make this into three 8-inch round layers or 28 cupcakes. To bake, begin checking for doneness at 30 minutes for layers and 20 minutes for cupcakes. For either layers or cupcakes, make an additional half batch of frosting.*

GRILLED PEACH SHORTCAKES

Shortcakes do not have the same luxurious margin of error that, say, pizza or ramen does. That is, bad versions, be they cups of ramen made at summer camp with hot water from the bathroom tap or frozen pizzas from gas stations, are still thoroughly enjoyable. But bad shortcakes aren't. At all.

In fact, I'll be so bold as to say that *most* shortcakes fall short in the worst way, which was a realization that came to me when I finally had a good one after decades on this earth. Suddenly I started questioning everything. What else is good that I've always thought was bad? Bananas? Game nights? *Lord of the Rings?* Great news: Our reality doesn't need to include bad shortcakes, because making them is not hard.

What gets most shortcakes in trouble is timing. They need to be fresh—no exceptions. Don't make them the day before your dinner party; don't even make them the morning of. Make them so they come out of the oven just before your guests arrive (you can shape the dough in advance and hold it in the freezer so they can be popped in the oven at the last minute) and eat them as soon as they're cool enough that they won't melt the whipped cream. After just a few hours, shortcakes start to lose hope—but that's what makes a good one like a unicorn sighting. Don't your guests deserve to have this revelation, too?

Use peak-season warm weather fruit (I'm a sucker for a peach, and a grilled one; thank you to my trusty assistant, Paige, for this idea! But of course the classic strawberry route will do, too) whose sweetness will just edge out the barely sweet, vanilla-heavy, buttery-as-heck cake and allow the most fantastic specimen of a simple pleasure to take hold of your life and turn your understanding of the world upside down. It may even make you forget that summer is the most garbage season.

Peaches

4 peaches, halved and pitted

2 tablespoons (25 grams) sugar, or more to taste

Shortcakes

4¼ cups (553 grams) all-purpose flour

½ cup sugar (100 grams) plus 1 tablespoon (13 grams), divided

2 tablespoons (28 grams) baking powder

1½ teaspoons kosher salt

1 cup (226 grams) cold unsalted butter, cut into ½-inch cubes, plus 1 tablespoon (13 grams) melted

1½ cups (360 grams) cold heavy cream

2 teaspoons pure vanilla extract

Whipped cream and assembly

1½ cups (360 grams) cold heavy cream

6 ounces (170 grams) cream cheese, room temperature

6 tablespoons (45 grams) powdered sugar

¾ teaspoon pure vanilla extract

Handful of fresh basil, torn or thinly sliced

IF you're intending to serve these immediately, start by grilling the peaches. If you're intending to prep the shortcake dough ahead of time, wait to grill the peaches until shortly before serving.

GRILL the peaches on an outdoor grill or grill pan over medium-high heat until char marks appear, a few minutes per side. Slice thinly and toss with the sugar in a medium bowl, adding more sugar to taste if desired. Let sit at room temperature for about 30 minutes (or for a few hours in the refrigerator) so the peaches release their juices, until ready to serve.

ARRANGE oven racks in the upper middle and lower middle positions and preheat the oven to 400°F. Line two sheet pans with parchment paper.

IN a large bowl, whisk together the flour, ½ cup (100 grams) of the sugar, the baking powder, and salt. Add the butter and use your fingers to incorporate it by smashing and rubbing it in with the dry ingredients until the pieces are evenly dispersed and the mixture is crumbly. (Don't try to make this mixture in a food processor; it's too big to fit in a standard one. Embrace how therapeutic it is to do this by hand.) Drizzle in the cream and vanilla and use a rubber spatula to gently incorporate it. Dump the mixture onto the counter and knead it a few times to bring the dough together into a mostly cohesive dough; don't overwork it.

DIVIDE the dough in half and pat each half into a 7-inch circle that's just under 1 inch thick, then cut each circle into 4 wedges. Space the wedges evenly on the sheet pans, brush with the melted butter, and sprinkle with the remaining 1 tablespoon (13 grams) sugar. (At this point you can freeze the dough for a few hours until ready to bake, or even for up to 3 months. Cover with plastic wrap if keeping for more than a day. Bake directly from frozen, adding a few more minutes to the baking time.)

BAKE only what you intend to eat immediately. Any remaining shortcakes should stay frozen until you plan to serve them. Bake until golden; begin checking for doneness after 20 minutes, switching each pan to the other rack and rotating the pans 180 degrees a little over halfway through the bake time. (If you're just baking one pan right now, bake in the center of the oven.) Let cool on the pans for 5 minutes, then transfer to a wire rack to cool completely.

TO make the whipped cream, in a stand mixer fitted with a whisk, combine the heavy cream, cream cheese, powdered sugar, and vanilla and beat on medium high until medium-stiff peaks form, 1 to 2 minutes.

SPLIT the shortcakes open and stack with whipped cream, peaches, and basil in the center. Serve immediately.

ALMOND BUTTER MINI CAKES WITH BERRY GLAZE

Here are some nutty little after-school cakes that channel PB&J energy but with slightly more sophistication, for days when Bernie has decided to don Aunt Ethel's giant dazzling clip-on earrings, sparkly heels, an updo, and a tiara. These cakes come together lightning fast, require no special tools, use the natural pink of strawberry jam for the glaze, and can certainly be made with pedestrian peanut butter for more casual days requiring fewer tiaras.

MAKES 6 MINI CAKES

Cakes

Nonstick spray

1 cup (200 grams) sugar

1 cup (130 grams) all-purpose flour

¾ teaspoon kosher salt

¾ teaspoon baking powder

¼ teaspoon baking soda

1 large egg

1 teaspoon pure vanilla extract

¾ cup (180 grams) milk

2 teaspoons lemon juice

¼ cup (50 grams) neutral oil

½ cup (128 grams) unsweetened unsalted almond butter (or peanut butter)

Glaze

1 cup (120 grams) powdered sugar

5 tablespoons (100 grams) strawberry jam, plus a little more as needed

PREHEAT the oven to 350°F. Grease 6 nonstick jumbo muffin wells.

IN a large bowl, whisk together the sugar, flour, salt, baking powder, and baking soda. In a medium bowl or large measuring cup, whisk together the egg, vanilla, milk, lemon juice, oil, and almond butter. Add the wet ingredients to the dry ingredients and whisk until just combined.

DIVIDE the batter evenly among the prepared muffin wells and bake until the tops are springy and a toothpick inserted into the center comes out clean; begin checking for doneness at 26 minutes. Let cool in the pan for 10 minutes, then use a butter knife or small offset spatula to help you transfer to a wire rack to cool completely.

TO make the glaze, in a medium bowl, combine the powdered sugar with the jam and mix until smooth, adding more jam as needed until the glaze is smooth and spreadable but thick enough that it will hold its shape when it drips.

TURN the cakes upside down so they're wide at the base. Top with the glaze, letting it drip down the sides.

FOR notes on storing leftover cake, see page 170.

THIS IS ALSO A WHEAT FARM

While sugar beets might be one of the most prevalent crops in the region, a lot of potatoes, corn, beans, sunflowers, canola, and grains rotate in with the beets; most farmers around here farm more than one crop for, among other reasons, risk management and crop health. I promise I didn't plan it this way, but Nick's rotational crop is wheat—that is, the other most common baking ingredient. So you could say we're kinda farm-to-cake.

Farming wheat is easier on the sleep schedule than beets. It also smells amazing, like pizza or fresh loaves of bread. Even though its harvest happens in the icky sticky heat of the summer, it's beautiful because when a wheat field is at maturity it is a stunning sea of gold. The way the huge combines chop off rows of the wheat in perfect lines before the wheat berries are separated from the chaff is very soothing to watch.

Wheat needs to be harvested when it's dry, so Nick drives his combine through the fields in the heat of the day. Then the berries are transported back to the farm, where they're stored in big cylindrical grain bins until the market price is right to sell them to the mill in town, which then turns them into flour. Nick grows hard red spring wheat, which does best in our cool climate, and generally produces a wheat with a higher protein level, meaning it's best for bread and bagels (!!). So a lot of the flour that he grows is shipped to New York.

Although they're not always the most practical ingredient prior to getting processed at the mill, wheat berries are fun to play around with! If I feel like a wheat berry salad or milling my own flour, I call up Nick and say, "Hi, you know of anywhere a girl can get some wheat berries?" And he says, "Yeah, I think I know a guy!" and then a few minutes later he shows up in the kitchen with a big bucket of wheat berries from the grain bins. For a wheat berry salad, you just simmer the berries for forever until they get soft and chewy, almost like farro. For turning into flour, I just toss some into the Vitamix and blend until fine. It's not the most practical ingredient because using only this flour would produce overly dense, hard results (it truly is a miracle we have all our teeth after making matzo with it a few years back). It's like your average grocery store whole wheat flour on steroids. So I just incorporate a little of this flour in the interest of flavor and farm-to-table novelty, and lighten it by adding all-purpose or cake flour.

At the mill, Nick's wheat gets combined with wheat from other farmers in the area and then the outer shell, called the bran, as well as the germ get separated from the endosperm inside, and the endosperm is used to produce flours like all-purpose, bread, and high-gluten. Sometimes the bran, germ, and endosperm are all used, and you get whole wheat flour. It gets packaged into sacks and brought to the grocery store where I buy my flour. Each time I get a sack, I like to look at it and envision that at least a few spoonfuls of it came from our backyard.

SALTED CHOCOLATE CHUNK WHOLE WHEAT SNACK CAKE

All the makings of a quality snack cake are present in this recipe: it has a vague nutritional angle with the inclusion of whole wheat flour and yogurt, it comes together with just a bowl and a whisk, and it wears a cool no-makeup makeup look that's sweatpants-casual but still manages to be interesting. The whole wheat flour is here not only to make you feel slightly less bad about eating cake for literally no reason at all; it also adds body to a style of cake that sometimes lacks heft. The yogurt glaze gets poured on top right when the cake comes out of the oven, so beyond the obvious perk of not needing this to cool before digging in, you also get to enjoy caramelized sticky edges and a hip semi-matte sheen.

Cake

¼ cup (50 grams) unrefined coconut oil, melted and cooled slightly

¼ cup (56 grams) unsalted butter, melted and cooled slightly

½ cup (100 grams) packed light brown sugar

½ cup (100 grams) granulated sugar

2 large eggs

1 tablespoon (13 grams) pure vanilla extract

¾ cup (180 grams) whole milk Greek yogurt

1 cup (130 grams) all-purpose flour

½ cup (65 grams) whole wheat flour

1½ teaspoons baking powder

¾ teaspoon kosher salt

6 ounces (170 grams) semisweet or milk chocolate, coarsely chopped

Glaze and assembly

¾ cup (90 grams) powdered sugar

2 tablespoons (30 grams) whole milk Greek yogurt

¼ teaspoon pure vanilla extract

Flaky salt

PREHEAT the oven to 350°F. Line an 8-inch square metal pan with enough parchment paper to allow for 1-inch wings on opposite sides.

IN a large bowl, whisk together the coconut oil, butter, granulated sugar, and brown sugar. Add the eggs one at a time, whisking well after each addition, then whisk in the vanilla. Whisk in the yogurt. Sprinkle the all-purpose flour, whole wheat flour, baking powder, and salt evenly over the top and give them a rough little whisk to combine before incorporating into the rest of the batter. Switch to a rubber spatula and fold in most of the chocolate, reserving a handful for the top.

TRANSFER the batter to the prepared pan, sprinkle the remaining chocolate on top, and bake until a toothpick inserted into the center comes out clean; begin checking for doneness at 28 minutes.

WHILE the cake is baking, make the glaze. In a medium bowl, combine the powdered sugar, yogurt, and vanilla and mix until smooth.

POUR the glaze over the cake while it's still hot in the pan. Sprinkle on a good pinch of flaky salt.

FOR notes on storing leftover cake, see page 170.

ELDERFLOWER STRAWBERRY BLØTKAKE

The original un-elderflowered version of this Bløtkake (BLOOD-ka-ka), scribbled on a battered old note card that I got from Nick's aunt Judie, seemed entirely too simple to create a celebration-worthy treat. Five ingredients, one being water, that come together all in one bowl to be baked in one pan and then covered with the plainest-ever whipped cream and super-basic berries? *Surely I'm missing something,* I thought the first time I attempted to bake it myself. How have the Hagens been getting away with this at the family Christmas?? But nope, that one-bowl cake baked up like a charm and the whipped cream was all I ever wanted, and I realized that this was a true testament to the power of simplicity. (The addition of salt has been my only change to the batter since, so now there are six ingredients. Judie, please forgive me.)

This is a light sponge cake, just one step heavier than angel food cake, and it's the type of thing you can have after a big meal or when it's hot out and everything that's not air-conditioning makes you cranky. It doesn't need the elderflower. No one needs elderflower. But no one needs a Parisian vacation either. If you happen to have St-Germain, or you feel like basking in a little luxury, go for it. The slightly citrusy floral atmosphere of a breezy summer afternoon will soak through your cake and your whip with no regrets. If not, skip the syrup or substitute simple syrup and you will still have a delicious treat.

MAKES ONE 2-LAYER 9-INCH CAKE

Cake

Nonstick spray

5 large eggs, room temperature

2 cups (400 grams) sugar

½ cup (120 grams) water

2½ cups (325 grams) all-purpose flour

2 heaping teaspoons baking powder

1 teaspoon kosher salt

Syrup

¼ cup (60 grams) elderflower liqueur or cordial

1 tablespoon (16 grams) lemon juice

Whipped cream and assembly

3 cups (720 grams) cold heavy cream

3 tablespoons (45 grams) powdered sugar

¼ cup (60 grams) elderflower liqueur or cordial

½ teaspoon pure vanilla extract

10 ounces (283 grams) strawberries, thinly sliced

PREHEAT the oven to 325°F. Grease a 9-inch springform pan and line the bottom with parchment paper.

IN a stand mixer fitted with a whisk, combine the eggs and sugar and beat on medium high until pale and fluffy, 3 to 4 minutes. Beat in the water. Remove the bowl from the mixer. Sift in the flour and baking powder, sprinkle on the salt, and fold together with a rubber spatula until just combined.

TRANSFER the batter to the prepared pan and bake until the top is springy; begin checking for doneness at 1 hour. Let cool completely in the pan. (It's okay if it sinks slightly in the center.)

TO make the syrup, combine the elderflower liqueur and lemon juice in a small bowl.

TO make the whipped cream, in a stand mixer fitted with a whisk, beat the heavy cream and powdered sugar on medium high until stiff peaks form, 1 to 2 minutes. Add the elderflower liqueur and vanilla and mix until just combined.

TO assemble, slice the cake in half crosswise using a serrated knife to create two layers. Place the bottom layer cut side up on a cardboard cake circle or directly onto a cake stand or serving platter. Brush with about half of the syrup. Spread on a thick layer of whipped cream and top with a layer of strawberries. Place the other half of the cake on top, cut side down, and brush on the remaining syrup. Spread the whipped cream on the top and sides of the cake to cover. Top with the remaining strawberries.

THIS cake is best eaten the day it's made, though leftovers can be covered and kept in the refrigerator for up to 3 days. My rule against cold cake gets an exception here, because bringing that much whipped cream to room temperature would be weird. So eat leftovers straight from the fridge, wash down with iced coffee or tea.

TOASTED SESAME CAKE

Between the heavy use of sesame in both Jewish and Chinese cooking and my mom's particular use of it in place of peanuts due to her peanut allergy, I feel like I have lived in a sea of sesame my whole life, which is a place I'd recommend. It also explains my family's perpetual paranoia that we have seeds stuck in our teeth. Something that I think makes sesame unique is the world of difference between raw sesame seeds and their dark toasted caramelly selves; you don't always see that kind of drastic transformation with other nuts or seeds. This cake highlights that wonderful toasty flavor in a cozy golden sheet with a sweet honey frosting that's fit for the Lunar New Year, the Jewish New Year, and anywhere in between.

MAKES ONE 9 × 13-INCH CAKE

Cake

Nonstick spray

1 cup (160 grams) plus 2 tablespoons (20 grams) toasted sesame seeds, divided, plus more for topping

3 cups (390 grams) all-purpose flour

1 tablespoon (14 grams) baking powder

1½ teaspoons kosher salt

¾ cup (180 grams) sour cream, room temperature

1½ cups (360 grams) heavy cream, room temperature

1 tablespoon (13 grams) pure vanilla extract

1 cup (226 grams) unsalted butter, room temperature

½ cup (100 grams) unrefined coconut oil, room temperature

1 teaspoon toasted sesame oil

1¼ cups (250 grams) sugar

Zest of 1 orange

½ cup (168 grams) honey

4 large eggs, room temperature

Frosting

1 cup (226 grams) unsalted butter, room temperature

½ cup (168 grams) honey

2 cups (240 grams) powdered sugar

⅛ teaspoon kosher salt

Zest of 1 orange

1 teaspoon pure vanilla extract

4 ounces (113 grams) cream cheese, room temperature

PREHEAT the oven to 350°F. Grease a 9 × 13-inch metal pan and line with enough parchment to allow for 1-inch wings on the long sides. (If you plan to serve the cake right out of the pan, you can forego the parchment.)

USING a spice grinder, finely grind 1 cup (160 grams) of the sesame seeds, in batches if necessary.

IN a medium bowl, sift together the flour and baking powder, then lightly stir in the ground sesame seeds, remaining 2 tablespoons (20 grams) whole sesame seeds, and the salt and set aside. In a medium bowl or large measuring cup, whisk together the sour cream, heavy cream, and vanilla and set aside.

IN a stand mixer fitted with a paddle, combine the butter, coconut oil, sesame oil, sugar, and orange zest and beat on medium high until pale and fluffy, 3 to 4 minutes. Beat in the honey, then add the eggs one at a time, mixing well after each addition and scraping down the sides of the bowl with a rubber spatula as needed to ensure that everything combines evenly. Reduce the speed to low and add the flour mixture and cream mixture in three alternating additions, mixing until mostly combined. Turn off the mixer and use your spatula to finish up the mixing by hand, making sure to combine thoroughly without overmixing.

TRANSFER the batter to the prepared pan, spreading it out evenly, and bake until the top is springy and a toothpick inserted into the center comes out clean or with just a few crumbs; begin checking for doneness at 35 minutes. Let cool completely in the pan.

TO make the frosting, in a stand mixer fitted with a paddle, combine the butter, honey, powdered sugar, salt, and orange zest and mix on low until you're confident that sugar won't fly everywhere, then gradually increase the speed to medium high and continue to mix until smooth and fluffy, about 2 minutes. Lower the speed to medium, add the cream cheese, and mix until just combined. Scrape down the sides of the bowl with a rubber spatula as needed to ensure that everything combines evenly.

TRANSFER the cake to a big serving platter or keep it in the pan to serve, and frost the top with big rustic swoops. Sprinkle with sesame seeds, and serve with a side of floss.

FOR notes on storing leftover cake, see page 170.

NOTE: *You can also make this into 28 cupcakes. To bake, begin checking for doneness at 20 minutes.*

BIG BUTTERY CHOCOLATE CAKE

This is sturdier, richer, and denser than your typical squishy oil-based back-of-the-Hershey's-box chocolate cake, and it's become the go-to for my niece's and nephew's birthdays, primarily because its stalwart nature makes it a great canvas for marzipan cows, superheroes, Ninja Turtles, and the like.

MAKES ONE 3-LAYER 8-INCH ROUND CAKE

Cake

Nonstick spray

1 cup (80 grams) Dutch-process cocoa powder

1 cup (240 grams) boiling water

3 cups (390 grams) all-purpose flour

1 tablespoon (14 grams) baking powder

1 teaspoon instant espresso powder

1½ teaspoons kosher salt

1½ cups (360 grams) heavy cream, room temperature

¾ cup (180 grams) sour cream, room temperature

4 teaspoons (16 grams) pure vanilla extract

1 cup (226 grams) unsalted butter, room temperature

½ cup (100 grams) unrefined coconut oil, room temperature

2 cups (400 grams) sugar

4 large eggs, room temperature

8 ounces (226 grams) milk chocolate, finely chopped (or 1⅓ cups chips) and then melted and cooled to room temperature

Frosting and assembly

1 cup (226 grams) unsalted butter, room temperature

8 ounces (226 grams) cream cheese, room temperature

½ cup (40 grams) Dutch-process or unsweetened cocoa powder

4 ounces (113 grams) semisweet chocolate, finely chopped (or ⅔ cup chips) and then melted and cooled to room temperature

1 teaspoon pure vanilla extract

¼ teaspoon kosher salt

4 cups (480 grams) powdered sugar

Marzipan shapes, for decor, optional (see page 249)

PREHEAT the oven to 350°F. Grease three 8-inch round cake pans and line the bottoms with parchment paper.

IN a medium bowl or large measuring cup, whisk together the cocoa and boiling water. Set aside to cool briefly.

IN a separate medium bowl, sift together the flour and baking powder, then lightly stir in the espresso powder and salt and set aside. Add the heavy cream, sour cream, and vanilla to the slightly cooled cocoa mixture, whisk to combine, and set aside.

IN a stand mixer fitted with a paddle, combine the butter, coconut oil, and sugar and beat on medium high until pale and fluffy, 3 to 4 minutes. Add the eggs one at a time, mixing well after each addition and scraping down the sides of the bowl with a rubber spatula as needed to ensure that everything combines evenly. With the mixer running, drizzle in the melted chocolate. Reduce the speed to low and add the flour mixture and cream mixture in three alternating additions, mixing until mostly combined. Turn off the mixer and use your spatula to finish up the mixing by hand, making sure to combine thoroughly without overmixing.

DIVIDE the batter among the prepared pans, spreading it out evenly with the back of a spoon or an offset spatula. Bake until the tops are springy and a toothpick inserted into the center comes out clean or with just a few crumbs on it; begin checking for doneness at 30 minutes. Let cool in the pans for 15 minutes, then transfer to a wire rack to cool completely.

TO make the frosting, in a stand mixer fitted with a paddle, combine the butter, cream cheese, cocoa, melted chocolate, vanilla, and salt and mix on medium until smooth. Reduce the speed to low, add the powdered sugar a little at a time, and continue to mix until you're confident that sugar won't fly everywhere, then increase the speed to medium and mix until combined and smooth, 1 to 2 minutes. Scrape down the sides of the bowl as needed to ensure that everything combines evenly.

TO assemble, level the cake layers and stack them up with a layer of frosting in between them. Frost the cake all over (see page 178) and decorate with marzipan shapes (if using).

FOR notes on storing leftover cake, see page 170.

NOTE: *You can also make this into 36 cupcakes or a 9 × 13-inch cake. To bake, begin checking for doneness at 22 minutes for cupcakes and 50 minutes for a 9 x 13-inch cake. The frosting amount will yield enough for a 9 x 13-inch cake and just enough for a thin layer on each cupcake. (If you're a big frosting person, make an additional half batch of frosting.)*

DECORATING WITH MARZIPAN

If you can play with Play-Doh, you can decorate with marzipan. Since I began decorating cakes, I've been drawn to the playful crisp, clean shapes and letters that you can easily cut out of marzipan—as well as its taste, of course. This is decor that anyone can make look good! Here are my tips:

- Store-bought marzipan is preferable to homemade for decorating, since the texture is usually smoother than what you can get when you make it from scratch.
- Make sure you're using marzipan and not almond paste, since almond paste can get oily if you work with it too much. (If almond paste is all you have, you can knead in powdered sugar until it's no longer oily.)
- To color marzipan, simply knead in drops of food coloring until you reach your desired shade. I recommend wearing gloves for this or putting the marzipan in a plastic bag so that your hands don't get dyed.
- Roll out the marzipan either on a surface dusted with powdered sugar (you can dust the top with powdered sugar, too, if it's getting too sticky) or between two pieces of parchment paper.
- If it's too sticky to work with even with powdered sugar and parchment, it may just be a little warm (often from kneading in food coloring). Simply let it sit and breathe for a few minutes uncovered, then try again.
- Use cookie cutters to cut out your desired shapes, then stick them directly onto your cake! If the cookie cutters stick to the marzipan, you can dust them with a little powdered sugar and/or use chopsticks to poke your shapes out.
- For cutting out letters, I recommend seeking out fondant letter cutters, which will poke the cutouts out of the cutters for you.

{ PIES }

If there is one table in the sugar-enthusiast cafeteria where I definitely do not belong, it is at the table of pie people. Am I friends with them, and do I love them? Absolutely. Do I identify with their general preference for fruit desserts, their talent for ~feeling~ when the dough is just the right consistency, and a free-spirited approach to a medium that looks like complete geometric perfection before baking but takes on a life of its own in the oven? Infrequently, at most. My reality is that I am part neurotic Jew/part Asian former mathlete, and the thrill I get from manipulating cake batters to the ⅛ teaspoon of baking soda paired with my obsession over the kind of stick-straight lines that can be achieved only by buttercream on a cake has forced me to accept that I am genetically predisposed to being on Team Cake. (See also Clara Dinowitz's 1924 op-ed in the *Forward*, "Why Don't We, Jews, Eat Pie?")

The pies you'll find in this small but mighty chapter are a slight departure from the more traditional use of pie crust as a way of showcasing special backyard seasonal fruit. Rather, they put slightly more emphasis on thick crusts with personality, fluffy puddings and creams, and cakes masquerading as pie fillings. If you're here for tradition, you're in the wrong place.

POPPY SEED HAND PIES WITH BLOOD ORANGE GLAZE

Every time I eat poppy seed–flavored desserts, I feel like I am preparing myself to be a Jewish grandma, and it makes me really happy. (It's like the thirtysomething version of when you'd drink Shirley Temples as a kid and pretend to be grown up.) I don't think anyone is born craving thick blobs of jet-black sweet goo, so I'm going to say that discovering how good it tastes is a sign of mature distinction. Poppy seeds are nutty, fruity, and make for a striking pie filling. And if you thought the filling was the only star of the show here, think again; this crust takes a cue from rugelach dough and gets a tender, tangy boost from cream cheese. If it's blood orange season where you are, enjoy the beautiful natural color of this glaze. If not, regular oranges will do.

MAKES 10 HAND PIES

Crust

2½ cups (325 grams) all-purpose flour, plus more for dusting

¼ cup (50 grams) sugar

¾ teaspoon kosher salt

1 cup (226 grams) cold unsalted butter, cut into ½-inch cubes

8 ounces (226 grams) cold cream cheese, cut into rough cubes

2 large egg yolks (reserve the whites for the egg wash)

1 teaspoon pure vanilla extract

Filling

½ cup (70 grams) poppy seeds, finely ground in a spice grinder

½ cup (120 grams) milk

⅓ cup (67 grams) sugar

¼ cup (84 grams) honey

Pinch of kosher salt

Zest and juice of ½ blood orange

½ teaspoon pure almond extract

Egg wash: the reserved egg whites beaten with a splash of water

Glaze and assembly

1½ cups (180 grams) powdered sugar

¼ cup (64 grams) blood orange juice, plus a little more as needed

Pinch of kosher salt

Sprinkles, optional but encouraged

TO make the crust, in a food processor, pulse together the flour, sugar, and salt. Scatter in the butter and cream cheese, distributing it all over the dry ingredients, and pulse until the butter and cream cheese are pea size. Add the egg yolks and vanilla and continue pulsing until larger clumps start to form. (You can also do this by hand in a big bowl, using your fingers to incorporate the butter and cream cheese by smashing and rubbing it in with the dry ingredients until it's evenly dispersed and pea size. Add the egg yolks and vanilla and use a spatula to gently mix into a shaggy mass.)

TURN out onto a work surface and press the dough together with your hands, divide the dough in half, and shape into two rectangles. Wrap tightly in plastic wrap and refrigerate for at least 1 hour or up to 2 days.

TO make the filling, in a small saucepan, combine the poppy seeds, milk, sugar, honey, salt, and orange zest and juice. Bring to a rapid simmer over medium heat and cook, stirring often, until thick and jam-like (if you draw a spoon across the bottom of the pan, you'll see a line), 6 to 8 minutes. Stir in the almond extract, transfer to a heat-safe bowl, and let cool completely. (You can expedite this in the fridge.)

ARRANGE oven racks in the upper middle and lower middle positions and preheat the oven to 375°F. Line two sheet pans with parchment paper.

WORKING with one dough rectangle at a time, roll out the dough on a lightly floured surface to ¼-inch thickness, dusting with a little more flour as needed to prevent sticking. Cut out 3¾- to 4-inch squares, rerolling the scraps to get 20 squares total. Place 10 of the squares on the pans, 2 inches apart, spacing out 5 squares per pan. Add a heaping tablespoon of filling to each of the squares on the pans, brush the edges with egg wash, place another square on top, and press the edges firmly with a fork to seal well. Brush the tops with egg wash and poke a few holes with your fork.

BAKE until golden brown; begin checking for doneness at 22 minutes. Switch each pan to the other rack and rotate the pans 180 degrees a little over halfway through the bake time. Let cool for 10 minutes on the pan, then transfer to a wire rack to cool completely.

TO make the glaze, in a medium bowl, whisk together the powdered sugar, orange juice, and salt until smooth and spreadable, adding more juice if necessary to make it smooth. Spread on top of the pastries and sprinkle with sprinkles (if using).

STORE in an airtight container at room temperature for 3 to 4 days.

PEANUT BUTTER (OR TAHINI) FUDGE PIE

The absence of peanut butter pie in my childhood was a teeny-tiny hole made by a peanut-allergic mom and a preference for other things in my Oreo crust, mainly mint chocolate chip ice cream. But after Nick's granny, whose specialty was peanut butter pie, passed away, I began my effort to see what this whole peanut butter pie thing was about. Oh, it's about something, all right. The luxurious trio of cream cheese, creamy peanut butter, and heavy cream, whipped into velvety stability. The crust that's a perfectly cast costar to the filling. And the chewy layer of fudge that hides in the middle, knowing coyly that he's a shoo-in for a supporting actor nomination.

With a draw to tahini in my DNA, I've made this with tahini in place of the peanut butter, and it is outstandingly good. But if forced to tattoo my preference across my face, peanut butter wins by the thinnest baby hair.

MAKES 1 PIE

Crust
Nonstick spray

30 Oreos

1 teaspoon instant espresso powder

Good pinch of kosher salt

6 tablespoons (85 grams) unsalted butter, melted

Fudge
½ cup (113 grams) unsalted butter

1 cup (80 grams) Dutch-process or unsweetened cocoa powder

1 cup (200 grams) sugar

1 teaspoon instant espresso powder

¼ teaspoon kosher salt

½ cup (120 grams) heavy cream

Filling and assembly
4 ounces (113 grams) cream cheese, room temperature

1½ cups (384 grams) unsweetened unsalted peanut butter (or tahini)

1½ cups (180 grams) powdered sugar

1 teaspoon pure vanilla extract

¼ teaspoon kosher salt

1½ cups (360 grams) cold heavy cream

Flaky salt, optional

PREHEAT the oven to 350°F. Grease a 9- to 9½-inch pie pan.

TO make the crust, combine the cookies, espresso powder, and salt in a food processor and blend until very finely ground. With the processor running, drizzle in the butter and blend until combined. Transfer the mixture to the prepared pan and pack it very firmly along the bottom and all the way up the sides.

BAKE until set; begin checking for doneness at 6 minutes.

TO make the fudge, combine the butter, cocoa, sugar, espresso powder, salt, and heavy cream in a medium saucepan and set over medium-low heat. Cook, whisking, until smooth and glossy, about 5 minutes. Remove from the heat.

WHEN the crust is done baking, pour most of the fudge into the crust and spread it evenly around the bottom, reserving a few spoonfuls to drizzle on top. Stick the crust in the fridge to cool completely.

TO make the filling, in a stand mixer fitted with a whisk, combine the cream cheese and peanut butter and beat on medium high until smooth, about 1 minute. Reduce the speed to low and add the powdered sugar, vanilla, and salt and beat until combined, increasing the speed when you're confident that sugar won't fly everywhere. (It's okay if it's crumbly.) With the mixer on low, drizzle in the heavy cream, then gradually increase the speed to high and mix until pale and fluffy, 1 to 2 minutes, scraping down the sides of the bowl with a rubber spatula as needed to ensure that everything combines evenly. Pour the mixture into the cooled crust, then drizzle with the reserved fudge (if it's firmed up by now, you can reheat it gently in a saucepan or microwave until it's drizzly), swirl it around, and sprinkle with flaky salt, if desired.

LET set in the fridge for 4 hours or up to overnight.

STORE, covered, in the refrigerator for up to 3 days.

BLUEBERRY SLAB PIE

Slab pies are the ultimate pies for crust lovers like myself because their ratio of crust to filling puts the emphasis where it deserves to be, on the buttery, flaky crust. I'm warning you now, though, your commitment to being a Crust Person may be tested, as assembling a slab pie is no small feat. It requires some grace and power (and fridge or freezer space) to handle such significant expanses of delicate dough, but I promise that the effort will pay off. What you get is a huge Pop-Tart-type thing that cuts into clean, satisfying slices that are crisp and crusty on the outside and juicy on the inside. A secret layer of speculoos spread prevents sogginess and contributes a hint of warm cinnamon depth that allows the blueberries to reach their full potential.

MAKES ONE 10 X 14-INCH PIE

Crust

2 cups (260 grams) all-purpose flour, plus more for dusting

1 cup (130 grams) whole wheat flour (or substitute all-purpose flour)

2 tablespoons (25 grams) sugar

1 teaspoon kosher salt

1¼ cups (283 grams) cold unsalted butter, cut into ½-inch cubes

½ cup (120 grams) ice water

1 tablespoon (15 grams) apple cider vinegar

Filling

4 cups (680 grams) blueberries (or juneberries, honeyberries, or similar)

½ cup (100 grams) sugar

¼ cup (32 grams) cornstarch

Zest and juice of ½ lemon

¼ teaspoon ground cardamom

½ teaspoon kosher salt

Assembly

½ cup (120 grams) speculoos spread

Egg wash: 1 egg beaten with a splash of water

Glaze

1½ cups (180 grams) powdered sugar

2 tablespoons (30 grams) milk, plus a little more as needed

Pinch of kosher salt

Coarsely crushed freeze-dried blueberries or sprinkles, optional

TO make the crust, in a food processor, pulse together the all-purpose flour, whole wheat flour, sugar, and salt. Add the butter and pulse until the butter is pea size, with a few larger bits. Drizzle in the water and vinegar and continue to pulse until the dough starts to clump together. It may still look crumbly but it's ready if you squeeze a handful of it and it sticks together. (You can also do this by hand in a big bowl, using your fingers to incorporate the butter by smashing and rubbing it in with the dry ingredients until it's evenly dispersed and pea size, with a few larger bits. Add the cold water and vinegar and use a spatula to gently mix into a shaggy mass.)

TURN out onto a work surface and press the dough together with your hands, divide the dough in half, and shape into two rectangles. Wrap tightly in plastic wrap and refrigerate for at least 30 minutes or up to 2 days.

TO make the filling, in a medium bowl, toss together the blueberries, sugar, cornstarch, lemon zest and juice, cardamom, and salt. (It will seem like there's too much powdery stuff, but it will cook together inside the pie.)

PREHEAT the oven to 425°F. Line a rimmed sheet pan with parchment paper.

ON a lightly floured surface, roll out half of the dough into a large rectangle, about 12 × 16 inches and about ⅛ inch thick, dusting with additional flour as needed to prevent sticking. (If it's a hot day or you're nervous about handling such a big expanse of dough, you can roll it out on a sheet of parchment.) Transfer to the prepared pan and freeze (or refrigerate if it won't fit in your freezer) while you roll out the other half of dough to roughly the same size. When the dough in the freezer is cold, gently (or it will tear) spread the speculoos in an even layer all over the surface, leaving a 2-inch border around the edges. Dump on the berry mixture and spread it out evenly over the speculoos.

BRUSH the border with egg wash, then cover with the other crust. Pinch the edges together firmly, roll them in, and then crimp. Brush egg wash over the entire surface, cut a few slits in the top, and bake until deep golden; begin checking for doneness at 30 minutes. Let cool completely on the pan.

TO make the glaze, in a medium bowl or large measuring cup, combine the powdered sugar, milk, and salt and mix until smooth and pourable, adding more milk little by little if necessary to achieve a pourable consistency.

POUR the glaze all over the pie and top with freeze-dried blueberries or sprinkles, if desired. When the glaze sets, slice into bars and enjoy.

STORE, covered, at room temperature for up to a couple of days.

MY DAD'S COCONUT CREAM PIE

The part of my personality that forces me to lean into anything that I'm a fan of one million and ten percent comes directly from my dad. See: my dad's extensive Bernie Sanders T-shirt collection, which is probably large enough for him to wear a different one every day for a month, his shelves of records that take up a quarter of the square footage of his house, my semipermanent butt-shaped divot that forms in the couch during the Grand Prix of Figure Skating, and I guess the fact that both of us turned our hobbies into full-time jobs. (When he was seventeen, my dad left pre-medical school to pursue music and two years later got his job with the Chicago Symphony, where he still plays today.) When we get into something, we get into it. We don't just want to be members of the Igor Stravinsky fan club; we want to be president.

So, while he might have taken the fake-it-till-you-make-it approach in calling his coconut cream pie "famous" before half his immediate family had even gotten a chance to taste it, he made it good enough to be famous. Well, Martha Stewart made it good enough to be famous, and then my dad made his own version, which is delightful in only the way that someone who does not really bake otherwise can achieve; it's now the taste of our family's annual Pi Day celebration. Until they were discontinued, my dad used the extra-crispy Trader Joe's cat cookies to make the crust, "Approximately eighty cats," according to him. He now says that "two cups of Teddies" is acceptable. Rather than making this in a pie plate, he insists on using a springform pan, which allows the pie to have a geometrically pleasing distribution of layers, striking height, and the ability to travel well, so it can accompany him easily on his Coconut Cream Pie for President campaign tour. It also shows some nice restraint in the sweetness department, using unsweetened coconut and unsweetened whipped cream to create a mouthful that doesn't mask the nutty toasted notes.

MAKES 1 PIE

Crust

Nonstick spray

2 cups (160 grams) chocolate Teddy Grahams

5 tablespoons (63 grams) unrefined coconut oil, room temperature

⅛ teaspoon kosher salt

⅓ cup (27 grams) unsweetened shredded coconut

Filling

⅔ cup (132 grams) sugar

⅓ cup (43 grams) cornstarch

¾ teaspoon kosher salt

4 large egg yolks

2¾ cups (660 grams) whole milk

2 teaspoons vanilla bean paste or extract

1¼ cups (100 grams) unsweetened shredded coconut

Topping

1½ cups (360 grams) cold heavy cream

½ cup (40 grams) unsweetened coconut flakes

Shaved chocolate or chocolate sprinkles, optional

TO make the crust, preheat the oven to 325°F. Grease a 9-inch springform pan and line the bottom with parchment paper.

IN a food processor, combine the Teddies with the coconut oil and salt and pulse until the mixture is sandy and starts to clump together. Add the coconut and pulse just a couple more times to evenly distribute it. Press the mixture firmly into the bottom of the pan and 1 to 1½ inches up the sides.

BAKE until set; begin checking for doneness at 20 minutes. Let cool.

TO make the filling, in a medium saucepan, whisk together the sugar, cornstarch, and salt, then whisk in the egg yolks and milk. Cook over medium heat, whisking continuously, until thickened, about 5 minutes. Stir in the vanilla and shredded coconut and pour into the cooled crust. Refrigerate until set, at least 2 hours or overnight.

TO make the topping, in a stand mixer fitted with a whisk, beat the heavy cream on medium high until stiff peaks form. Spread it over the pie. Toast the flaked coconut in a dry skillet over medium heat, stirring often, for 2 to 3 minutes, to your desired toastiness. Let cool and sprinkle on the pie. Top with shaved chocolate or chocolate sprinkles, if desired, and refrigerate until ready to serve.

WHEN you're ready to take the pie out of the pan, run a small offset spatula around the edge and carefully remove the sides. Slice and serve.

STORE, covered, in the refrigerator for up to 3 days.

MAZARIN PIE

When I had my first bite of mazarin tart, probably twenty years ago at IKEA, I braced myself, expecting some kind of fruit layer to disrupt the soft cakey almond filling, but was pleasantly surprised to learn that it was sweet buttery almond all the way through. Cha-ching! I still sometimes think that mazarin tarts are too good to be true, because I live with this perpetual insecurity over the fact that my deep love for almond things may in fact be too much. I should really go to Sweden.

Mazarin tarts are typically individually sized, but shaping individual tart shells stresses me out, so this is a giant pie. And its large size appropriately represents my love for it!

MAKES 1 PIE

Crust

1¼ cups (165 grams) all-purpose flour, plus more for dusting

2 tablespoons (25 grams) sugar

¼ teaspoon kosher salt

½ cup (113 grams) cold unsalted butter, cut into ½-inch cubes

1 large egg

Filling

1½ cups (168 grams) fine almond flour

1 cup (200 grams) sugar

3 tablespoons (24 grams) all-purpose flour

¾ teaspoon kosher salt

½ cup (113 grams) unsalted butter, room temperature

1½ teaspoons pure almond extract

3 large eggs

Glaze and assembly

¼ cup (60 grams) heavy cream or 2 tablespoons (30 grams) cranberry juice, plus a little more as needed

1 cup (120 grams) powdered sugar, plus a little more as needed

¼ teaspoon pure almond extract

Pinch of kosher salt

Toasted sliced almonds, for topping

TO make the crust, in a food processor, pulse together the flour, sugar, and salt. Add the butter and continue to pulse until mealy. Add the egg and pulse until larger clumps start to form. (You can also do this by hand in a big bowl, using your fingers to incorporate the butter by smashing and rubbing it in with the dry ingredients until it's evenly dispersed and the mixture is mealy. Add the egg and use a spatula to gently mix into a shaggy mass.) Turn the dough out onto a piece of plastic wrap and press it into a disk. Wrap tightly and refrigerate for at least 1 hour or overnight. (If refrigerating overnight, remove it from the fridge 10 minutes or so before you want to roll it.)

TO make the filling, in the food processor, blend to combine the almond flour, sugar, all-purpose flour, salt, and butter. Add the almond extract and eggs and continue to blend until smooth and combined. Set aside while you roll out the crust. (You can also make this by hand using a rubber spatula and mixing vigorously until smooth, or in a stand mixer fitted with a paddle.)

ON a lightly floured surface, roll out the dough to a large circle that's about ¼ inch thick, dusting with additional flour as needed to prevent sticking. Press into a 9-inch metal pie pan and trim off any excess dough. Freeze for 15 minutes.

PREHEAT the oven to 425°F.

LINE the pie crust with parchment paper and fill with baking beans or pie weights. Bake until the edges are set, about 12 minutes. Carefully remove the parchment and weights and bake until the bottom no longer looks raw, about 3 minutes more.

REDUCE the oven temperature to 325°F. Spread the filling in the crust and bake until the top is browned and the filling is set; begin checking for doneness at 30 minutes and cover loosely with foil if it's browning too much for your liking. Let cool completely in the pan.

MAKE the glaze. You can use heavy cream for a white glaze, cranberry juice for a pink glaze, or make half batches of each for a two-toned look as pictured. In a medium bowl or large measuring cup, combine the sugar, heavy cream or cranberry juice, almond extract, and salt until smooth. Add more powdered sugar or heavy cream or cranberry juice as needed to achieve a thick yet pourable consistency. Spread the glaze over the pie and sprinkle with the almonds. Let the glaze set at room temperature (or get kinda sloppy and slice immediately because how can you resist that almond aroma?).

STORE, covered, at room temperature or in the fridge for up to 4 days.

PUMPKIN JAM AND GOAT CHEESE BOUREKAS

Pumpkin season overlaps completely with harvest season, which might feel like an obvious statement to anyone who has ever operated under the impression that all that "harvest" means is that PSLs are now at Starbucks and sweater weather has arrived. (I'm describing me until I moved here.) But now when I say "harvest," I mean, like, muddy twenty-hour shifts of Nick sitting in a tractor, yanking beets from the ground, barely having enough time to eat, and when he does the food has to be in handheld form so he can continue to drive a tractor with his other hand, and me covered in yogurt and oatmeal and in need of a nap because someone's gotta take over the roughhousing responsibilities while Nick is away. So I stuff things into pastry pockets (or "bourekas" when I want to feel like I am my younger self eating cheese-filled pastries on the streets of Tel Aviv, carbo loading for a long night of dancing ahead) during this season to send out in his field lunches because they're fun to make, easy to keep on hand in the freezer, and intriguing for picky toddlers. Never mind that Nick will get covered in crumbs—he's already covered in a thin layer of soil, so what's one more topping?

This pumpkin jam pocket sits in the middle of sweet and savory thanks to the addition of herby goat cheese. It's a lovely combination that encourages a vision of pumpkin beyond pairing it with the same old cinnamon and allspice (not that those are bad).

MAKES 12 BOUREKAS

Filling

One 15-ounce can pumpkin puree

1 cup (200 grams) sugar

1 teaspoon smoked paprika

¼ teaspoon ground cardamom

¼ teaspoon kosher salt

Assembly

All-purpose flour, for dusting

2 sheets (one 17.3-ounce package) puff pastry, thawed overnight in the fridge or for about 45 minutes at room temperature

8 ounces (226 grams) herbed goat cheese, room temperature

Egg wash: 1 egg beaten with a splash of water

¼ cup (50 grams) turbinado sugar

LINE two sheet pans with parchment paper.

IN a large pot, combine the pumpkin, sugar, paprika, cardamom, and salt and cook over medium-high heat, stirring continuously with a heat-safe spatula, until the liquid is cooked out and the mixture is thick and jam-like, 5 to 8 minutes. Remove from the heat and let cool completely.

ON a lightly floured surface, roll one sheet of puff pastry out into a 10 × 15-inch rectangle, dusting with more flour as needed if it gets sticky. Cut the pastry into 6 squares and transfer to one of the prepared pans. Repeat with the other sheet of pastry on the other pan.

PUT the goat cheese in a piping bag or large zip-top bag and knead to soften it a bit. Snip off the corner to make an opening that's a little smaller than ½ inch and pipe a circle of goat cheese in one diagonal half of the pastry, leaving a ¾-inch border around the adjacent edges, creating what looks like a kiddie pool made of goat cheese. Fill the kiddie pool with the pumpkin jam. Brush the edges of the pastry with the egg wash. Fold the pastry over and press the edges firmly with a fork to seal well. Repeat with the remaining pastry squares. Brush the tops with egg wash and sprinkle each with 1 teaspoon turbinado sugar.

REFRIGERATE for 30 minutes. (Or freeze up to 3 months! Cover with plastic wrap if you do this and add a few minutes on to the bake time.)

ARRANGE oven racks in the upper middle and lower middle positions and preheat the oven to 375°F.

BAKE until golden brown; begin checking for doneness at 28 minutes. Switch each pan to the other rack and rotate the pans 180 degrees a little over halfway through the bake time. Let cool slightly and brace yourself for pastry crumbs.

THESE are best the day they're baked but leftovers can be stored in an airtight container in the fridge for up to 3 days. Reheat in the microwave or oven.

CHOCOLATE CHUNK CHERRY COBBLER

The best part about a cobbler is not the actual fruit or the actual topping; it's that moment in the middle where the topping soaks up the fruit juices and is so soft and comfortable. As someone whose first choice for dessert isn't typically a fruity thing, this layer wins me over every time. But just like you can't have a muffin top without a muffin bottom, you can't have cobbler innards without cobbler outtards, so let's make it the best it can be. Cherries, great. (Fresh or frozen, convenient!) Buttery drop biscuit that's dressed up like a chocolate chip cookie, also great. Put 'em together, and yeah, this'll do.

SERVES 6 TO 8

Filling

1 tablespoon (14 grams) unsalted butter, room temperature, for greasing the dish

4 cups (720 grams) fresh or frozen pitted cherries, thawed, juices reserved (if using frozen)

1 tablespoon (8 grams) cornstarch

½ cup (100 grams) sugar

¼ teaspoon kosher salt

Zest of ½ lemon

2 tablespoons (30 grams) lemon juice

¼ teaspoon pure almond extract

Topping and assembly

2 cups (260 grams) all-purpose flour

6 tablespoons (75 grams) granulated sugar, divided

¼ cup (50 grams) packed light brown sugar

1 tablespoon (14 grams) baking powder

½ teaspoon kosher salt

½ cup (113 grams) cold unsalted butter, cut into ½-inch cubes

6 ounces (170 grams) semisweet chocolate, coarsely chopped

1 large egg

½ cup (120 grams) cold heavy cream

1 teaspoon pure vanilla extract

Vanilla ice cream, for serving

PREHEAT the oven to 375°F. Butter a 9-inch cake pan or high-sided pie dish.

TO make the filling, measure out the reserved cherry juice to get ⅓ cup (80 grams), supplementing with water if the juices come up short. (If you're using fresh cherries, use ⅓ cup/80 grams water.) In a large bowl, whisk together the cherry juice (or water) and cornstarch until smooth. Add the cherries, sugar, salt, lemon zest, lemon juice, and almond extract and toss to combine. Transfer to the prepared pan and set aside.

TO make the topping, in a large bowl, whisk together the flour, ¼ cup (50 grams) of the granulated sugar, the brown sugar, baking powder, and salt. Scatter on the butter, then use your fingers to incorporate it by smashing and rubbing it in with the dry ingredients until it's evenly dispersed and pea size. (You can also pulse this together in a food processor and then dump into a large bowl.) Add most of the chocolate chunks, reserving a handful to sprinkle on top, and toss to combine.

IN a small bowl or measuring cup, whisk together the egg, heavy cream, and vanilla. Pour the mixture over the dry ingredients and mix with a spatula just until the dough comes together. (You may have to finish the last few mixes with your hands—just take care not to overwork it.)

USE a ¼-cup ice cream scoop to scoop the topping over the cherries in about 10 mounds. Top with the reserved chocolate and the remaining 2 tablespoons (25 grams) sugar. Place the pan on a parchment-lined rimmed sheet pan to catch any drips. Bake for 40 minutes, then tent with foil and continue to bake until golden brown, cooked through, and the cherries are bubbling; begin checking for doneness after another 10 minutes.

LET cool for about 20 minutes and then serve with ice cream.

THIS is best served warm shortly after it's made, but leftover cobbler will keep, covered, in the fridge for up to 2 days. Rewarm before serving.

FROZEN AND NO BAKE

While I was in music school, one of the big things that drew me to baking in my little apartment was the instant, tangible satisfaction, which I often didn't get from being trapped in a practice room with a xylophone. Four hours of practicing the same xylophone excerpt improved my note accuracy so that I could *maybe* not miss any notes at a mock audition and then *maybe* that would earn me the chance to play the snare drum part instead of the triangle part in an orchestra concert in a few months . . . maybe? Whereas four hours in my tiny kitchen could leave me with a big, beautiful almond cake that I could share with my friends and devour immediately.

Even if the cake wasn't perfect, it was still something that I'd built start to finish and could reap the benefits of that day. I got such a high off that! My friend Rob, who actually preferred the slow-burn delayed satisfaction of learning one new xylophone note a day and eventually went on to win his dream orchestra job, was the first one who noticed my impatient love of instant satisfaction. He never judged me for it; he just said, "You like this and I like that. And that's okay!" and that was a significant turning point in my internal journey of embracing my life in the kitchen.

So imagine the satisfaction I get when I can watch sweets come together before my very eyes without having to shut them away in an oven for a period of time. Oh yeah, it's a lot! Living in a place that is winter for what seems like a vast majority of the year, I don't have a major need for recipes that avoid turning on the oven and heating up the kitchen, but boy, they are hella good.

From puppy chow to buckeyes, there's a lot of instant satisfaction in this chapter. If the recipes happen to require prolonged chill times before they're done, there's no risk of salmonella to prevent you or your toddler from taste testing whatever pudding you're making before it's fully set. So while this chapter is small, it's wild and varied. It's got the requisite snow recipe, salty ingredients you never thought you'd see in sweets, and one life-changing, earth-shattering tiramisu.

PROCESSED CHEESE FUDGE

I truly thought we'd reached peak Church-Cookbook-Recipe-as-Stripper-Name after spotting the title "Chinese Hotdish" a decade ago, but then *Velveeta fudge* entered the picture, and I want to say, "You can't make this stuff up," but then I remember that somebody did make this up and I want to know who that person was. Did they forget to put their reading glasses on before they went to reach for the butter and accidentally got Velveeta? Did this person's child create a concoction that somehow caught on? Or was it a ploy by the Velveeta marketing team? We could Google it, but that's not how rumors start, that's how rumors die, and one of those options is way more fun than the other.

Let's address the cheesy elephant in the room: it's, uhhhhh, actually good! You don't taste the Velveeta. You really don't. What you might detect is a slight salty depth akin to what you'd get from salted caramel. The chief role of the Velveeta is texture. When it combines with pounds (yes, plural) of sugar and cocoa powder, it firms up easily and reliably into a classic fudgy texture that, in the absence of Velveeta, would require way more time, attention, and tools at the stove.

Make it for your friends, with a prize for who can name the secret ingredient.

MAKES 36 LITTLE SQUARES

Nonstick spray

8 ounces (226 grams) Velveeta, cut into ½-inch cubes

1 cup (226 grams) unsalted butter, cut into ½-inch cubes

2 pounds (908 grams/7½ cups) powdered sugar

½ cup (40 grams) unsweetened cocoa powder

2 teaspoons pure vanilla extract

1 cup (104 grams) roasted pecans, coarsely chopped

GREASE an 8- or 9-inch square pan and line with enough parchment paper to allow for 1-inch wings on opposite sides.

IN a large pot, melt the Velveeta and butter over medium-low heat, whisking to combine. It will look curdly at first but keep on whisking, putting some elbow grease into it, until smooth, about 5 minutes. Reduce the heat to low and add the powdered sugar, cocoa, and vanilla and whisk until combined, switching to a stiff rubber spatula as needed. Fold in the pecans and scrape into the prepared pan, spreading it out evenly.

LET set in the fridge until firm, about an hour. Remove from the pan and cut into 36 little squares.

STORE in an airtight container in the fridge for up to a couple of weeks.

MACADAMIA PUDDING POPS

Pistachio is typically the queen of the pudding mix aisle, but if you want to up the ante for any pudding connoisseur, bring in the macadamias. They're buttery, they're creamy, and they make you think for one second that you're in Hawaii watching your children build sand cakes on the beach.

This recipe requires you to make roasted macadamia milk, and unfortunately grocery store macadamia milk cannot be substituted because making it fresh is the only way to get enough actual macadamia flavor.[*] Macadamia's BFF, white chocolate, brings in sweetness and body, just a few sprinkles go a long way in terms of festivity, and the pops' freezer-friendly lifespan makes for an ideal standby dessert, fit for surprise guests and play dates that happily go longer than expected.

MAKES 8 POPS

1½ cups (210 grams) roasted unsalted macadamia nuts

3 cups (720 grams) water

3 tablespoons (24 grams) cornstarch

2 tablespoons (25 grams) sugar

¼ teaspoon kosher salt

6 ounces (170 grams) white chocolate, finely chopped, or 1 cup chips

1 teaspoon pure vanilla extract

Sprinkles, optional

SOAK the macadamias in the water for at least 2 hours or overnight.

ADD the macadamias and their soaking water to a high-speed blender and blend until very smooth, then strain through a nut milk bag to yield about 2¼ cups (540 grams). Voilà, macadamia nut milk! You can reserve any excess milk for another use (put it in your coffee!), and the pulp can be given to the chickens or tossed into pancake batter.

IN a medium saucepan, whisk together the cornstarch, sugar, and salt. Add ½ cup (120 grams) of the macadamia milk and whisk until smooth. Add the remaining milk and whisk until smooth. Cook over medium heat, whisking continuously, until the mixture is thickened enough to coat the back of a spoon, about 5 minutes. Remove from the heat, add the chocolate and vanilla, and continue to whisk until the chocolate is melted.

DIVIDE the mixture among eight 3-ounce paper cups or ice pop molds. Place ice pop sticks into the centers, add sprinkles if desired, and freeze until firm, at least 4 hours or overnight.

STORE in the freezer for up to a few weeks.

---

[*] *This is based on the current macadamia nut milk market in East Grand Forks, Minnesota. If you live near a fancy grocery store that carries fancy macadamia milk that bursts with macadamia flavor, then that would probably work . . . but, making nut milks is satisfying, so . . .*

PEANUT BUTTER HALVA

As a longtime enthusiast of Middle Eastern–style halva, my favorite halva breakthrough came when I discovered that if you swap out the typical tahini for peanut butter, you get a confection that tastes just like the inside of a Butterfinger, but slightly softer. A whole dang pan of Butterfinger innards!! If you cut up this pan and coated the bars in chocolate for a pile of homemade Butterfingers, I would 100 percent eat them all, but I'd also encourage you to just try it with the cacao nibs as written here, which lend an awesome bitter, crunchy counterpoint to the sweet, crumbly, melt-in-your-mouth halva. And it's just easier. Moreover, this is the only time I'm going to insist that you use a peanut butter with oil added in the ingredients, because the oil prevents the final texture from being overly crumbly.

MAKES ABOUT 36 LITTLE SQUARES

Nonstick spray

1½ cups (384 grams) unsweetened unsalted peanut butter (preferably a kind with palm oil)

½ teaspoon kosher salt

1 teaspoon pure vanilla extract

⅔ cup (76 grams) cacao nibs

2 cups (400 grams) sugar

½ cup (120 grams) water

GREASE an 8-inch square pan and line with enough parchment paper to allow for 1-inch wings on two opposite sides.

IN a large heat-safe bowl, whisk together the peanut butter, salt, and vanilla until smooth. Stir in the cacao nibs.

IN a small saucepan fitted with a candy thermometer, combine the sugar and water and set over medium-high heat, whisking to dissolve the sugar. Once it bubbles, stop whisking and allow it to continue to heat until the mixture reaches 245°F. Carefully pour the sugar mixture into the peanut butter mixture with one hand while quickly but carefully stirring with a heat-safe spatula with the other hand until just combined, 10 to 15 seconds. Pour it into the prepared pan and flatten it out evenly.

LET cool completely at room temperature, about 1 hour. Remove from the pan and cut into 36 little squares. Some may break while cutting and that's okay, eat those first.

STORE in an airtight container at room temperature for up to several weeks.

BUTTERY CRACKER ICEBOX CAKE

My ideal afternoon as a tween included *Lizzie McGuire* marathons and stacks of Ritz crackers dragged through whipped cream cheese. The slight sweetness of the crackers with the tang of the cream cheese was a combo that just wouldn't quit—it was the best and so addictive. Here is a cake made in honor of that iconic duo that allows the crackers to soften but still maintain their salty souls, and it introduces some fruity, snacky excitement in the form of strawberry jam.

SERVES 8 TO 10

8 ounces (226 grams) cream cheese, room temperature

2 cups (480 grams) cold heavy cream

1 cup (120 grams) powdered sugar

80 Ritz crackers (about 2½ sleeves from a regular-size box)

¾ cup (240 grams) strawberry jam

LINE a 9-inch springform pan with enough plastic wrap to hang over the edges. (This will make the cake a little easier to remove.)

IN a stand mixer fitted with a whisk, combine the cream cheese, heavy cream, and powdered sugar and beat on medium high until medium-stiff peaks form, 1 to 2 minutes.

USING a small offset spatula, spread a thin but even layer of the cream mixture in the bottom of the prepared pan. Top with a layer of crackers, as close together as possible without overlapping. Spread with one-third of the remaining cream mixture. Dollop on ¼ cup (80 grams) of the jam all over.

TOP with another layer of crackers, another one-third of the cream, and ¼ cup (80 grams) of the jam. Finish with another layer of crackers, the remaining cream, and the remaining jam. Rap the pan on the counter a few times to settle the layers. Coarsely crush the remaining crackers and sprinkle on top, pressing down lightly to adhere. Refrigerate at least 4 hours or overnight.

TO serve, lift out of the pan, cut into wedges and embrace the rusticness.

STORE, covered, in the fridge for up to 3 days.

FURIKAKE PUPPY CHOW

According to my good friends and Maui natives Lily and Alana, I could pass for a Maui local . . . until I open my mouth to reveal my nasally midwestern *a*'s. Nevertheless, my love for Hawaii runs deep, and on multiple occasions I've happily gone into sodium overload there from my powerlessness against furikake snack mix. Furikake is a Japanese seasoning blend that is primarily composed of sesame seeds and nori seaweed. It's typically sprinkled on savory things like rice balls and veggies, but the salty, fresh sea quality of the nori also lends extra personality to a sweet snack mix. A midwestern favorite like puppy chow is perfect for this challenge, because the peanut butter bridges the gap between the savory and sweet.

For this purpose, look for a furikake with as few additives as possible and one that doesn't include fish flakes.

MAKES ABOUT 9 CUPS

¼ cup (56 grams) unsalted butter

½ cup (112 grams) unsweetened unsalted peanut butter

6 ounces (170 grams) bittersweet chocolate, finely chopped, or 1 cup chips

¼ teaspoon kosher salt

1½ teaspoons pure vanilla extract

6 cups (192 grams) Chex cereal

2 cups (90 grams) pretzels

1 cup (140 grams) roasted salted macadamia nuts

1½ cups (180 grams) powdered sugar

¼ cup (28 grams) furikake

IN a medium saucepan, combine the butter, peanut butter, chocolate, salt, and vanilla and set over low heat, stirring, until the chocolate is melted and everything is combined and smooth. Remove from the heat and cool briefly.

IN a large container or bowl with a lid, combine the Chex, pretzels, and nuts. Pour the peanut butter mixture over the top and fold gently to combine. Fold in about half of the powdered sugar and all the furikake until evenly distributed, and then dump in the rest of the powdered sugar. Snap on the lid and shake, shake, shake!

STORE in an airtight container at room temperature or in the fridge (cold puppy chow is so good!) for up to a few weeks.

CASHEW COCONUT BUCKEYES

The Cleveland Orchestra. A place that will put pierogi on your grilled cheese. Our friends Luke and Annika, who are the godparents to our chickens. Buckeyes. Those right there are my favorite things about Ohio.

Buckeyes are cute spherical no-bake treasures that resemble the nut of the Ohio state tree, the buckeye. They are easy to make, easy to eat, and easy to keep on hand in the fridge for when you need just two bites of something sweet. The ratio of innards to chocolate is key here because, while something like a peanut butter cup has a chunk of chocolate that you have to gnaw through in order to get to the filling, the buckeye gives you a lot of its bulbous superior interior with just a thin coating of chocolate exterior to complement but not overshadow. I may be overstepping my non-Ohioan boundaries here by incorporating Rice Krispies for crunch, but they're pleasing! And the combination of cashews, almonds, lots of cinnamon, and coconut is inspired by one of the greatest nut butters of all time, Ground Up's Snickerdoodle butter.

MAKES ABOUT 22 BUCKEYES

¼ cup (64 grams) unsweetened unsalted cashew butter

¼ cup (64 grams) unsweetened unsalted almond butter

¼ cup (56 grams) unsalted butter, room temperature

¼ teaspoon ground cinnamon

¼ teaspoon kosher salt

½ teaspoon pure vanilla extract

1 cup (120 grams) powdered sugar

½ cup (40 grams) unsweetened shredded coconut

¾ cup (24 grams) crispy rice cereal

4 ounces (113 grams) dark chocolate, finely chopped, or ⅔ cup chips

2 teaspoons unrefined coconut oil

Flaky salt, optional

LINE a quarter sheet pan with parchment paper.

IN a stand mixer fitted with a paddle, combine the cashew butter, almond butter, butter, cinnamon, salt, and vanilla and mix on medium until smooth and creamy, 1 to 2 minutes. Stop the mixer, scrape down the sides with a rubber spatula, add the powdered sugar and coconut, and turn the mixer back on low. Once you're reasonably confident that powdered sugar won't fly everywhere, you can increase the speed to medium and continue mixing, scraping down the sides of the bowl as needed, until everything is combined into a soft dough. Add the crispy rice cereal and mix a couple of times just until combined; try not to overmix and crush the cereal.

ROLL 1-inch balls of the dough until smooth and place them on the prepared sheet pan. Freeze for 20 minutes.

IN a small bowl or mug, combine the chocolate and coconut oil and microwave in 30-second increments, stirring after each, until melted and smooth.

PICK up a buckeye ball by poking the top with a toothpick or wooden skewer and dipping it into the chocolate about three-quarters of the way, leaving the top exposed. Scrape excess chocolate off the bottom using the side of the bowl, return the buckeye to the sheet pan, remove the toothpick, and smooth over the tiny hole with a knife or small offset spatula. Repeat to make the rest of the buckeyes. Sprinkle with flaky salt if desired. Refrigerate until set, about 15 minutes.

STORE in an airtight container in the fridge for up to a few weeks.

ALMOND BUTTER-STUFFED DATES

THE EASIEST EVER NON-RECIPE TO KEEP IN THE FRIDGE AT ALL TIMES FOR ANY TIME YOU NEED A SLIGHTLY VIRTUOUS HIT OF SWEETNESS

IN a bowl, combine a large (½ cup-ish/128 grams-ish) plop of almond butter with a pinch of salt, splash of vanilla, and honey or maple syrup or brown sugar to taste. Add in a couple of handfuls of whatever odds and ends you have lying around, like seeds, chopped nuts, chopped leftover candy bars, cacao nibs, rainbow candy-coated chips, you get the idea. Taste! Adjust as desired. Spoon into pitted dates (depending on the size of the date and amount of mix-ins, this can range from around 12 to 20 dates), sprinkle with flaky salt, and keep in a container in the fridge for up to several weeks for when you need something sweet that also gives you energy.

WHAT DO SUGAR BEET FARMERS DO IN THE WINTER?

1. **FIX MACHINERY.** If there's an equipment breakdown during the farming season, there's a chance that Nick just (metaphorically) duct-tapes it together so that it can keep on functioning. Time is always of the essence, and full repairs have to wait for the winter months, when he can bring the tractor into the workshop, put on some pop tunes, take it all apart, and put it back together again.

2. **GO TO DIRT CAMP.** The preferred term is "soil seminar," and it's where farmers learn about taking care of the dirt and making sure that it's healthy for generations to come. Sometimes dirt camp is in a fun place like Sioux Falls, South Dakota, and we get to go with Nick and explore the cute town while he learns about dirt.

3. **DO PAPERWORK.** Farmers are business owners, too. And business owners have to do a lot of paperwork.

4. **GO TO WARM CLIMATES.** Arizona, usually.

5. **TAKE UP HOBBIES, MAKE FRIENDS.** Preferably rejoin the brass quintet that rehearses in our garage. Preferably not broomball again; I worry about frostbite.

6. **DO OTHER JOBS.** Sometimes farmers take on seasonal office jobs or undertake other business ventures, like opening a bakery café.

7. **COACH YOUTH BASKETBALL?? TAKE THE KIDS SLEDDING! PLAY IN THE SNOW.** I'll stay inside and make the soup.

BLACK SESAME SNOW ICE CREAM

What this region lacks in the way of Asian shaved ice shops serving frosty mountains of machine-made snow drizzled with condensed milk and dotted with nuggets of mochi, it makes up for in mountains of actual snow that fall every winter and, coincidentally, an old-school practice of mixing that snow with sweetened condensed milk to make "snow ice cream."

Snow ice cream, typically containing just those two ingredients, is surprisingly fluffier and sturdier than the sweet soupy mess I envisioned before I actually tried it, and so long as you don't lollygag, it will actually hold up long enough for you to eat it in the warmth of your home. My flavor of choice when it comes to either iteration of creamy snow is black sesame, whose bitterness softens when paired with anything creamy. And also because, while you can't order black sesame ice cream over the internet, you sure can order black sesame paste.

SERVES 4

Half of one 14-ounce can sweetened condensed milk or sweetened condensed coconut milk (see Note)

1½ tablespoons (23 grams) black sesame paste or 2 heaping tablespoons (23 grams) black sesame seeds, finely ground in a spice grinder

Pinch of kosher salt

Freshly fallen snow

Mochi Bits (recipe follows, or store-bought), for topping, optional

Red Bean Paste (homemade, page 37, or store-bought), for topping, optional

Black and/or white sesame seeds, for topping

IN a large metal or other lightweight bowl, combine the condensed milk, black sesame paste, and salt and mix with a rubber spatula until smooth. Get your boots on, go outside with the bowl and a 1-cup measuring cup, and scoop in 4 heaping cups of snow. Go back inside (or stay out there if it's pleasant) and fold the snow with the black sesame mixture until combined. Top with mochi bits (if using), red bean paste (if you'd like), and sesame seeds. Eat immediately!

NOTE: *If you don't want to be left with half a can of sweetened condensed milk, go ahead and make a double batch in the biggest bowl you've got. (But if you don't mind the leftover milk, use it in French toast or an egg cream, or drizzle it into coffee.)*

MOCHI BITS

1 cup (140 grams) mochiko sweet rice flour

1 cup (240 grams) water

⅓ cup (66 grams) sugar

¼ teaspoon kosher salt

1 teaspoon matcha powder, optional

Potato starch (or cornstarch), for dusting

IN a medium saucepan, whisk together the rice flour, water, sugar, salt, and matcha (if using) until smooth. Cook over medium-low heat, stirring continuously with a heat-safe spatula, until you have a thick sticky dough that pulls away from the sides and bottom of the pan, 8 to 10 minutes.

TURN out the dough onto a cutting board that is dusted liberally with potato starch. Dust the top and pat out the dough until it's ¼ to ½ inch thick. Let cool completely at room temperature, about 20 minutes.

DUST off the excess starch and chop into bite-size bits, dusting the newly cut ends with more starch.

STORE in an airtight container in the fridge for 4 to 5 days.

SAFFRON AND CARDAMOM TIRAMISU

There is this subset of people who are completely obsessed with tiramisu and make a sport out of who can get more excited at the very mention of it. I'm not one of these people, because mixing liqueur and strong coffee in one bite after dinner when I'm already full and wanting to go to bed has never appealed to me. *But.* I have to tell you about this tiramisu, which has brought me as close to being one of these tiramisu fanatics as I ever will be. It is adapted from a recipe I tasted in Berlin at the most beautiful Shabbat feast, cooked by sisters Sophie and Xenia von Oswald. The ingredients list alone is profound, and when you put them all together, you have a reimagined tiramisu that is in an entirely new league. It may seem like there's a lot going on between the Earl Grey, the saffron, the cardamom, and the rosewater, but each player does its part to transport you to total tiramisu perfection.

SERVES 8 TO 12

Custard

1 cup (240 grams) whole milk

⅛ teaspoon saffron threads

⅛ teaspoon ground turmeric

4 large egg yolks

⅓ cup (67 grams) sugar

2 teaspoons cornstarch

¼ teaspoon kosher salt

½ teaspoon pure vanilla extract

Soaking liquid

1½ cups (360 grams) water

5 Earl Grey tea bags

2 tablespoons (25 grams) sugar

2 tablespoons (30 grams) vanilla liqueur (or ½ teaspoon pure vanilla extract and 1 additional tablespoon [13 grams] sugar)

Mascarpone layer and assembly

1¼ cups (300 grams) cold heavy cream

⅓ cup (40 grams) powdered sugar

1 pound (454 grams) mascarpone, room temperature

1 teaspoon ground cardamom

⅛ teaspoon kosher salt

2 tablespoons (30 grams) rosewater

½ teaspoon pure vanilla extract

24 ladyfingers

Chopped roasted salted pistachios and candied or dried rose petals, for topping

TO make the custard, in a small saucepan, bring the milk to a bare simmer. Remove from the heat and add the saffron and turmeric. Let steep for 10 minutes, then strain into a medium measuring cup. In the same saucepan (make sure it's cooled by now so it won't scramble the eggs), whisk together the egg yolks, sugar, cornstarch, and salt, and then drizzle in the steeped milk while whisking continuously until smooth.

SET over medium-low heat and cook for a few minutes, whisking continuously, until the mixture thickens enough to coat the back of a spoon. Remove from the heat and whisk in the vanilla. Pour into a heat-safe bowl and cover with plastic wrap so that the wrap touches the surface of the custard so a skin doesn't form. Refrigerate for at least 1 hour or overnight.

TO make the soaking liquid, in a small saucepan, bring the water to a simmer. Remove from the heat and add the tea bags. Let steep for 5 to 6 minutes, then remove the tea bags, pressing to extract the liquid. Stir in the sugar to dissolve and the liqueur (or vanilla plus additional sugar). Let cool completely.

IN a stand mixer fitted with a whisk, beat the heavy cream and powdered sugar on medium high until medium stiff peaks form, about a minute. Stop the mixer and add the mascarpone, cardamom, salt, rosewater, and vanilla and mix on medium until just combined.

TO assemble, quickly dunk the ladyfingers, one at a time, in the cooled tea and use them to line the bottom of an 8-inch square pan, breaking them up if necessary. (Don't soak them too long or they'll fall apart.) Spread half of the mascarpone mixture over the ladyfingers. Spread all the custard over the mascarpone and soak and layer the rest of the ladyfingers on top. Spread the remaining mascarpone mixture on top.

REFRIGERATE at least 4 hours or up to overnight. Top with pistachios and rose petals before serving.

STORE, covered, in the refrigerator for up to 3 days.

DRINKS

There's a lot of nostalgia in the act of drinking a dessert. Cookie dough milkshakes and shoestring fries at the Steak 'n Shake after marching band competitions, spiking 7-Eleven Slurpees with the percussionists after hours of orchestra rehearsal, washing down schnitzel with overflowing egg creams at Sammy's Roumanian Steakhouse, and driving through McDonald's for Shamrock Shakes after school on the way to figure skating. Being a kid just makes it easier to take in sugar via a format that's one step away from an IV, apparently. Today I need to lie down if I steal too many sips of Nick's bubble tea. But that clearly doesn't stop me from knocking back a marzipan soda or a grapefruit float. What makes it all taste better is the very specific pleasure in hanging out with the kids after a hot day in the kiddie pool, listening to the sounds of their thirsty little gulps, and watching them resurface with grins the size of Texas and big silly milkshake mustaches.

TAHINI CAKE SHAKE

By far the most annoying thing about tahini milkshake recipes on the internet is that they usually contain bananas. F*** bananas! What did tahini do in a past life to make everyone think that if someone wants a tahini milkshake, they actually want a dumb kinda-healthy banana smoothie in disguise? When I want a tahini milkshake, I want real blended-up ice cream. I want to feel a little bad after drinking it. To really stick it to those health nuts, I'm drawing inspiration from the uncontested best milkshake in the universe according to anyone who has ever spent time in Chicago, Portillo's cake shake, which has straight-up cake tossed right into the blender. The mashed cake and ice cream scenario yields a milkshake you can chew. Get in my belly.

MAKES 4 MEDIUM OR 2 LARGE SHAKES

2 cups (400 grams) vanilla ice cream

½ cup (120 grams) milk

½ cup (112 grams) tahini

½ teaspoon pure vanilla extract

Pinch of ground cinnamon

1¼ cups (133 grams) crumbled chocolate cake (fresh or a few days old)

Drizzle of chocolate syrup, optional

Fresh whipped cream

Rainbow sprinkles and/or toasted sesame seeds

IN a blender, combine the ice cream, milk, tahini, vanilla, and cinnamon and pulse to mostly combine. Add the cake and pulse to combine until smooth but still with a few chunky cakey bits. Pour into glasses and top with a drizzle of chocolate syrup (if using), whipped cream, and sprinkles or toasted sesame seeds or both and guzzle.

GRAPEFRUIT SLUSHY FLOAT

My lifelong habit of second-guessing myself wreaked total havoc on my pregnancy cravings. If I needed fries at the beginning of the Sonic drive-through line, how could I be so sure that I wouldn't instead need tots by the end of the Sonic drive-through line? If I needed a bagel and cream cheese on the way to Panera, what's to say I wouldn't prefer a bacon, egg, and cheese bagel on the way home? Nine times out of ten, I just ordered both, ate however much I wanted, and pawned the rest off on Nick. I'm still determining how embarrassed I should be about this, and now I'm officially second-guessing whether I should have admitted this to you.

I found the most convenient solution to this conundrum on a trip to Dairy Queen with Bernie one hot summer day, when I discovered that there was an actual menu item that cured both my slushy craving and my anxiety about missing out on vanilla soft serve in one convenient cup: the float! I thought it was so cool that you could get something both fruity and icy, and creamy and sweet, all at the same time and not have to choose one or the other. The high school kid at the cash register looked at me like I was born yesterday for making this float "discovery" at the ripe age of thirtysomething, but whatever, let me enjoy this!! This version brings in another pregnancy craving, grapefruit, and a hint of fresh mint classes the whole place up—and hopefully redeems me from discussing so much fast food in two paragraphs.

MAKES 4 FLOATS

3 cups (720 grams) grapefruit juice, divided, plus a little more as needed

6 tablespoons (108 grams) Mint Simple Syrup, plus more to taste (recipe follows)

Vanilla ice cream

DIVIDE 2 cups (480 grams) of the grapefruit juice between 2 standard-size ice cube trays and freeze solid, at least a few hours or overnight.

ADD the cubes to a high-speed blender with the remaining 1 cup (240 grams) grapefruit juice and mint simple syrup. Blend on high until smooth, adding more juice if needed. Taste and add more simple syrup, if desired. Scoop 1 or 2 scoops of ice cream into glasses and pour the grapefruit slushy over. Slurp!

MINT SIMPLE SYRUP

1 cup (200 grams) sugar
1 cup (240 grams) water

A handful of fresh mint leaves

IN a medium saucepan, combine the sugar and water and bring to a boil over high heat, whisking to dissolve the sugar. Remove from the heat, add the mint, and cover. Steep for 20 to 30 minutes. Remove and discard the mint. Let cool. Use immediately or store in the refrigerator for up to 1 month. (The syrup can also be used to sweeten cocktails or iced tea!)

MARZIPAN SODA

Here's a frothy, milky, creamy soda that's as dazzling as it is boring looking, and it brings us one step closer to the dream in which everything is available in marzipan flavor. This is great as a stand-alone afternoon treat, but the syrup is also nice when paired with shrubs or mixed into cocktails.

MAKES ENOUGH SYRUP FOR ABOUT 18 GLASSES OF SODA

1½ cups (228 grams) blanched unsalted almonds

¾ cup (90 grams) powdered sugar

1 teaspoon almond extract

¼ teaspoon kosher salt

1 cup (240 grams) water

Ice cubes

Chilled plain seltzer

IN a food processor, blend the almonds, scraping down the sides and bottom with a rubber spatula occasionally, until creamy and spreadable, about 10 minutes. Add the powdered sugar, almond extract, and salt and continue to process until very creamy, scraping down the sides and bottom as needed to ensure that everything combines evenly, about 5 minutes. With the processor running, drizzle in the water and continue to process to make a thick, very smooth, and creamy syrup, about 2 minutes.

TO assemble, in a tall glass, add 2 tablespoons (30 grams) of the syrup. Add ice cubes. Fill the glass with about 6 ounces (170 grams) of chilled seltzer. Swirl with a straw, taste, and add more syrup if desired. Drink immediately.

STORE the syrup in an airtight container in the refrigerator for up to a week. (It may thicken a bit; stir in a tablespoon or so of water if needed to thin it out.)

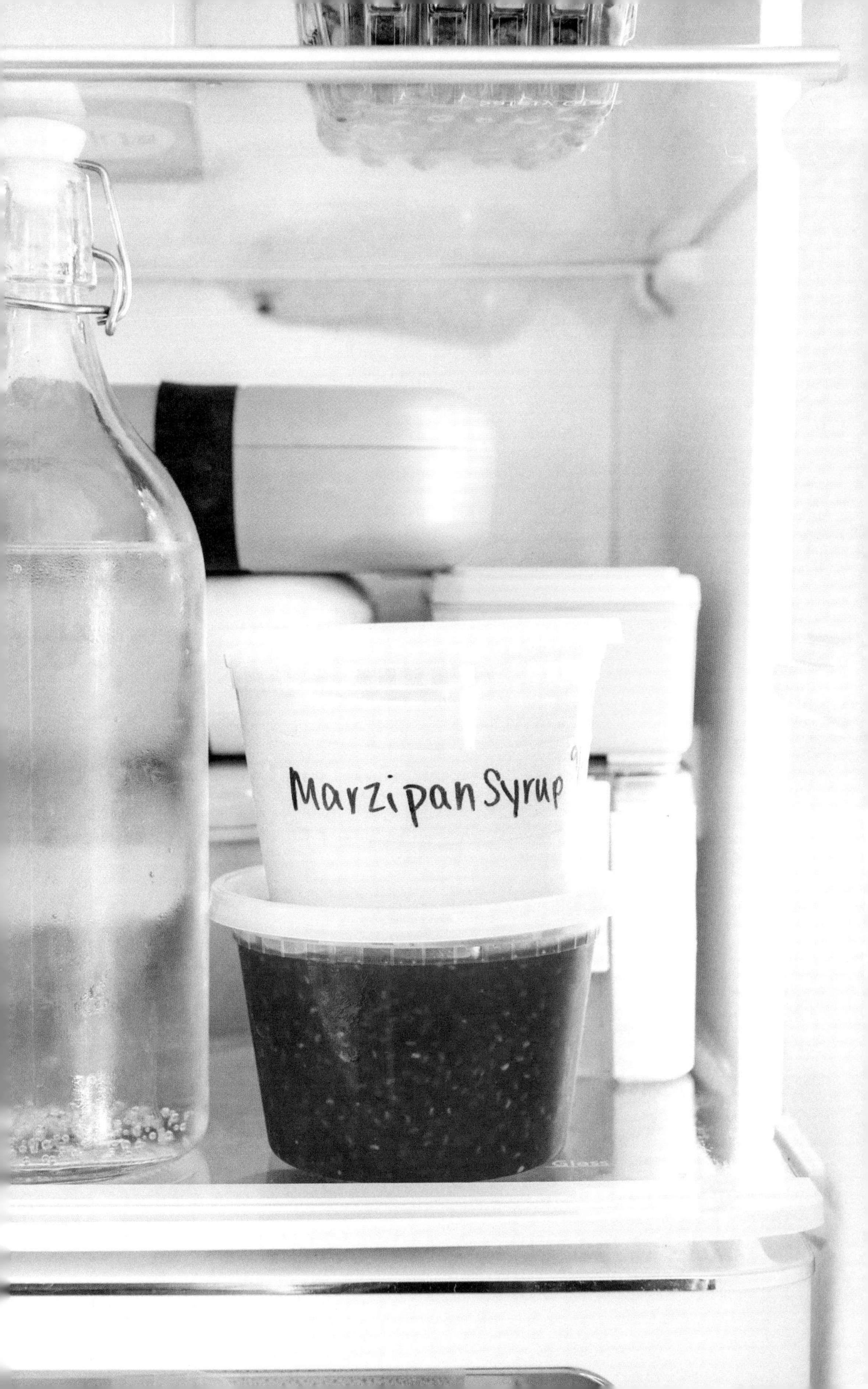
Marzipan Syrup

CARDAMOM FROZEN COFFEE

Cardamom, coffee, and speculoos: a throuple made in caffeine heaven, with Turkish, Belgian, and Delta airlines heritage.

MAKES 2 COFFEES

2 cups (480 grams) milk

2 tablespoons (42 grams) honey

1 tablespoon (6 grams) whole green cardamom pods, crushed

1 tablespoon (5 grams) Dutch-process or unsweetened cocoa powder

2 teaspoons instant espresso powder

1 teaspoon whole black peppercorns

Pinch of kosher salt

¾ cup (180 grams) cold brew or cooled coffee

3 tablespoons (45 grams) speculoos spread

IN a medium saucepan, whisk together the milk, honey, cardamom, cocoa, espresso powder, peppercorns, and salt. Bring to a gentle bubble over medium heat, remove from the heat, cover, and steep until the mixture cools to room temperature, about 1 hour.

STRAIN, pour into an ice cube tray, and freeze until solid, at least 4 hours or overnight.

IN a high-speed blender, combine the frozen cubes, coffee, and speculoos spread and blend until smooth. You may need to stop the blender and scrape down the sides a couple of times. Pour into 2 glasses and caffeinate!

FRESH MINT COCONUT SHAKE

I've been making variations on this recipe since I lived in Brooklyn and wanted to create a wholesome-ish version of the Shamrock Shakes I grew up getting from McDonald's every March. I kept up my no-fast-food-except-for-road-trips-and-during-pregnancy streak going pretty well until my mom introduced Bernie to the wonders of the Happy Meal, and now there's no undoing that. So I don't have too much of a need for a homemade slightly-better-for-you Shamrock Shake these days, but maybe you do! Or maybe you just need a way to use up all your garden mint. (It really does take over the plot, doesn't it?) This shake is extra creamy and smooth, has a nice balance of sweetness and mint flavor, and happens to be vegan.

MAKES 2 SHAKES

One 13.5-ounce can full-fat coconut milk

½ cup (72 grams) raw cashews

¼ cup (50 grams) sugar

½ cup (12 grams) lightly packed fresh mint leaves

¼ teaspoon pure vanilla extract or vanilla bean paste

Pinch of kosher salt

1 cup (about 226 grams) ice cubes

IN a high-speed blender, combine the coconut milk, cashews, sugar, mint, vanilla, and salt and blend on high until very smooth, 1 to 2 minutes. Add the ice and blend until smooth. Pour into glasses.

STRAWBERRIES AND CREAM FROZEN COCKTAIL

Part smoothie, part milkshake, part take the edge off your twelve-septillionth time watching *Frozen*.

MAKES 2 COCKTAILS

Drizzle of honey

Finely chopped or ground raw or roasted unsalted pistachios and freeze-dried strawberries, for the rim

2 cups (280 grams) frozen strawberries

¼ cup (50 grams) sugar

¼ cup (60 grams) whole milk

¼ cup (60 grams) heavy cream

¼ cup (60 grams) vodka

½ teaspoon pure vanilla extract

⅛ teaspoon ground cardamom, plus more for garnish

Dried rose petals, for garnish, optional

APPLY a thin even layer of honey around the rim of two glasses (I find it's easiest to drizzle it directly on the top outside edge of the glass and then use a small rubber spatula or knife to spread it all around), then coat the rims with the pistachios and freeze-dried strawberries. Set the glasses aside.

IN a high-speed blender, combine the strawberries, sugar, milk, cream, vodka, vanilla, and cardamom and blend until smooth. Pour into glasses and top with dried rose petals (if using), and another tiny pinch of cardamom. Cheers!

MACADAMIA MATCHA LATTE

While Grand Forks may be big enough to have a superb Super Target, multiple axe-throwing places, and an airport that Delta services, it's still small enough that if you have a weird Starbucks order, word will eventually get around through the town gossip line that you have a weird Starbucks order, and then it will eventually get back to you that people have been talking smack about your weird Starbucks order. (A matcha latte made with water is just an iced tea, girls!!!!!) Where does that leave us? It leaves us at the less weird, very creamy, totally nuanced, perfectly sweet matcha latte that I *would* order if it were a menu option. But baristas can't be expected to make their own roasted macadamia milk when they have a packed schedule of shade throwing!

MAKES 2 LATTES

¼ cup (35 grams) roasted unsalted macadamia nuts

1½ (360 grams) cups water, just under boiling temperature

1½ teaspoons matcha powder

1 tablespoon (20 grams) sweetened condensed coconut milk, or more to taste (or regular condensed milk)

Tiny pinch of kosher salt

IN a high-speed blender, combine the macadamia nuts, water, matcha, condensed milk, and salt and blend on high until smooth, 1 to 2 minutes. Carefully strain through a nut milk bag, pressing on the solids to extract every drop of liquid, and enjoy. (This is also good iced!)

BLACK SESAME EGG CREAM

I like to believe that the fact that I haven't gotten any angry letters about my matcha egg cream in *Home Is Where the Eggs Are* (which uses sweetened condensed milk and matcha in place of the requisite Fox's U-Bet Chocolate Syrup) is because people liked it. Not because the intersection of People Who Feel Strongly About Egg Creams and People Who Got That Far in My Book is nonexistent. Since it's probably the latter, consider this another cry for attention.

This black sesame version works so well because black sesame and cream are as great a duo as cookies and cream, and if you've ever thought to yourself, "Hmmm, I'd like a milkshake, but I don't want something so heavy, and also a sparkle of effervescence might be nice," then an egg cream was made for you.

MAKES 1 EGG CREAM, EASILY MULTIPLIABLE

2 tablespoons (40 grams) sweetened condensed milk or sweetened condensed coconut milk

1 teaspoon black sesame paste or 1½ teaspoons black sesame seeds, finely ground in a spice grinder

¼ cup (60 grams) whole milk, straight out of the fridge (you want it cold!)

Plain seltzer, straight out of the fridge

IN a 12-ounce glass, combine the sweetened condensed milk and black sesame, stirring with a long spoon or metal straw. Pour in the whole milk. Mix vigorously with the spoon or straw as you assertively and quickly pour the seltzer in, stopping when you're an inch from the top of the glass. Continue stirring until you have a nice layer of foam. (Did it overflow? L'Chaim!) Drink immediately.

ACKNOWLEDGMENTS

They say that birthing a book is like birthing a baby, and now after two human babies, I can safely say that this was way (*way*) harder. And the gestation took more than three times as long. It was a labor of love but it was also a lot of labor (!!), and it truly was the work of a massive, skilled village. I could not have ever come close to doing this without them. To this village: Thank you, thank you, *thank you*. I am endlessly grateful for your hard work.

To Cassie Jones, Jill Zimmerman, Nicole Braun, Liate Stehlik, Ben Steinberg, Anwesha Basu, Melissa Esner, Rachel Meyers, Ploy Siripant, Renata De Oliveira, Heather Rodino, and Anna Brower at William Morrow. You are an absolute dream team, and I feel honored that the spine of this book bears the William Morrow badge.

PAIGE, my right-hand lady. I don't even want to imagine what it would have been like to write this book without you by my side. You are a recipe-testing machine, a cake-decorating wizard, a buttered-potato-dough genius, and the calm, collected, precise presence that this book required. Thank you for your amazing work ethic, and for never batting an eyelash at the excessive amount of retests that I asked you to do.

To Jonah Straus, Andy Stabile, Lanie Ragsdale, Max Nagler, Amanda Paa, Tara Melega, Rikki Kyle, and Kayla Inanc Musto. I've got the greatest team in the business and your support means the world.

To Amy Stevenson, who tirelessly tested every single recipe in this book and provided the greatest wealth of expertise.

To my trusty squad of recipe testers, taste testers, advisers, developers, inspirers, and those who happily (or "happily") accepted random cakes and cookies that I forced them to take home even when they were very, very sick of sugar: Jenna Yeh, Amy Stevenson, Courtney Roker, Hannah Aufmuth,

Paige Greene, Hayden Haas, Sandra Trippichio, Jenny Kirsten, Allie Shern, My Cookbook Club ladies, Zoe Huston, Kristen Tomlan, Anna Sather, Jason Sather, Cliff Sather, Bette Sather, Sandi Sather, Kristiana Sather, Christian Matthews, Kelsey Sather, Jay Sather, Elaine Ramstad, Judie Kanten, Margarette Rue, Roxanne Hagen, Roger Hagen, Mom, Dad, Teresa, Mia.

To Bobie Brown, Matt Talley, Max Van Blarcom, Elisa Nowatzki, Aspen Moreland, Kylie Stover, David Davis, and our bakers and management team past and present at Bernie's. You are a brilliant team, and you bring so many of these recipes to life in the most beautiful way.

To Mark Bliven, for generously lending your knowledge of sugar beets, farming, and Hagen family history to my research (and Janice Rost for making this connection).

To the unstoppable team that brought these photos and illustrations to life: Chantell and Brett Quernemoen, Lisel Jane Ashlock, Ewa Perry, Barrett Washburne, Amelia Arend, Laura Evavold, Maren Ellingboe King, Sunny Cho, Vanesa Santana, Chris Wrobleski, Brianna Beaudry, Courtney Fuglein, Hayley Lukaczyk. Working with all of you is such a joy.

And last but not least, the humans who keep me going: Nick, Bernie, and Ira. I love you sooo *soooo* much!

BIBLIOGRAPHY

Campos, Adriane. "Cane vs. Beet Sugar: A Difference?" *What Sugar Blog*, July 14, 2022. whatsugar.com/post/difference-between-cane-and-beet-sugar.

Kenney, Lynda. *The Past Is Never Far Away: A History of the Red River Valley Potato Industry*. East Grand Forks, MN: Red River Valley Potato Growers Association, 1995.

Olson, David. "A Brief History of American Crystal Sugar Co." *Fargo Forum*, January 15, 2012. inforum.com/business/a-brief-history-of-american-crystal -sugar-co.

Strand, Philip. *A Heritage of Growth: American Crystal Sugar Company and the First Hundred Harvests*. Moorhead, MN: American Crystal Sugar Company, 1998.

Ware, Lewis S. *The Sugarbeet: History of the Beet Sugar Industry in Europe*. Philadelphia: Henry Carey Baird & Co., 1880.

"Sugarbeet History." American Sugarbeet Growers Association. 2023. Americansugarbeet.org.

UNIVERSAL CONVERSION CHART

OVEN TEMPERATURE EQUIVALENTS

250°F = 120°C   350°F = 180°C   450°F = 230°C

275°F = 135°C   375°F = 190°C   475°F = 240°C

300°F = 150°C   400°F = 200°C   500°F = 260°C

325°F = 160°C   425°F = 220°C

MEASUREMENT EQUIVALENTS

Measurements should always be level unless directed otherwise.

⅛ teaspoon = 0.5 mL

¼ teaspoon = 1 mL

½ teaspoon = 2 mL

1 teaspoon = 5 mL

1 tablespoon = 3 teaspoons = ½ fluid ounce = 15 mL

2 tablespoons = ⅛ cup = 1 fluid ounce = 30 mL

4 tablespoons = ¼ cup = 2 fluid ounces = 60 mL

5⅓ tablespoons = ⅓ cup = 3 fluid ounces = 80 mL

8 tablespoons = ½ cup = 4 fluid ounces = 120 mL

10⅔ tablespoons = ⅔ cup = 5 fluid ounces = 160 mL

12 tablespoons = ¾ cup = 6 fluid ounces = 180 mL

16 tablespoons = 1 cup = 8 fluid ounces = 240 mL

SCONE
MUFFIN

ALMOND
COOKIE BAR

TAHINI MONSTER

SUGAR COOKIE

INDEX

NOTE: Page references in *italics* indicate photographs.

A

Accordion pastry cutter, xxix
Almond Butter
    Blossoms, Giant, 8–9, *10*
    Cashew Coconut Buckeyes, 284–85,
      285
    Fairy French Toast, 146–47, *148*
    Mini Cakes with Berry Glaze,
      234–35, *235*
    –Stuffed Dates, 286, *286*
Almond paste
    about, xxiv–xxv
    Italian Rainbow Cookie Dough, *44*,
      45–46
    Jam Bars, Three Ways, 70–71, *71*
    Marzipan Cake, *202*, 203–5
Almond(s)
    Jam Bars, Three Ways, 70–71, *71*
    Mandel Bread Cereal, 140–41, *142*
    Marzipan Soda, 300
    Mazarin Pie, 264–65, *266*
    Stone Fruit Streusel Cake, *197*,
      198–99
    Sugar Cookie Bars, Soft, *53*,
      54–55
Apples
    Classic Candy Bar Salad, 89
    Overachiever's Candy Bar Salad,
      90–92, *92*

B

Babka, Black Sesame, *129*, 130–31
Babka Muffins, Marzipan Poppy Seed,
    117–19, *118*
Bagel Chip(s)
    Blueberry Cream Cheese Salad,
      96–97, *98*

Sorta Weird Seven-Layer Bars, *56*,
    56–57
Bake times, xxxviii–xxxix
Bars, list of recipes, viii
Basbousa, Pistachio, 194–95, *196*
Beet(s)
    (Sugar) Chocolate Muffins, 166–67
    Naturally Colored Rainbow Cake,
      206–8, *208*
    Red-ish Velvet Cake, 191–93, *193*
    sugar, about, xxvii
Bench scraper, xxix
Berries. *See also* Raspberry(ies);
    Strawberry(ies)
    Blueberry Cream Cheese Bagel Chip
      Salad, 96–97, *98*
    Blueberry Slab Pie, 258–59, *260*
    Naturally Colored Rainbow Cake,
      206–8, *208*
    Stollen Bars, 78–79, *80*
Black-and-White Cookies, Earl Grey,
    24–26, *26*
Black-and-White Cookie Salad, 104–5,
    105
Black Sesame
    Babka, *129*, 130–31
    Egg Cream, *310*, 311
    Snow Ice Cream, 288, *289*
Blender, xxix
Bløtkake, Strawberry Elderflower, 240–41,
    242
Blueberry(ies)
    Cream Cheese Bagel Chip Salad,
      96–97, *98*
    Naturally Colored Rainbow Cake,
      206–8, *208*
    Slab Pie, 258–59, *260*

Bourekas, Pumpkin Jam and Goat Cheese, *267*, 268–69
Breads
    Black Sesame Babka, *129*, 130–31
    Fairy French Toast, 146–47, *148*
    Halva, Walnut, and Chocolate Chunk Scone Loaf, 134–35, *136*
Breakfast dishes, list of recipes, viii–ix
Buckeyes, Cashew Coconut, 284–85, *285*
Buns
    Cardamom, 124–25, *125*
    Chocolate Swirly, 126–27, *128*
    Pineapple, 152–55, *153*
Butter
    cold, cubing, xix
    European-style, xviii
    room temperature, xviii–xix
    unsalted, xviii
Buttermilk
    Classic Cookie Salad, 85, 86
    for recipes, xxv
Butterscotch chips
    Sorta Weird Seven-Layer Bars, 56, 56–57

c
Cacao nibs
    Peanut Butter Halva, *278*, 279
Cakes
    general notes on, 170–71
    how to frost, 178
    list of recipes, ix
Cake Shake, Tahini, *295*, 296
Cake wheel, xxxiv
Candy Bar Salads
    Classic, 89
    Overachiever's, 90–92, *92*
Candy thermometer, xxxv
Cane sugar, xxvii
Caramels
    Overachiever's Candy Bar Salad, 90–92, *92*
Cardamom
    Buns, 124–25, *125*
    Frozen Coffee, *302*, 303
    Jam Bars, Three Ways, 70–71, *71*
    and Saffron Tiramisu, *291*, 292–93
    Stollen Bars, 78–79, *80*

Carrot(s)
    Hawaij Cake with Orange Blossom Cream Cheese Frosting, 180–82, *182*
    Naturally Colored Rainbow Cake, 206–8, *208*
Cashew(s)
    Coconut Buckeyes, 284–85, *285*
    Fresh Mint Coconut Shake, 304
Cereal, Mandel Bread, 140–41, *142*
Challah Hotteok, *156*, 157–58
Cheese. *See also* Cream Cheese
    Black-and-White Cookie Salad, 104–5, *105*
    Goat, and Pumpkin Jam Bourekas, *267*, 268–69
    Jam and Mozzarella English Muffin Rolls, *137*, 138–39
    Processed, Fudge, *273*, 274–75
    Saffron and Cardamom Tiramisu, *291*, 292–93
Cherry(ies)
    Chocolate Chunk Cobbler, *270*, 270–71
    Mahlab Linzers, 27, *28–29*
    Stone Fruit Streusel Cake, *197*, 198–99
Chex cereal
    Furikake Puppy Chow, *282*, 283
Chips, Rainbow, 190
Chocolate. *See also* White chocolate
    (Sugar) Beet Muffins, 166–67
    Beet Red-ish Velvet Cake, 191–93, *193*
    buying, xix
    Cake, Big Buttery, 246–47, *248*
    Cashew Coconut Buckeyes, 284–85, *285*
    Chip Potato Chip Cookies, 18–19, *20*
    Chocolate Halva Walnut Cookies, *21*, 22–23
    Chunk, Halva, and Walnut Scone Loaf, 134–35, *136*
    Chunk Cherry Cobbler, *270*, 270–71
    Chunk Whole Wheat Snack Cake, Salted, *238*, 238–39
    Cinnamon Sugar Rugelach, 30–32, *33*

Coffee Cake with Fresh Mint
 Frosting, 209–10, *211*
-Dipped Brown Sugar Animals, *41,*
 42–43
Earl Grey Black-and-White Cookies,
 24–26, *26*
Fairy French Toast, 146–47, *148*
filling for doughnuts, 123
Furikake Puppy Chow, *282, 283*
Giant Almond Butter Blossoms, 8–9,
 10
Italian Rainbow Cookie Dough, *44,*
 45–46
Larder Cabinet Cookies, 49, *49–51*
Mandel Bread Cereal, 140–41, *142*
Miso Toffee Crackers, 72–73, *74*
Orange Pistachio Scone Muffins, *149,*
 150–51
Overachiever's Candy Bar Salad,
 90–92, *92*
Overachiever's Cookie Salad, 87–88
Peanut Butter Cake, 216–17, *218*
Peanut Butter (or Tahini) Fudge Pie,
 255, 256–57
Processed Cheese Fudge, *273,*
 274–75
Rosemary Potato Loaf Cake, 212–13,
 213
Sandwich Cookies, Big Soft, 38–39,
 40
S'mores Bars, 67, *68–69*
Sorta Weird Seven-Layer Bars, *56,*
 56–57
Swirly Buns, 126–27, *128*
Tahini Cake Shake, *295, 296*
Tahini Fudge Cake with Tahini Whip
 and Halva, 200–201, *201*
Yellow Cake Cookie Bars, *81,*
 82–83
Cinnamon
 Jam Bars, Three Ways, 70–71, *71*
 Stollen Bars, 78–79, *80*
 Sugar Chocolate Rugelach, 30–32,
  33
Cobbler, Chocolate Chunk Cherry, *270,*
 270–71
Cocktail, Strawberries and Cream Frozen,
 306, 307
Cocoa powder, xix

Coconut
 Cashew Buckeyes, 284–85, *285*
 Cream Pie, My Dad's, *261,*
  262–63
 Fresh Mint Shake, 304
 Jam Bars, Three Ways, 70–71, *71*
 Larder Cabinet Cookies, 49, *49–51*
 milk, buying and using, xix
 Pistachio Basbousa, 194–95, *196*
 Pomegranate Coconut Gelatin Mold,
  106–7, *108*
 Pomegranate Gelatin Mold, 106–7,
  108
 Raspberry Rose Pistachio Cake,
  176–77, *179*
 Sorta Weird Seven-Layer Bars, *56,*
  56–57
 Ube Fluff, *109,* 110–11
Coconut oil, xx
Coffee
 Cake with Fresh Mint Frosting,
  209–10, *211*
 Cardamom Frozen, *302, 303*
Cookie cutters, xxxv
Cookie Dough, Italian Rainbow, *44,*
 45–46
Cookies, list of recipes, viii
Cookie Salads
 Black-and-White, 104–5, *105*
 Classic, *85,* 86
 Overachiever's, 87–88
Cookie scoop, xxix
Cool Whip
 Classic Candy Bar Salad, 89
 Classic Cookie Salad, *85,* 86
Cracker(s)
 Buttery, Icebox Cake, 280, *281*
 Miso Toffee, 72–73, *74*
Cranberries
 Mandel Bread Cereal, 140–41, *142*
Cream Cheese
 Beet Red-ish Velvet Cake, 191–93,
  193
 Big Buttery Chocolate Cake, 246–47,
  248
 Big Soft Chocolate Sandwich
  Cookies, 38–39, *40*
 Blueberry Bagel Chip Salad, 96–97,
  98

Cream Cheese (*continued*)
    Buttery Cracker Icebox Cake, 280,
        281
    Cinnamon Sugar Chocolate Rugelach,
        30–32, *33*
    Coconut Raspberry Rose Pistachio
        Cake, 176–77, *179*
    Cutouts, Thick Soft, *14,* 15–17
    Jumbo Thumbprints, *47,* 47–48
    mixing, for frosting, xx–xxi
    Naturally Colored Rainbow Cake,
        206–8, *208*
    Orange Blossom Frosting, Hawaij
        Carrot Cake with, 180–82, *182*
    Overachiever's Cookie Salad, 87–88
    Poppy Seed Hand Pies with Blood
        Orange Glaze, 252–53, *254*
    Roasted Squash Cake with Brown
        Sugar Frosting, *219,* 220–21
    Soft Almond Sugar Cookie Bars, *53,*
        54–55
    Sprinkle Cake 2.0, 186–89, *187*
    Stollen Bars, 78–79, *80*
    storing, xx
    Yellow Cake Cookie Bars, *81,* 82–83
Crispy rice cereal
    Cashew Coconut Buckeyes, 284–85,
        285
Cupcakes, Vanilla, with Vanilla Frosting,
    172–75, *173*

D
Dates, Almond Butter–Stuffed, *286, 286*
Decorating with marzipan, 249
Digital instant-read thermometer, xxx
Digital scale, xxxiv, xxxviii
Dough, Buttered Potato, 114–16
Doughnuts
    Puffy Potato, 120–23, *121*
    Sprinkle Cake, *159,* 159–61
Drinks, list of recipes, ix

E
Earl Grey
    Black-and-White Cookies, 24–26,
        26
    Saffron and Cardamom Tiramisu,
        291, 292–93
Egg Cream, Black Sesame, *310,* 311

Egg(s)
    large, for recipes, xxi
    room temperature, xxi
    whites, beating, xxi
Elderflower (liqueur)
    about, xxiii
    Strawberry and Raspberry Jam, *132,*
        133
    Strawberry Bløtkake, 240–41,
        242
English Muffin Rolls, Jam and Mozzarella,
    137, 138–39
Extracts, xxi

F
Financiers, Rainbow Chip, *214,* 215
Flaky salt, xxvi
Float, Grapefruit Slushy, 297, *298*
Floral flavors, xxi–xxiii
Flours, xxiii
Fluff, Ube, *109,* 110–11
Food coloring, xxiii
Food processor, xxx
French Toast, Fairy, 146–47, *148*
Frosted Tahini Cookies, Chewy, 5–7, *7*
Frosting, applying to cake, 178
Frozen and no bake, list of recipes, ix
Fruit, xxiv. *See also* Berries; *specific fruits*
    Chewy Nutty Fruity Granola Bars,
        75, 76–77
Fudge, Processed Cheese, *273,* 274–75
Furikake Puppy Chow, *282,* 283

G
Gelatin Mold, Pomegranate Coconut,
    106–7, *108*
Gel coloring, xxiii
Goat Cheese and Pumpkin Jam Bourekas,
    267, 268–69
Graham crackers
    S'mores Bars, *67,* 68–69
Granola Bars, Chewy Nutty Fruity, 75,
    76–77
Grapefruit Slushy Float, 297, *298*
Grape Salad, *102,* 103

H
Halva
    about, xxiv

Chocolate Chocolate Walnut Cookies, *21*, 22–23

Larder Cabinet Cookies, *49*, 49–51

Peanut Butter, *278*, 279

and Tahini Whip, Chocolate Tahini Fudge Cake with, 200–201, *201*

Walnut, and Chocolate Chunk Scone Loaf, 134–35, *136*

Hand Pies, Poppy Seed, with Blood Orange Glaze, 252–53, *254*

Hawaij Carrot Cake with Orange Blossom Cream Cheese Frosting, 180–82, *182*

Hazelnuts and hazelnut butter

Fairy French Toast, 146–47, *148*

Jam Bars, Three Ways, 70–71, *71*

Stone Fruit Streusel Cake, *197*, 198–99

Hotteok, Challah, *156*, 157–58

I

Ice Cream

Grapefruit Slushy Float, 297, *298*

Snow, Black Sesame, 288, *289*

Tahini Cake Shake, *295*, 296

Ice pop molds, xxxv

Ingredients, xviii–xxviii

notes on, xxxvii–xxxix

substituting, xxxvii

temperatures, xxxvii

weighing, xxxvii–xxxviii

Italian Rainbow Cookie Dough, *44*, 45–46

J

Jam. *See also* Raspberry jam; Strawberry jam

Bars, Three Ways, 70–71, *71*

Jumbo Thumbprints, *47*, 47–48

Marzipan Cake, *202*, 203–5

and Mozzarella English Muffin Rolls, *137*, 138–39

Strawberry, Raspberry, and Elderflower, *132*, 133

K

Kitchen ruler, xxx

Knives, xxxi

L

Larder Cabinet Cookies, *49*, 49–51

Latte, Macadamia Matcha, 308, *309*

Lavender

about, xxi–xxiii

Lemon Loaf, 183–84, *185*

Lemon

Lavender Loaf, 183–84, *185*

Preserved, Yogurt Whip, Fresh Mint Olive Oil Cake with, 222–24, *223*

Linzers, Cherry Mahlab, 27, 28–29

M

Macadamia(s)

Furikake Puppy Chow, *282*, 283

Matcha Latte, 308, *309*

Pudding Pops, *276*, 276–77

Mahlab Cherry Linzers, 27, 28–29

Mandel Bread Cereal, 140–41, *142*

Marshmallow(s)

Classic Cookie Salad, 85, *86*

Overachiever's Candy Bar Salad, 90–92, *92*

S'mores Bars, *67*, 68–69

Ube Fluff, *109*, 110–11

Marzipan

about, xxiv–xxv

Cake, *202*, 203–5

decorating with, 249

Poppy Seed Babka Muffins, 117–19, *118*

Soda, 300

Stollen Bars, 78–79, *80*

Mascarpone

Black-and-White Cookie Salad, 104–5, *105*

Saffron and Cardamom Tiramisu, *291*, 292–93

Matcha Macadamia Latte, 308, *309*

Matzo meal

Sorta Weird Seven-Layer Bars, *56*, 56–57

Mazarin Pie, 264–65, *266*

Measuring spoons and cups, xxxi

Microplane, xxx

Milks, xxv

Mint
    Fresh, Coconut Shake, 304
    Fresh, Olive Oil Cake with Preserved
        Lemon Yogurt Whip, 222–24,
        223
    Frosting, Fresh, Coffee Cake with,
        209–10, *211*
    Naturally Colored Rainbow Cake,
        206–8, *208*
    Simple Syrup, 299
Miso Toffee Crackers, 72–73, *74*
Mixing bowls, xxix
Mochi Bits, 289, *289*
Mozzarella and Jam English Muffin Rolls,
    137, 138–39
Muffins
    Chocolate (Sugar) Beet,
        166–67
    Marzipan Poppy Seed Babka,
        117–19, *118*
    Orange Chocolate Pistachio Scone,
        149, 150–51

N
Newtons, Red Bean, 34–35, *36*
Nut butters. *See also* Almond Butter;
    Peanut Butter
    about, xxv
    Chewy Nutty Fruity Granola Bars,
        75, 76–77
    Fairy French Toast, 146–47,
        148
    One-Bowl Any-Butter Cookie Bars,
        64–65, *66*
Nut milk bags, xxxv
Nuts. See also specific nuts
    Chewy Nutty Fruity Granola Bars,
        75, 76–77
    storing, xxv
    toasting, xxv

O
Oats
    Chewy Nutty Fruity Granola Bars,
        75, 76–77
Offset spatulas, xxxi
Oils, xxvi
Orange blossom water
    about, xxi

    Hawaij Carrot Cake with Orange
        Blossom Cream Cheese Frosting,
        180–82, *182*
Orange(s)
    Black Sesame Babka, *129*, 130–31
    Blood, Glaze, Poppy Seed Hand Pies
        with, 252–53, *254*
    Chocolate Pistachio Scone Muffins,
        149, 150–51
    Classic Cookie Salad, 85, *86*
    Mandarin, and Toasted Sesame Bars,
        58–59, *60*
    Overachiever's Cookie Salad, 87–88
Oven racks, xxxviii
Oven thermometer, xxxi

P
Pancakes
    Challah Hotteok, *156*, 157–58
    Wild Rice, with Poached Rhubarb,
        143, 144–45
Pans, xxxii
Parchment paper, xxxii
Pastry cutter, xxix
Peach(es)
    Grilled, Shortcakes, *230*, 231–33
    Stone Fruit Streusel Cake, *197*,
        198–99
Peanut Butter
    Chocolate Cake, 216–17, *218*
    (or Tahini) Fudge Pie, *255*, 256–57
    Furikake Puppy Chow, *282*, 283
    Halva, *278*, 279
    Overachiever's Candy Bar Salad,
        90–92, *92*
Peanuts
    Classic Candy Bar Salad, 89
    Overachiever's Candy Bar Salad,
        90–92, *92*
    Pomegranate Coconut Gelatin Mold,
        106–7, *108*
Pecans
    Processed Cheese Fudge, *273*,
        274–75
Pies, list of recipes, ix
Pineapple
    Buns, 152–55, *153*
    Classic Cookie Salad, 85, *86*
    Overachiever's Cookie Salad, 87–88

Piping bags, xxxii
Piping tips, xxxii–xxxiv
Pistachio(s)
    Basbousa, 194–95, *196*
    Beet Red-ish Velvet Cake, 191–93,
        193
    Coconut Raspberry Rose Cake,
        176–77, *179*
    Hawaij Carrot Cake with Orange
        Blossom Cream Cheese Frosting,
        180–82, *182*
    Larder Cabinet Cookies, *49*, 49–51
    Orange Chocolate Scone Muffins,
        149, 150–51
    Rose Shortbread Delight, *99*,
        100–101
    Saffron and Cardamom Tiramisu,
        291, 292–93
    Sandwich Cookies, *11*, 12–13
    Stollen Bars, 78–79, *80*
    Strawberries and Cream Frozen
        Cocktail, *306*, 307
Plum jam
    Jam Bars, Three Ways, 70–71, *71*
    Marzipan Cake, *202*, 203–5
Pomegranate Coconut Gelatin Mold,
    106–7, *108*
Poppy Seed(s)
    Hand Pies with Blood Orange Glaze,
        252–53, *254*
    Marzipan Babka Muffins, 117–19,
        118
    Sorta Weird Seven-Layer Bars, *56*,
        56–57
Potato
    Dough, Buttered, 114–16
    Doughnuts, Puffy, 120–23, *121*
    Rosemary Loaf Cake, 212–13, *213*
Potato Chip Chocolate Chip Cookies,
    18–19, *20*
Pretzel(s)
    Furikake Puppy Chow, *282*, 283
    Streusel, Yogurt Whip, and
        Sumac, Roasted Rhubarb and
        Strawberries with, 93–95, *94*
Processed Cheese Fudge, *273*, 274–75
Pudding
    Classic Candy Bar Salad, 89
    Classic Cookie Salad, 85, 86

Overachiever's Candy Bar Salad,
    90–92, *92*
Overachiever's Cookie Salad, 87–88
Pistachio Rose Shortbread Delight,
    99, 100–101
Pudding Pops, Macadamia, *276*, 276–77
Pumpkin Jam and Goat Cheese Bourekas,
    267, 268–69
Puppy Chow, Furikake, *282*, 283

R
Rainbow Cake, Naturally Colored, 206–8,
    208
Rainbow Chip Financiers, *214*, 215
Rainbow Chips, 190
Rainbow Sprinkles, 189–90
Raisins
    Hawaij Carrot Cake with Orange
        Blossom Cream Cheese Frosting,
        180–82, *182*
    Stollen Bars, 78–79, *80*
Raspberry(ies)
    Coconut Rose Pistachio Cake,
        176–77, *179*
    Larder Cabinet Cookies, *49*, 49–51
    Pistachio Rose Shortbread Delight,
        99, 100–101
    Strawberry, and Elderflower Jam, *132*,
        133
Raspberry jam
    Italian Rainbow Cookie Dough, *44*,
        45–46
    Jam Bars, Three Ways, 70–71, *71*
    Marzipan Cake, *202*, 203–5
Red Bean
    Newtons, 34–35, *36*
    Paste, 37
Rhubarb
    Poached, Wild Rice Pancakes with,
        143, 144–45
    Roasted, and Strawberries with
        Yogurt Whip, Pretzel Streusel,
        and Sumac, 93–95, *94*
    Rose Bars, *61*, 62–63
Rice, Wild, Pancakes with Poached
    Rhubarb, *143*, 144–45
Rolling pin, xxxiv
Rolls, Jam and Mozzarella English Muffin,
    137, 138–39

Rosemary Potato Loaf Cake, 212–13, *213*
Rose Rose Cake, 225–29, *226–27*
Rosewater
    about, xxi
    Coconut Raspberry Rose Pistachio
        Cake, 176–77, *179*
    Larder Cabinet Cookies, *49*, 49–51
    Pistachio Basbousa, 194–95, *196*
    Pistachio Rose Shortbread Delight,
        99, 100–101
    Pomegranate Coconut Gelatin Mold,
        106–7, *108*
    Rhubarb Rose Bars, *61*, 62–63
    Roasted Rhubarb and Strawberries
        with Yogurt Whip, Pretzel
        Streusel, and Sumac, 93–95, *94*
    Rose Rose Cake, 225–29, *226–27*
    Saffron and Cardamom Tiramisu,
        291, 292–93
Rugelach, Cinnamon Sugar Chocolate,
    30–32, *33*
Ruler, xxx

S
Saffron and Cardamom Tiramisu, *291*,
    292–93
Salads, dessert, list of recipes, viii
Salt, xxvi–xxvii
Salted Chocolate Chunk Whole Wheat
    Snack Cake, *238*, 238–39
Sandwich Cookies
    Big Soft Chocolate, 38–39, *40*
    Cherry Mahlab Linzers, *27*, 28–29
    Pistachio, *11*, 12–13
Scale, xxxiv, xxxviii
Scone Muffins, Orange Chocolate
    Pistachio, *149*, 150–51
Seed butters. *See also* Tahini
    One-Bowl Any-Butter Cookie Bars,
        64–65, *66*
    for recipes, xxv
Seeds. *See also* Poppy Seed(s); Sesame
    seeds
    Chewy Nutty Fruity Granola Bars,
        75, 76–77
    Classic Candy Bar Salad, 89
    storing, xxv
    toasting, xxv–xxvi
Serving temperatures, xxxix

Sesame seeds
    Black Sesame Babka, *129*, 130–31
    Black Sesame Egg Cream, *310*, 311
    Black Sesame Snow Ice Cream, 288,
        289
    Mandarin Orange and Toasted
        Sesame Bars, 58–59, *60*
    Sorta Weird Seven-Layer Bars, *56*,
        56–57
    Toasted Sesame Cake, *243*, 244–45
Shakes
    Fresh Mint Coconut, 304
    Tahini Cake, *295*, 296
Shortcakes, Grilled Peach, *230*, 231–33
Sieve or sifter, xxxiv
Simple Syrup, Mint, 299
Slab Pie, Blueberry, 258–59, *260*
Slushy Float, Grapefruit, *297*, *298*
S'mores Bars, *67*, 68–69
Snow Ice Cream, Black Sesame, 288, *289*
Soda, Marzipan, 300
Sour cream
    Grape Salad, *102*, 103
    for recipes, xxvi
Spice grinder, xxxv
Spices, xxvi
Spoonulas, xxxv
Sprinkle Cake 2.0, 186–89, *187*
Sprinkle Cake Doughnuts, *159*, 159–61
Sprinkles, Rainbow, 189–90
Squash, Roasted, Cake with Brown Sugar
    Frosting, *219*, 220–21
Stand mixer, xxxv
Stollen Bars, 78–79, *80*
Stone Fruit Streusel Cake, *197*, 198–99
Strawberry(ies)
    Black-and-White Cookie Salad,
        104–5, *105*
    and Cream Frozen Cocktail, 306,
        307
    Elderflower Bløtkake, 240–41, *242*
    Raspberry, and Elderflower Jam, *132*,
        133
    Roasted, and Rhubarb with Yogurt
        Whip, Pretzel Streusel, and
        Sumac, 93–95, *94*
Strawberry jam
    Almond Butter Mini Cakes with
        Berry Glaze, 234–35, *235*

Buttery Cracker Icebox Cake, 280, *281*
Sugar
    and nutrition, note about, xxxix
    for recipes, xxvii
Sugar beets
    Chocolate (Sugar) Beet Muffins, 166–67
    history of, xiii
    planting and harvesting, 162–64
Sugar Cookies, Big Craggly, 2–4, *3*
Sumac, Yogurt Whip, and Pretzel Streusel, Roasted Rhubarb and Strawberries with, 93–95, *94*
Sweeteners, xxvii
Syrups
    Marzipan Soda, 300
    Mint Simple, 299

T
Tahini
    Cake Shake, *295*, 296
    Chewy Nutty Fruity Granola Bars, *75*, 76–77
    Chocolate Fudge Cake with Tahini Whip and Halva, 200–201, *201*
    Cookies, Chewy Frosted, 5–7, *7*
    (or Peanut Butter) Fudge Pie, *255*, 256–57
Tapioca
    Ube Fluff, *109*, 110–11
Thermometers
    candy, xxxv
    digital instant-read, xxx
    oven, xxxi
Thumbprints, Jumbo, *47*, 47–48
Tiramisu, Saffron and Cardamom, *291*, 292–93
Tools, xxix–xxxv

U
Ube Fluff, *109*, 110–11

V
Vanilla bean paste, xxi
Vanilla beans, xxi

Vanilla Cupcakes with Vanilla Frosting, 172–75, *173*
Vanilla extract, xxi
Vegetables, xxiv
Violet flowers, buying, xxiii
Violet syrup, about, xxiii
Vodka
    Strawberries and Cream Frozen Cocktail, *306*, 307

W
Walnut
    Chocolate Chocolate Halva Cookies, *21*, 22–23
    Halva, and Chocolate Chunk Scone Loaf, 134–35, *136*
Wheat farming, 236
Whisks, xxxv
White chocolate
    Chocolate Chocolate Halva Walnut Cookies, *21*, 22–23
    Macadamia Pudding Pops, *276*, 276–77
    Rainbow Chips, 190
Whole Wheat Chocolate Chunk Snack Cake, Salted, *238*, 238–39
Wild Rice Pancakes with Poached Rhubarb, *143*, 144–45

Y
Yeast, xxviii
Yellow Cake Cookie Bars, *81*, 82–83
Yogurt
    for baking, xxviii
    buying, xxviii
    Pistachio Rose Shortbread Delight, *99*, 100–101
    Preserved Lemon Whip, Fresh Mint Olive Oil Cake with, 222–24, *223*
    Whip, Pretzel Streusel, and Sumac, Roasted Rhubarb and Strawberries with, 93–95, *94*

Z
Zester, xxx

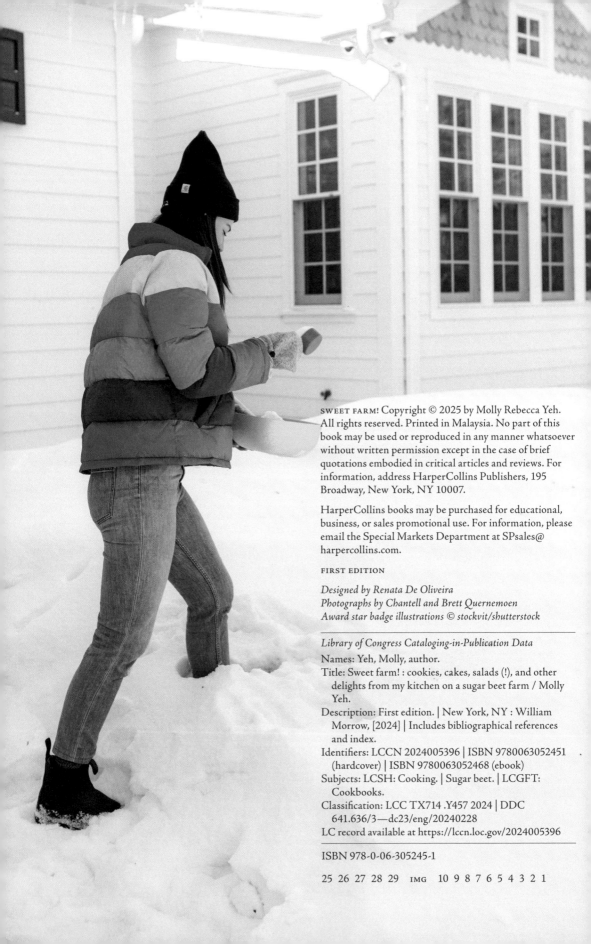

HarperCollins books may be purchased for educational, business, or sales promotional use. For information, please email the Special Markets Department at SPsales@harpercollins.com.

FIRST EDITION

Designed by Renata De Oliveira
Photographs by Chantell and Brett Quernemoen
Award star badge illustrations © stockvit/shutterstock

Library of Congress Cataloging-in-Publication Data
Names: Yeh, Molly, author.
Title: Sweet farm! : cookies, cakes, salads (!), and other delights from my kitchen on a sugar beet farm / Molly Yeh.
Description: First edition. | New York, NY : William Morrow, [2024] | Includes bibliographical references and index.
Identifiers: LCCN 2024005396 | ISBN 9780063052451 (hardcover) | ISBN 9780063052468 (ebook)
Subjects: LCSH: Cooking. | Sugar beet. | LCGFT: Cookbooks.
Classification: LCC TX714 .Y457 2024 | DDC 641.636/3—dc23/eng/20240228
LC record available at https://lccn.loc.gov/2024005396

ISBN 978-0-06-305245-1

25 26 27 28 29   IMG   10 9 8 7 6 5 4 3 2 1